Charles Thomas Wilson, Robert William Felkin

Uganda and the Egyptian Soudan

Charles Thomas Wilson, Robert William Felkin

Uganda and the Egyptian Soudan

ISBN/EAN: 9783743349681

Manufactured in Europe, USA, Canada, Australia, Japa

Cover: Foto ©ninafisch / pixelio.de

Manufactured and distributed by brebook publishing software (www.brebook.com)

Charles Thomas Wilson, Robert William Felkin

Uganda and the Egyptian Soudan

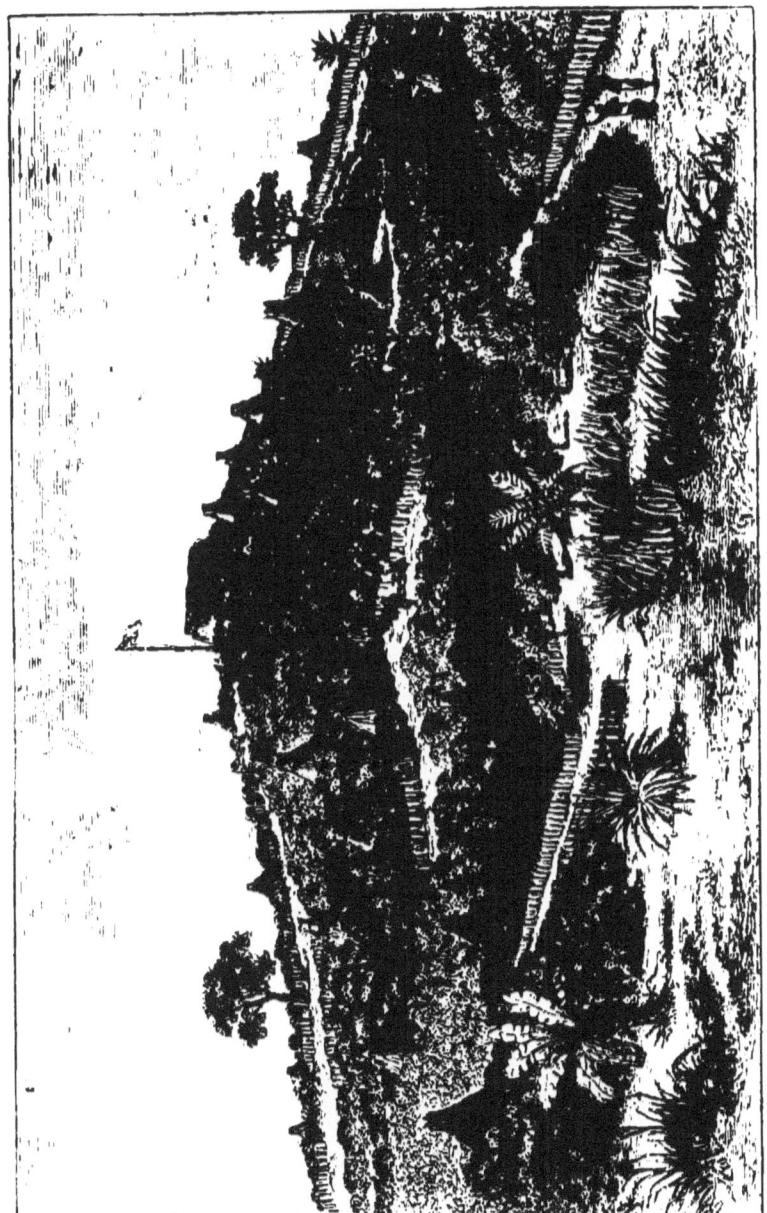

MTESA'S PALACE FROM MY VERANDAH.

UGANDA

AND

THE EGYPTIAN SOUDAN.

BY THE

REV. C. T. WILSON, M.A., F.R.G.S.,
MEMBER OF THE SOCIETY OF ARTS;
CORRESPONDING FELLOW OF THE CAIRO GEOGRAPHICAL SOCIETY;

AND

R. W. FELKIN, F.R.G.S.,
MEMBER OF THE ANTHROPOLOGICAL INSTITUTE OF GREAT BRITAIN AND IRELAND;
CORRESPONDING FELLOW OF THE BERLIN ANTHROPOLOGICAL SOCIETY;
MEMBER OF THE SOCIETY OF ARTS, ETC.

IN TWO VOLUMES.

VOL. I.

LONDON:
SAMPSON LOW, MARSTON, SEARLE, & RIVINGTON,
CROWN BUILDINGS, 188, FLEET STREET.
1882.

[*All rights reserved.*]

PREFACE.

In March 1875 the well-known American traveller, Stanley, while staying in Uganda, wrote a letter which, after several narrow escapes, reached England, and was published in the English newspapers in November of that year. In this letter Stanley spoke of the promising field for missionary labour which Uganda, with its enlightened ruler and intelligent people, afforded, and made an earnest appeal to the English nation to evangelize this place; giving at the same time a list of articles required as outfit, and stating the probable expense of such an expedition. Within a few days large donations were offered to the Church Missionary Society if they would commence a Mission in Mtesa's country. The Society accepted the responsibility, and asked for volunteers to go out to the Victoria Lake to establish two stations, one in Karagwe, the other in Uganda. A well-equipped party, under the direction of Lieut. G. Shergold Smith, R.N., proceeded to Africa in the Spring of 1876. In May 1877 four men were on the southern shores of the Victoria Nyanza; one of whom, Dr. Smith, died there. Two, Lieut. Smith and Mr. Wilson, crossed the Lake, and were cordially received by Mtesa on July 2nd. Subsequently the fourth, Mr. O'Neill, and Lieut. Smith were killed by the natives of Ukeréwe, a large island in the Lake, and Mr. Wilson was thus left alone. He was afterwards joined by Mr. Mackay, one of the original party, and in the meanwhile a party by the Nile route had been sent to his aid. This consisted of the Rev. G. Litchfield, Mr. C. W. Pearson, Mr. R. W. Felkin, medical missionary, and Mr. J. W. Hall. The latter was taken ill at Suakim, and obliged to return to England, but the other three reached Uganda safely in February 1879.

A few months later the Rev. C. T. Wilson and Mr. Felkin started for Europe, to take charge of three ambassadors whom Mtesa, king of Uganda, was anxious to send to England to see her Majesty the Queen.

The following pages must not be supposed to be an account of the Mission, but simply as intended to give a description of the countries visited, and especially of Uganda, where Mr. Wilson resided for two years, and the work of the Mission will only be alluded to so far as is necessary for the connection of the narrative.

The Committee of the Church Missionary Society

while sanctioning the publication of this book, are not in any way responsible for it. At the same time it will be borne in mind, that the authors were agents of the Society; and the work, of which the results are embodied in the following pages, was undertaken in addition to their ordinary labours as Missionaries, and must be judged accordingly.

As will be seen from the title-page, the book is the joint work of the Rev. C. T. Wilson and Mr. R. W. Felkin. The first part of it is by the former, with the exception of the chapters on the manners and customs of the Waganda, in which Mr. Felkin has given some help. The second part, in like manner, is the work of Mr. Felkin, Mr. Wilson having contributed a few suggestions. It is not intended to claim literary merit for the following pages; the desire of the authors being to state as simply and truthfully as possible what they observed in a part of the earth till now little known; but which, given good roads and a just and unambitious government, will offer a field for religious and mercantile enterprises of the utmost importance to the human race.

August 24*th*, 1881.

CONTENTS.

REV. C. T. WILSON'S NARRATIVE.

CHAPTER I.
	PAGE
ZANZIBAR	1

CHAPTER II.
BAGAMOYO TO MPWAPWA	27

CHAPTER III.
UGOGO AND IRAMBA TO NG'URU	53

CHAPTER IV.
NG'URU TO KAGEI AND UKEREWE	76

CHAPTER V.
LIFE IN UGANDA	98

CHAPTER VI.
KAGEI TO TABORA AND BACK	126

CHAPTER VII.
UGANDA AND THE WAGANDA	143

CHAPTER VIII.
GOVERNMENT AND LANGUAGE OF THE WAGANDA	193

CHAPTER IX.
Voyage to Kagei and Shipwreck 228

CHAPTER X.
Farewell to Uganda 257

MR. R. W. FELKIN'S NARRATIVE.

CHAPTER I.
Suakim to Dufli 285

CHAPTER II.
Dufli to Rubaga 303

APPENDIX I.
On Trade, by Rev. C. T. Wilson 337

APPENDIX II.
List of Plants collected by Rev. C. T. Wilson 346

APPENDIX III.
Itinerary of Journey from Bagamoyo to Kagei, by Rev. C. T. Wilson 349

APPENDIX IV.
Vocabularies of Luganda, Fur, Madi, and Kederu Languages 351

APPENDIX V.
Mr. Wilson and Mr. Felkin's Meteorological and Hypsometrical Observations, by E. G. Ravenstein, F.R.G.S. 355

Index 369

LIST OF ILLUSTRATIONS.

MTESA'S PALACE. By Rev. C. T. Wilson	*Frontispiece*
NG'AMBO, ZANZIBAR	6
MPWAPWA. By Rev. C. T. Wilson	53
KAGEI. By Rev. C. T. Wilson	84
DR. SMITH'S GRAVE. By Rev. C. T. Wilson	95
UKEREWE AND VEZI. By Rev. C. T. Wilson	122
UGANDA CANOE AND FISH-TRAP. By Rev. C. T. Wilson	204
MOUNT MKONO. By Rev. G. Litchfield	260
THE NILE AT FOWEIRA. By Rev. C. T. Wilson	266
MISSION HOUSE, RUBAGA. By R. W. Felkin	276
SKETCH MAP OF ALBERT LAKE	309
MURCHISON FALLS. From a photograph by Buchta	317

UGANDA

AND

THE EGYPTIAN SOUDAN.

CHAPTER I.

ZANZIBAR.

Welcome, welcome, ye dark blue waves!
And when you fail my sight,
Welcome, ye deserts and ye caves!
My native land—Good night!
Childe Harold.

"LAND HO!" sung out the officer of the watch about eleven o'clock on the morning of June 24, 1876, as the mail steamer *Putialla* was ploughing her way through the Indian Ocean. All eyes were at once turned eagerly to the west, where upon the distant horizon was a dim grey line which was said to be the island of Zanzibar. Soon the island of Pemba was sighted, and, as the day wore on, the more prominent features were gradually made out; then the cocoanut palms could be distinguished, and the white line of surf which marked the coral reefs on which the ocean billows break their force. An hour or two later, the strait between Zanzibar and Pemba was threaded, the island of Tumbati rounded, and we were steaming along within a stone's-throw of the coral strand of one of the loveliest of the many lovely islands of the Indian Ocean. The view which here met our eyes—the first glimpse to many of us of real tropical scenery—was one of indescribable beauty. The shore was lined with vast groves of feathery date and cocoanut palms, relieved here and there by masses of the sombre foliage of the mango; groups of native huts were seen at intervals, surrounded by their gardens of oranges, pomegranates, bananas, cassava, and many other plants strange to an English eye; the comparatively still waters were dotted with picturesque little fishing-boats, and in mid-channel were seen the huge white sails of one or two dhows; while the air was heavy with the scent of orange-groves and clove-gardens, and musical with the song of birds and the hum of insects.

Two hours of such scenery, the same—though ever varying—brought us in view of the town of Zanzibar. First, an irregular mass of white buildings was seen, with the masts of H.M.S. *London* towering above them; then slowly the Sultan's palace, the minarets of some mosques, the houses of the various consuls, the saluting battery, the rows of dhows drawn up on the beach, and the ships in the harbour, gay with the flags of various nations, became distinctly visible. The narrow channel into the harbour was threaded, the flag run up to the mast-head, two guns fired as a salute, and the anchor went with a rattling plunge into the blue waters, just as the glowing sun sank behind the far-off purple hills of Africa.

A crowd of small boats soon gathered round the steamer, waiting for passengers; then a man-o'-war's boat, pulled by sturdy blue-jackets, came bounding across the harbour, and a smart-looking officer tripped up the gangway, and demanded the *London's* mail-bag. As we were watching the lively scene, a man informed us in broken English that "de mission boat was comed," and looking over the ship's side, I saw one of the boats belonging to the *Highland Lassie*, the little mission steamer, and in it two of our party who had preceded us to Zanzibar. After some delay we entered the boat and rowed across the harbour to our house, which was situated in the suburb of Gulioni, and had formerly been the residence of Dr. Livingstone. It was quite dark when we left the *Putialla*—one of those glorious starlight nights such as one only sees in the tropics: the Southern Cross blazed ever over our heads, and was reflected from the smooth surface of the sea, with but slightly diminished brilliancy; in the north the familiar Pleiades,

> Like a swarm of fire-flies tangled in a silver braid,

shone clear and distinct; the wake of our boat was marked with phosphorescent light, which also sparkled on our oars as they rose from the water. On we glided, past curiously-built native craft, which loomed dim and mysterious through the darkness till, on rounding a point, a bright light shone out across the water; in a few minutes more we had set foot on the sandy shore, and had received a hearty English welcome from our comrades who were awaiting us. We were a merry party that night. Those of us who had just arrived had many loving messages from home for those who had preceded us, and they had many things to tell about the new life which was before us.

The island of Zanzibar is of coral formation, and one of a chain of islands which, like a great natural breakwater, runs down the eastern coast of Africa about thirty miles from the mainland. It is remarkable for its fertility, being a perfect garden from end to end, and few places in the world can rival it in the variety of fruits and vegetables which it produces. Limes, lemons, shaddocks, oranges of several sorts, papaws, custard apples, guavas, jackfruit, grapes, mangoes, pineapples, dates, cocoanuts, and a number of other fruits whose names even are unknown to Europeans, abound; while cassava, ginger, sugarcane, sweet potatoes, ground-nuts, tomatoes, cloves, nutmegs, and various other plants, are largely cultivated by the natives.

The chief town of the island is also called Zanzibar, this name being a corruption of the Arabic words "Zang," a negro, and "barr," coast, or mainland. This name is, however, unknown to the natives, who invariably call it Unguja.

Gulioni, the suburb in which our house is situated, consisted principally of a straggling bazaar, where dealers in fruit and vegetables congregate in the early morning. A walk through this bazaar well repays any one who has never seen such a sight. The market-people usually squat upon the ground with mats spread out before them on which their goods are displayed: little heaps of limes, flanked by rough-skinned, strong-smelling jackfruit, each one a load for a man; or tall baskets made of the fronds of the cocoa-palm, filled with golden-yellow oranges, and often ornamented with flowers; heaps of groundnuts, and bundles of cassava or sweet juicy sugarcane. There is a woman with a pile of creamy custard-apples; and here, one with a basket of guavas, smelling like strawberries and cream. At little stalls shaded by low-thatched roofs are the vendors of cocoanuts, or of dried shark—the odour of which informs the passer-by of its whereabouts long before he sees it.

Leaving Gulioni, and taking our way through the suburb of Ng'ambo, we enter a long, narrow, winding street with low, filthy houses on either side, inhabited by Hindus, who earn a scanty living by selling miscellaneous articles of European manufacture, cocoanut oil, tobacco and drugs; these shops are chiefly attended to by women who, with henna-dyed nails and bejewelled noses squat on the ground behind their wares nursing their babies. Crowds of negroes, clad in all the colours of the rainbow, are coming and going; strings of pannier-laden donkeys carrying sand or stone for building purposes

NG'AMBO, ZANZIBAR, FROM DR. LIVINGSTONE'S OLD HOUSE.

crawl in a dejected manner along the streets; stalwart hammalis or coolies, staggering under sacks of cloves or bales of merchandise, pass at a rapid trot, shouting to the crowd to make way; then a well-dressed slave, his long shirt tucked up into his girdle that he may run better, threads his way quickly among the groups of buyers, calling out "Simila, similla punda!"—"Out of the way, out of the donkey's way!"—and the people stand aside as a well-to-do Arab canters past on his handsome Muscat donkey. Then we reach the bridge connecting the suburb of Ng'ambo with the town itself, and spanning the creek, which at high-tide makes the town almost an island. Here are crowds of beggars, dirty and disgusting in the extreme, and suffering from all manner of loathsome diseases; some are seated on the ground reciting prayers, while others hold out their hands to every passer-by, whining out "Maskini"—"I am poor."

Just beyond the bridge, turning down to the left, we come to the residences of several Arab physicians, with their apothecaries' shops in the basement, showing an imposing array of medicines and long pompous inscriptions in Arabic, setting forth that the hakim inside has most marvellous drugs which will cure all the diseases under the sun; and on which the suffering crowd we have just passed forms a keen satire. Making our way towards the centre of the town, we pass through narrow shady streets with tall well-built houses on either side, from the basements of which comes the musical clink of the coppersmith's hammer fashioning the copper and brazen vessels which are universally employed by the Arabs and Hindus; there also may be seen the goldsmiths at work on the delicate jewelry so much worn by the Hindu women. A little beyond this the hum of many voices strikes the ear, and we pause opposite an Arab school; here some thirty or forty youngsters are squatting on the ground, reciting passages from the Koran in a monotonous chant, swaying their bodies to and fro as they read; while at one end a long-bearded, spectacled Mwalimu, or dominie, presides. Presently an unlucky urchin makes a false quantity, and promptly receives a dig in the chest from the dominie's cane, and is sent sprawling on his back, but he quickly rights himself, and proceeds with his reading in the same dismal strain. Threading our way through the narrow winding streets, passing the shops of the ivory dealers, where piles of the huge tusks, which first saw the light in some far-off forest on the shores of the Nyanza or banks of the Lualaba, lie waiting for shipment to Europe, watched over by solemn-faced, placid Hindus or Banyans, we turn down into the soko, or market-place. Here an animated scene meets the eye: dealers in almost every imaginable thing that can be bought or sold are here to be found with their wares. The whole of the large open space extending from the custom-house between the Fort and the Sultan's palace to the centre of the town is filled with a dense crowd, bargaining, chaffering, arguing, quarrelling, and minding every one's business except their own. Round every group of sellers a throng of people is gathered, the greater number being merely onlookers who have no intention of buying, but, attracted by the chink of money, must have their say about the bargain to be made. Carpenters, blacksmiths, sandal-makers; dealers in calico, Manchester goods, iron, &c., retailers of food, fruit, medicine, tobacco and various odds and ends, gun-menders, barbers, tailors, and letter-writers—form part of the motley crowd.

Leaving this Babel we enter the custom-house yard, where a different, though scarcely less animated, scene meets the view. Two or three steamers are lying in the harbour discharging or embarking cargo, and half a score of dhows left high and dry by the receding tide are undergoing the same operations. Heavily-laden lighters are passing to and fro between the steamers and the custom-house quay, if we may dignify the primitive landing-stage in front of the custom-house with that name; the coolies engaged in loading or emptying these lighters chant a monotonous sort of chorus as they move the heavy bales. Large tusks of ivory are being unshipped from some dhows which have just arrived from Dar-es-salaam, Bagamoyo, Sadaani or some other of the ports on the mainland, and are taken to one side of the custom-house, where they are weighed and marked by the Banyan clerks who manage the business of the place. Within the precincts of the custom-house are sundry sheds and warehouses belonging to various European merchants, and here, book in hand, may be seen their Parsee clerks checking off the bales of goods as they arrive from the steamers. It being now the close of the clove harvest, in every corner of the yard are huge piles of matting bags full of this fragrant spice, filling the air with its aromatic smell, in pleasing contrast to the odours from the beach close by, which are not exactly suggestive of the "isles of the blessed."

Turning our backs on the custom-house, and proceeding along the beach, we pass under the black muzzles of the saluting battery, where a few filthy Balooch soldiers, clad in soiled and tattered uniforms, are lounging about. Along the shore are a few dhows embarking goods and passengers for the mainland. Leaving these we pass the various consulates, the English consul-general's house being the most imposing and having the best situation; then we reach Shangani Point, which is slowly disappearing beneath the waves of the Indian Ocean. Beyond Shangani Point is another harbour, or rather roadstead, where powder-ships lie when discharging their cargoes. Turning into the town at this place, we pass through one of the quarters inhabited by negroes. The houses here are of wattle-and-daub, with sloping thatched roofs, which are very inflammable, and fires are of frequent occurrence among them; the houses stand close together, with crooked, filthy lanes between.

Leaving the negro quarter we enter the better-built part of the town. On turning a corner the sound of singing comes from the roof of a house, accompanied by a regular stamping sound somewhat resembling that made by a troop of soldiers on the march; and on looking up we see a crowd of girls on the roof of a newly-built house treading and stamping the cement with which it is covered with wooden rammers, the blows keeping time to a chorus they are singing. This process is continued for three days, to consolidate the newly-made roofs and to prevent their cracking while drying. In this part of the town we pass a shop kept by a Goanese where all kind of European goods can be purchased, and where Crosse and Blackwell's pickles, Huntley and Palmer's biscuits, somebody else's tooth-paste, and patent medicines are advertised; but the genuineness of aught save the labels is rather doubtful. Bearing round to the left, a short distance brings us again to the bridge by which we entered the town, and we make our way home again through Ng'ambo to Gulioni.

The island of Zanzibar, which is growing in importance year by year as its trade increases and the attention of Europe is turned to the opening-up and civilisation of those districts of Central Africa which are best reached from the East Coast, comprises an area of about 400,000 acres, and its population in 1871 was estimated at 150,000, the chief town being Zanzibar, containing 80,000 inhabitants. The town of Zanzibar with its suburbs is comprised in a very small area, the people being crowded closely together. There are no good streets, but in the best parts of the town are some well-built stone houses of two and three stories in height, inhabited by Europeans and the more wealthy Indian and Arab traders. The houses of the poorer class of Indians and the wattle-and-daub huts of the negro population have already been mentioned. The town and suburbs of Zanzibar are divided into numerous mita or quarters, having each its own name, which is frequently derived from some particular feature connected with it: e.g. Forthâni, " at the custom house;" Gerazani, " at the fort;" Mnazi moja, " the one cocoanut palm ;" Mzambarauni, " at the mzambarau tree," and so on.

The population of Zanzibar is composed of representatives of a considerable variety of nationalities—Arabs, Hindus, Banyans, Persians, Negroes, Waswahili, Malagasies, Europeans, Americans and Goanese.

The most important class are the Arabs, as to them the island belongs, and many of them are large landed proprietors, possessing extensive mashamba or plantations, and great numbers of slaves. They are also the principal traders with the interior of the continent of Africa, and considerable numbers of them leave Zanzibar every year for the mainland with large caravans and a numerous retinue, and, settling down at Unyanyembe, Ujiji, or other trade centres of the interior, send out their principal slaves to buy ivory and slaves, which they gradually collect at their headquarters, returning after a lapse of several years to Zanzibar to dispose of their merchandise and to lay in a fresh stock of goods with which to renew their trading. It not unfrequently happens that the head slaves who are sent in this way to trade by the Arab merchants, squander or lose the goods entrusted to them, and being afraid, under such circumstances, to return to their master's house or to Zanzibar, they settle down in the country where they happen to be, and form small colonies, keeping to a great extent aloof from the natives of the country. Such colonies may be found in Karagwe, Uganda, and all the more distant countries to which the Arab traders have penetrated, and have been useful in preparing the way for the explorer and the missionary by disseminating the knowledge of the Swahili language. The most wealthy class in Zanzibar is that of the Banyans: they are the bankers and money-lenders of the place, and advance money to the Arab merchants at enormous rates of interest to purchase the goods with which they trade. The Hindus are a considerable body as far as numbers go, and may generally be found in the coast towns of the mainland, where they are usually engaged in buying bees'-wax, orchilla weed, indiarubber, copal, etc., from the natives, who collect these articles; in Zanzibar they are for the most shopkeepers or hucksters, and but rarely amass any wealth. Both Banyans and Hindus are British subjects, and consequently are not allowed to keep slaves.

The negroes are by far the most numerous body in the island, forming fully two-thirds of the entire population. The greater number of them are slaves, only a comparatively small percentage having become free by the death of their masters or in some other way. It is from the ranks of these negroes that the so-called Wang'uána or Seedees are drawn, who form an indispensable part of the caravan of every traveller in East Central Africa, and to whom frequent reference will be made hereafter. The word Wang'uána means gentlemen, and has been appropriated by these negroes to distinguish themselves from the slaves who work on the mashamba or plantations. These Wang'uána are not, as a rule, natives of Zanzibar, but slaves who have been brought from the interior when young, and have become to a great extent naturalised, and who have learnt Kiswahili (the language of Zanzibar). A few of them have obtained their freedom, but the majority are still slaves, allowed by their owners, on condition of their receiving a part of their wages, to engage in the service of European travellers. They are all professedly Mohammedans, having been circumcised by their Arab masters that they may be "clean" to slaughter animals for food; it being unlawful for a Mohammedan to eat meat killed by an "infidel." Most of them, however, have little acquaintance with the tenets of the religion which they profess, and rarely if ever repeat the prescribed prayers; I had many of them in my service for more than two years, and never knew any of them to pray except on one occasion, when we were overtaken by a terrific storm on the Victoria Lake and our boat was in imminent danger of being swamped. Although most of them have been brought from the interior as slaves, they look down with infinite contempt upon their brethren of the mainland, calling them Washenzi or savages. The Wang'uána are as improvident a class as it is possible to find anywhere, and never give a thought to the future; consequently it is no punishment to them to stop their pay for misconduct or breaches of discipline. When a Mng'uána returns from the interior with his pocket full of money he buys a brand-new suit of clothes and a cane and is quite the elegant gentleman for a short time, eating and drinking of the best, and indulging in nightly carouses with his boon companions. But when his money is all gone, as it usually is in a few weeks, he sells his clothes, and when the proceeds have all disappeared he is reduced to rags and is glad to engage again for another two or three years' journey into the interior. On the march they are always trying to shirk their work, and are perpetually concocting dodges with the object of obtaining more food and drink. If any complication arise with the natives and an attack be feared, they are very brave and boast loudly of what they will do as long as the enemy are at a distance, but should fighting become imminent none are so ready as they to show the enemy a clean pair of heels. In the capacity of personal servants they are, as a rule, by no means satisfactory. The cook has a deeply-rooted conviction, which it is impossible to eradicate, that a little dirt rather improves the flavour of food than otherwise, and he stares with astonishment if you object to his wearing the table-napkins as a loincloth; he drinks your tea out of the spout of the teapot, and uses the dinner-knives as razors. The Wang'uána, moreover, have very little regard for truth, and their ideas of the difference between meum and tuum are often hazy in the extreme.

Still there are some noble exceptions to the picture which I have drawn of the Wang'uána, and I have had splendid servants and brave and faithful followers among them. As a rule also they are warm-hearted, and if properly treated become much attached to their employer, showing their affection often in very unexpected ways. I have known them march many miles after a long day's journey to fetch their master a drink of water, and if he is stricken down with fever they will nurse him as tenderly as a woman, and sit up night after night to watch him and give him food and water. It must never be forgotten that the Wang'uana are really great children, and what they need is gentle but firm treatment, and in cases where punishment is considered necessary great care should be taken to make sure that it is justly inflicted, as they have a keen sense of unjust chastisement and strongly resent it.

Another class found in Zanzibar, and consisting chiefly of negroes, are the so-called mafundi, or skilled workmen, some of whom are usually found in an explorer's caravan. They are mostly masons, carpenters, ship-builders and blacksmiths, and we had several of them attached to our party to assist in building boats and houses when we arrived at our destination in the distant interior. The rate of pay which these men receive is decidedly high compared with wages generally at Zanzibar, being, during the whole of the time they are in the interior, ten dollars per month besides their food. Some of them are really good workmen, but the majority are idle, careless fellows whose object is to shirk their work as far as possible, and who consequently need constant supervision. The carpenters sit down to do almost everything, and use their tools generally in exactly the opposite way to English workmen, pulling the plane towards them and having the teeth of their saws set the reverse way to ours. They have as great an aversion to a straight line as nature is usually supposed to have, and if a log is given them to cut up into planks every one of the boards has to be gone over carefully with the adze before it becomes of anything approaching a uniform thickness throughout. In the use of this latter tool, the adze, the Zanzibar carpenters are wonderfully expert, and turn out extremely neat work with its aid. It is impossible, however, to get anything like a real day's work out of them under ordinary circumstances. Indeed all negroes seem incapable of sustained exertion, and require constant watching if anything is to be done in reasonable time.

Besides the negroes already mentioned there are the Wahudimu (lit. servants), the original inhabitants of Zanzibar, and who were the possessors of the island at the time it was conquered by the Arabs. They are scattered about in small villages in various parts of the island, and speak a dialect differing considerably from that of the town. There are a few Goanese who have settled down in the town of Zanzibar, and who are mostly shopkeepers and washermen. A small number of Baluch soldiers are kept by the Sultan as a sort of bodyguard.

The present Sultan of Zanzibar, Seyyid Burgash, is a pure Arab, and, for a Mohammedan, wonderfully liberal in his views; he seems anxious to improve his dominions and to adopt European inventions and customs. He has lately organised a small body of negro soldiers, with the aid of one of the officers of H.M.S. *London*, and has armed them with breech-loading rifles.

There is no distinctive coinage in Zanzibar, and consequently an immense variety of coins pass current there. In former times mtama, a species of millet, was employed as small change, but some thirty or forty years ago pice were introduced from India, by one of our Consuls, and are now universally used in the island and the towns of the coast opposite Zanzibar. The rupee and anna are also largely circulated in the island, besides which English, French, and American coins are frequently met with. English gold is always at a premium, and when I was in Zanzibar in 1876, the sovereign was worth about twenty-two shillings in silver. The Maria Theresa dollar (the Abu Nuktar, Father of dots, of Egypt), which is here called Fetha ya Sham, is the principal coin in circulation, and is supposed to be the standard of value, the price of goods and servants' wages being always calculated in dollars; but the number of pice which will be given for one of these coins varies according to the quantity of pice in the market: when they are plentiful the dollar, of course, is worth more than when they are scarce; the amount varying, under ordinary circumstances, from 112 to 140 pice per dollar. The Mexican pillar dollar is also used, and is known as Fetha ya mzinga, or the cannon dollar, the pillar on the coins being supposed to resemble a cannon. The multiplicity of coins is very puzzling at first to a traveller, and it is often no easy matter for him to ascertain the relative value of each.

There is, considering the size of the island, a tolerably large trade, and one which is ever increasing, carried on between Zanzibar and Europe and America. Cotton goods, prints, handkerchiefs, beads, brass and copper wire, arms, ammunition, and Birmingham goods are imported by the English and American houses there. The trade in the first-mentioned article (cotton goods) is almost entirely in the hands of the Americans, very little of the unbleached calico ("domestics" is, I believe, the proper term for it) which constitutes the principal article of barter in the interior of Africa being imported from England; indeed, the name by which it is universally known is merikáni, from the country where it is manufactured. The beads, which, next to merikáni, form the most important article of barter, are for the most part of Venetian manufacture, and are imported direct from Venice. Switzerland, India, Persia, and Muscat supply various kinds of cloth used in the trade carried on with the interior; while the trade in gunpowder, which is a monopoly of the Sultans, is carried on almost entirely with Germany. The exports consist of cloves, which are largely cultivated in the island, cocoanuts, cinnamon, pepper, cocoanut oil, ivory, gum copal, orchilla weed, hides, indiarubber, and tortoiseshell. The total value of the imports in 1871 was £429,053, while the value of the exports in the same year amounted to £495,789.

There is also a small amount of trade carried on with India and the Persian Gulf, by means of native vessels called Bagala and Bedeni. These are two-masted craft owned generally and manned by Arabs; they come down to Zanzibar with the north-east monsoon, making the return voyage with the south-westerly one.

A large local traffic is carried on between the island of Zanzibar and the mainland, the principal centres being Dar-es-Salaam, Bagamoyo, Sadaani, Whindi, Lamu, Tanga and Mombasa. The whole of this trade is conducted by means of native craft, all the ivory, copal gum, orchilla weed and indiarubber being thus brought to the island for shipment to Europe.

There is, too, in spite of all precautions, a considerable trade still carried on in slaves. There is little doubt but that a large number of regular slave cargoes are run by the Arab slave-dealers in spite of the vigilance of the officers of H.M.S. *London*, and the various gunboats which are employed to stop this nefarious traffic. I believe, however, that many more are smuggled over in the trading dhows (of which a great number run daily between the mainland and Zanzibar) under the guise of sailors, passengers, and servants. Certain it is, at least, that the slave population of the island still keeps up, though the number of births among the slave population falls far below the deaths in any given period. And although large numbers of dhows pass daily between Zanzibar and the mainland, carrying ostensibly passengers only, yet no watch seems ever to be exercised over them, or any means employed to ascertain whether they are *bonâ fidê* passengers or only slaves in disguise. As will be seen also in the sequel, large gangs of slaves are still sent from the interior to the coast; so that, putting these various facts together, the conclusion is inevitable, even if there were no direct proof in support of it, that there is still a very considerable trade in slaves carried on between Zanzibar and the East Coast of Africa.

There are two missions established at Zanzibar, one English and the other French. The English is under the auspices of the Universities' Mission, Bishop Steere having the general direction. There is a large school for freed slaves who have been rescued by Her Majesty's cruisers, under the management of this Mission, and the missionaries also act as chaplains to the English church, which has been built on the site of the old slave market, but they do not profess to work amongst the people of Zanzibar, their mission being to the continent of Africa. The French mission belongs to a Romish fraternity, and is managed by a number of priests with *frères* and nuns who teach in the schools, instruct the freed slaves entrusted to them in various trades, and tend the sick. They have a hospital in the town of Zanzibar, and capital workshops, while at Bagamoyo they have a large estate which they have purchased, and where a number of the boys are employed in tilling the ground.

Our party was now all gathered at Zanzibar, and preparations for the start were vigorously pushed on. Our instructions were to establish a station at a place called Mpwapwa, on the western side of the Usagara Mountains, one of our number taking charge of this post while the rest proceeded to the Victoria Lake with the view of taking up stations in the countries of Karagwe and Uganda. It had been suggested by Stanley and others that the Wami river, which rises in the Usagara Mountains, might prove a useful waterway to the interior, and in hopes that this might be so, we were ordered to explore the Wami river, and should it not turn out to be navigable, to try the Kingani, another river which falls into the Indian Ocean opposite to the island of Zanzibar, and which takes its rise from the same district as the Wami. The former of these rivers was explored for a short distance from its mouth by Lieutenant Smith, the leader of our party, and Mr. Mackay; and the latter by Mr. Mackay accompanied by Vice-Consul Holmwood, who, during the whole of our stay in the island, showed us the greatest kindness. Both rivers, however, proved useless as waterways, being excessively winding, and only to be navigated during the close of the rains, and then, owing to the force of the current, only by a powerful steam-launch.

When it became known in Zanzibar that our party was going up into the interior, we received visits and applications from various Arab and Hindu merchants who, knowing that we should require a considerable amount of barter goods, were anxious to secure our custom. We obtained tenders from these men for the goods we required, and chose that of a Hindu named Isa Sulimani. The piles of domestics, kaniki (a thin indigo-blue material from India), prints, coloured cottons and gorgeous gold fringed cloths from Muscat and the Persian Gulf, were brought to our house by a large body of coolies, and stacked in huge piles in the outhouses opening into the courtyard. Then ensued a busy scene. The packers, sent by the merchant, laying on the ground a piece of stout calico, which was to form a covering for the bale of cloth, placed on it a bolt of American sheeting, then pieces of kaniki, prints, etc., then more sheeting, and again kaniki and cloths, another bolt of merikáni concluding the pile; this when fastened up forming a bale of the regulation weight, viz., about seventy pounds, and of the size of a stout bolster. The outer cloth was then folded over the whole, and a long rope of cocoanut fibre wound tightly round it at frequent intervals. Then one of the packers taking the first coil of the rope in his hands and steadying the bale with his feet, pulls hard at it while another man beats the bale rapidly with a heavy piece of wood; the slackened rope is pulled tight, and the next coil treated in a similar manner. By this means the whole bale is powerfully compressed, and becomes as hard and rigid as a board, and will stand an immense amount of knocking about without becoming unfastened; moreover, should a shower of rain come on at any time during the march, the wet does not penetrate to any depth. The bales are then sewn up in matting bags, and are then numbered and lettered, after which they are ready to be handed over to the porters who have to carry them.

We had at first intended to form one large caravan, and that the whole of our party should proceed together to the interior, but by the time that I had reached Zanzibar the height of the travelling season was come, and it was found to be impossible to collect at one time or place the number of porters we required. So after consideration it was decided to despatch a number of small caravans, as porters could be procured, under one or two of our number, and to meet at some convenient place in the interior. O'Neill was selected as the leader of the first caravan, and about July 10th he left for the town of Bagamoyo, Lieutenant Smith accompanying him to that place to assist in the work of hiring porters and getting the caravan ready. In a few days more O'Neill got fairly off, having about sixty men in all with him.

It was decided that I was to have charge of the second caravan; so immediately on O'Neill's departure I began preparing for a start, and for a fortnight Dr. Smith and I were busily employed unpacking the goods brought from England and repacking them in suitable loads for transport into the interior.

CHAPTER II.

BAGAMOYO TO MPWAPWA.

On July 22nd, all preparations on the island of Zanzibar being finished, I bid adieu to my various friends and took my place on board a dhow which was bound for Bagamoyo and now lay anchored off the custom house. The hold of the dhow was nearly filled with my goods, boxes of clothes, books and other personal property; bundles of iron rods and steam piping; sacks of nails, screws and bolts, packages of tools, anvils, grindstones, portions of lathes, cases of ammunition and miscellaneous goods, and last, but not least, a good riding donkey.

The dhow was a clumsy craft of some thirty tons measurement, with a "shetri," or small poop, at the stern, on which a motley group of passengers, Arabs, Hindus, Banyans, Negroes, half-breeds, and a solitary European (myself) were huddled; the hold was covered with a sloping thatched roof, and a small platform, or deck, in the bows accommodated the two or three sailors who worked the huge calico sail. The timbers of this singular-looking craft were sewn together and caulked with a chunam of lime and fat, which not being in the best possible condition, combined with the straining of the dhow, caused her to leak considerably, and gave constant employment to two men in baling out the water. The mast was placed very far forward, and carried one large square sail, but no jib. The cargo was badly stowed, and the vessel had a considerable list to starboard, which, however, did not appear to interfere with her speed. Just as we were about to start, a venerable-looking Hindu with a magnificent white beard brought a woman and three little children on board, and requested me to look after them as far as Bagamoyo, which, of course, I consented to do. At length, after waiting some three hours doing nothing, the captain, who was also owner, quartermaster, supercargo, and steward all in one, came on board, the order to hoist sail, "Tweka tanga," was given, the sailors replied with " Ewála, é wála," the anchor was hauled up, the huge yard went creaking and groaning up the mast, and we were at last fairly on our way towards the continent of Africa. There was a strong breeze blowing, and the town and island of Zanzibar faded rapidly from our view, as we flew over the reefs, whose snowy masses of coral were distinctly visible several fathoms below, with shoals of rainbow-hued fishes swimming in the clear, cool depths. We bounded merrily on over the blue waters, the coast of Africa, which at starting had been but a grey line on the horizon, grew clearer and clearer till the belt of feathery cocoanut palms which fringes the shore could be plainly distinguished, broken here and there with the sombre foliage of the mango, and relieved by the white walls and straggling streets of Bagamoyo.

The sun was low in the west when the dhow grounded on the coral shore of Africa, the run of over thirty miles having been accomplished in a little less than four hours.

The town of Bagamoyo consists of two or three irregular streets of low white stone houses running parallel to the beach, interspersed with cocoanut palms and mango trees, and here and there on the outskirts a large baobab (*Adansonia digitata*) with its gouty-looking limbs, now bare of leaves, but hung with large green bottle-shaped fruit. There is a dirty little bazaar with a few shops kept by Hindus, a few good stone houses belonging to Arab merchants, and some wretched little huts, hardly as large as an English pigstye, where whole families of negroes live, or rather exist.

In a tolerably good stone house in the centre of the town I found Lieutenant Smith busily engaged in hiring wapagazi or porters, assisted by an Arab interpreter and a dirty little Hindu, who, perpetually chewing betel nut and tobacco, was measuring out calico and other materials for the hire of Wanyamwézi porters, a crowd of whom were squatted at the lower end of the room watching with interest the doings of the strange man with the pale face. In the courtyard at the back of the house some donkeys and a fine sheep were tethered, the latter being a present from the Wali or Governor of Bagamoyo; a few Wanyamwezi porters were cooking their evening meal of beans or mtama (millet) in little earthenware pots, placed on three stones over a small fire of sticks, and others were tying up goods into the long sausage-shaped bundles which are the favourite form for loads. In front of the house a motley group of Arabs, Wanyamwezi, coast Negroes (Wamerima), and a few dirty Beluch soldiers blocked up the narrow street.

After the day's work was over we strolled round the town, passing the neat grounds of the French mission, where a troop of boys returning home from their day's work passed us with a polite "Bon soir, messieurs." Then on to the beach, alive with burrowing crabs, and when the tide was out showing a large expanse of mud and sand strewn with shells and haunted by curlews, sandpipers, and other wading birds. Towards the mouth of the Kingani, a mile or two from the town, dense masses of mangrove shrubs are found growing in the water, while here and there a stranded dhow left by the receding tide lay high and dry out of water. Then, as the sun has set and the grey twilight is rapidly stealing over all, and the white line of breakers on the coral reefs out at sea grows dim, the stars come twinkling out in the deep blue sky, the bats flit about with their sharp, ear-piercing " tweet, tweet," the goat-sucker floats by on silent wings, and the murmur of the waves on the coral strand is borne softly to our ears, we turn our steps homewards, and our first day on African soil is over.

A week of constant toil followed, repacking loads, breaking in refractory donkeys, hiring porters, teaching our servants to pitch tents, paying and receiving visits, and getting all ready for the long march into the interior, and finally writing letters for the monthly mail which was about to leave for England.

At length on July 28th the last loads were packed, the runaways collected, and Smith and I set off for Shimba Gonéra, the first camp from Bagamoyo, but distant only three miles. I was delayed at Shámba Gonéra, till August 14th, when my Mswahili interpreter having arrived, I moved on, bidding a long farewell to civilisation and taking a last look at the ocean. We only succeeded in crossing the Kingani river that day, our donkeys being terribly hindered by the numerous swamps, and encamped on a low sandy clearing on its northern bank. The Kingani is at this point a tidal river, and swarms with hippopotami and crocodiles. I tried a few shots unsuccessfully at the hippopotami; but next morning I got some good rifle practice at the crocodiles as they lay asleep on a sandbank on the opposite side of the river, though it was impossible to secure any of them, as, owing to the remarkable tenacity of life for which these creatures are celebrated, they always managed to get into the water, and were swept away by the rapid current to the sea.

Leaving our camp, we kept for some distance along the banks of the Kingani, among noble forest trees, through large fields of sugarcane just ready to cut, and over treacherous black swamps. Then we crossed undulating ground covered with open jungle consisting of thorny acacias, candelabra, euphorbiæ, aloes and other tropical plants, till the village of Kekoka was reached. This was a straggling hamlet of a few huts scattered about a small clearing in the jungle. Large flocks of parrots and pigeons frequented the gardens, and as no meat was to be obtained here, I had resort to my gun, and in a couple of hours had bagged a sufficient number of pigeons to make several good meals. Six marches from Kekoka in a W.N.W. direction brought us to the Póngwe hills. The country was for the most part open forest or jungle with grassy valleys at intervals, and now and then villages, which were generally surrounded by dense thorny hedges as a protection against enemies and wild beasts; one of the prettiest of these villages being Rosako, two days from Kekoka. Streams were tolerably frequent, the water being sometimes brackish, and on their banks Indian corn, tobacco, ground-nuts (*Arachis hypogæa*), sweet potatoes, and a few bananas were grown. There were no cattle to be found, goats and a few sheep being the only domestic animals seen, so that meat was scarce and very dear, and we had to depend largely on our guns for our supplies of food. The country between the Kingani and the Póngwe hills was undulating, and more or less densely covered with forest, any distant view revealing nothing but a waving sea of foliage broken here and there by a few low hills. The country around the Póngwe hills is more open; the soil is a tenacious red clay, which is used by the natives to plaster the walls of their houses, the flat roofs being formed of the same material, a thick layer of it being laid upon a foundation of mtama stalks. Enormous quantities of the castor-oil tree, (*Ricinus communis*) are found here; the natives collect the seeds, dry them in the sun, and after pounding them in a mortar, boil them in water and skim off the oil which comes to the top. This oil they use for anointing their persons, and as it soon becomes rancid, the odour of a crowd of natives who have been indulging in its use is better imagined than described. The two Póngwe peaks were fine bold hills rising several hundred feet above the sea-level, and formed useful landmarks for a considerable distance; they were for the most part covered with trees, and were said to be infested by lions.

On this part of the journey small-pox broke out

in my caravan, and in spite of all precautions, seven Wanyamwézi porters fell victims to it before it could be eradicated.

Three days' journey from Póngwe brought us to the valley of the Wami. On the first day we stopped at a village called Fúni, situated on the banks of a considerable stream of the same name which flowed to the Wami. Here we were delayed several days by sickness, and did not reach the latter river till August 21st. The Wami at this point certainly looked like a river which could be navigated by small steamers of light draught, though it had not proved so nearer its mouth. It was here some eighty yards wide, muddy, and with a strong current of about two miles an hour; its depth I could not ascertain, but as it was not fordable, it must be at least five feet. The scenery here was quite different to any we had hitherto passed through. There was a broad grassy valley with a scanty growth of thorny acacias, while on the river-bank the constant supply of water produced a dense growth of tropical vegetation. Gigantic trees upwards of one hundred feet in height, festooned with huge rope-like creepers, overhung the stream and dipped their branches in its waters; a species of white jasmine filled the air with its sweet scent; large black kingfishers, looking as if carved out of ebony, sat motionless, watching for their prey; here and there little islands covered with tall grass and bright green palms, broke the monotony of the stream; now and then a solitary crane would fly slowly by, doves cooed in the thick shade, while in the evening the red rays of the setting sun as it sank behind the purple mountains of Ng'úru formed a picture of surpassing beauty. One tree in the Wami valley struck me particularly; it had a large white-barked trunk, which grew straight as an arrow to a height of eighty or ninety feet without throwing out a single branch, till it ended in a large dome-shaped head of dark-green foliage. For three days we followed the valley of the Wami in a N.W. direction, occasionally leaving its banks and plunging into the forest, when the river made a detour to the N., and on the third day we reached the village of Kwedibago, about a quarter of a mile from the river-bank. This village was conspicuous from some large fig-trees which grew near it, and which, though bare of leaves, were covered with small figs which were just ripe, and attracted large flocks of pigeons and parrots.

At this point the Wami had to be crossed, and on August 26th we accomplished this feat. At an early hour the caravan had reached a spot on the banks of the river where a bridge had been constructed. The banks here were about fifteen feet high, and two stout creepers had been carried across and secured to trees on either side; strong cross-pieces were fastened to these at intervals, and on them long poles were tied; a third layer of short sticks were placed transversely over these, and formed the floor of the bridge. Substantial stakes were driven into the bed of the river on either side of the bridge, and fastened to the two creepers to steady and strengthen the whole, and finally two other long creepers had been passed over the branches of trees on either side to serve as handrails and give additional support. As originally designed, it showed no small amount of ingenuity and skill, and must, when new, have been strong and reliable; but now it was old, the sticks of the floor were smooth and polished by the naked feet of countless passengers, many of the supports were broken, and there were great gaps in it here and there which told the traveller plainly that a false step must send him into the boiling water beneath, while the whole structure shook and vibrated to such a degree that one had to hold on firmly to keep one's balance. At length, however, all were safely over with the exception of the donkeys, and how were they to be transported across? They certainly could not walk over the bridge, and the river lay deep in its banks, which were very steep, and was foaming along with a powerful stream; also there were probably crocodiles, though the wapagazi made noise enough to have frightened away any ordinary crocodile within several miles of us. The river being the only alternative, ropes were procured, tied together, and passed across the stream; one of the donkeys was then caught and the rope fastened round him, and he was pushed and dragged down the bank; when, however, he was halfway down he lost his footing and rolled over into the water; the rope getting unfastened in the fall, he was swept away by the stream, and I thought he would have been drowned; but he was carried to the opposite bank, and was hauled out by the tail and ears by a number of the porters on the other side, who were howling like madmen. It was evident that this place would not do, and further search revealed a sloping spot a little lower down the stream. The approach, however, was blocked up by a fallen tree, but an axe was sent for, and as I made it a rule that a felling axe, hatchet, and crosscut saw should always form part of the donkeys' loads, it was ready to hand at a moment's notice: a road was quickly cleared, and the four remaining donkeys were soon hauled over. Leaving the bank of the river, we entered a large flat grassy plain, which extended right up to the foot of the Usagara Mountains, several miles away, and encamped a few hundred yards from the belt of forest which fringes the river, the crossing of the Wami having taken nearly four hours. A herd of giraffes was feeding at the edge of the plain as the caravan emerged on to it, and made off with their rapid swinging trot before I could get a shot at them.

Leaving the Wami valley, we continued for a whole day's march along the plain which was under water to a great extent, and where large herds of buffaloes and various species of antelopes were seen, and encamped in the evening in a forest near the foot of the Usagara Mountains. On this march we passed an old camp, where in a hut lay the body of a man who had died of small-pox. At this part of the journey numerous old bomas or ring fences of camps were found, as many as fourteen and fifteen being passed in a single day's march.

The water at this camp in the forest was horrible. On first reaching it none could be found, so the Wanyamwézi porters began digging holes in a slight hollow by loosening the earth with their spears and scoping it out with their hands to a depth of two or three feet, and into the holes so formed a liquid drained, closely resembling soap-suds both in taste and appearance.

For two days more our road lay through the plains at the foot of the Usagara Mountains, passing large villages with extensive fields of mtama, pumpkins, tobacco, sweet potatoes, etc., with small quantities of ground-nuts, rice and bananas. Pigeons were abundant, and were a great boon to us, as meat was not to be had, except at a prohibitive price. On August 30th, our last night in the plains, the first death from small-pox occurred in the caravan. On August 31st we entered the mountains. Our road on leaving the camp was nearly due west for a mile or two, then we struck off in a northerly direction, crossing a steep stony ridge covered with open jungle, consisting mainly of ebony trees, into a beautiful valley with bright green grass, luxuriant vegetation, and the same tall white-stemmed tree which I had seen in the Wami valley. Soon afterwards we reached the Mkúndi river, a broad shallow stream flowing over a clean sandy bottom, and along its bed we waded for a mile or more, when we encamped on the farther side on some rising ground, from which we had a glorious view of the Usagara Mountains, which rose, peak after peak and range after range, to a distant purple mass behind which Mpwápwa was said to lie. Two more days' march through magnificent mountain scenery brought us to the district of Magubíka, containing a number of villages and plenty of cultivation. The next three days' marches were very hard ones, and the pack-donkeys gave us much trouble. The road lay over steep forest-clad ridges and through deep gullies and ravines. At the top of one of the latter one of the donkeys lost his footing and fell, rolling over and over to the bottom, a depth of 200 feet. I thought he was killed, but he got up, shook himself, and walked off apparently none the worse. Many of these ravines were very beautiful. Streams of clear cool water murmured along the stony bottom or fell in miniature cascades from masses of rocks; the steep banks were adorned with a variety of ferns and rich velvety clumps of dark-green moss; overhead tall graceful bamboos bent, swaying to and fro with every breeze, while high over all the boughs of the forest trees intermingled, forming a perfect arch, and shutting out the burning rays of the midday sun : flocks of bright-coloured parrots darted past, and troops of monkeys chattered and screamed among the boughs.

Towards the end of the third day's march the forest grew thinner, till at last it disappeared altogether, and we emerged on to the edge of a broad valley with wide expanses of grassland scorched to a dazzling whiteness by the fierce glare of a tropical sun, and looking like desert sand in the distance. Red-walled tembes were visible here and there, and, pleasantest sight of all, herds of cattle were roaming about or lay sleepily chewing the cud under the scanty shade of some mimosas. We descended rapidly, passing one or two large villages, and pitched our camp by the dry bed of a stream about the centre of the valley. We soon had crowds of natives round us, attracted by the Wazúngu (white men), bringing mtama, beans, pumpkins, goats, fowls, eggs, and, last but not least, milk both fresh and sour. This sour, or, rather, curdled milk is generally preferred by negroes to fresh, and is much the same as curds and whey, and if the watery part is poured off, the solid residue forms a nice dish with sugar or some flavouring matter. At this place, which is called Kitánge, we made the acquaintance of the Wahúmba, a sub-tribe of the Masái. The great Masái tribe occupy nearly the whole of the territory lying between the Victoria Lake and the East Coast of Africa, extending as far as is known from the equator to about the seventh parallel of south latitude. The Wahúmba are the most southerly division of the Masái, and must be carefully distinguished from the Wahúma, who will be met with farther inland. These Wahúmba are much dreaded by the Arab traders and the tribes who live near them, as they are very brave and warlike, and often make raids on their neighbours, and on passing caravans if insufficiently armed. They are also great hunters, and use bows and poisoned arrows hideously barbed, and carry long shields of buffalo hides. Their women used frequently to visit our camp at Kitánge, bringing milk for sale in long narrow cylindrical gourds closely resembling German sausages in appearance; they wore huge coils of thick brass wire on their arms, extending up to the elbow, and large flat coils of the same material round their necks.

The view from our camp at Kitánge was a very fine one, the valley at this point being a large basin with a perfect panorama of hills, through which there was no apparent outlet. Some of the hills were barren, or covered only with short grass and a few stunted shrubs, while others were clothed to their summits with forest, consisting chiefly of a kind of ebony. We were delayed at Kitánge nearly a week by the sickness of some of our porters, five or six of them being down with small-pox. Provisions were very cheap here, and I purchased eleven fowls and a large basket of beans for a dóti (four yards) of merikani or unbleached calico.

Before, however, going any further it will be well to describe more minutely the mode of travelling in this part of Africa, and the system of barter. The travelling had almost entirely to be done on foot, on account of the existence in many districts between the East Coast and the Victoria Lake of the terrible tsetse fly (*Glossina morsitans*), whose bite is fatal to horses, camels, mules, and oxen, so that none of these animals can be used as beasts of burden; donkeys are more or less employed, as they are hardier than the others, but sooner or later they almost invariably fall victims to the tsetse. The wapagazi or porters, who are almost the only means of transport in Central Africa, come chiefly from a large tribe, called Wanyamwézi, who inhabit a country called Unyamwézi, to the south of the Victoria Lake. Every year thousands of these people come down to the coast, either carrying the ivory of Arab traders, or on their own account, to engage as porters in up-going caravans. They come in parties of ten, twenty and upwards from the various districts and towns, each being under a niampára (lit. grandfather) or local chief, through whom they are engaged, and who receives the food allowance for his gang of men, every day when on the march. Most of these porters are young men who undertake the journey in order to get sufficient cloth to buy a wife and begin housekeeping; and very often they change their names as a memorial of their visit to the coast. They are paid in cloths, guns and ammunition, and the hire for the journey from the East Coast to Unyanyembe, Uyui or Ng'úru, is about fifty shillings. When the caravan is made up, one of their number, generally a niampára, is chosen as kilangózi or guide, and if the caravan is a large one there are often two or more vilangózi. My caravan consisted of 120 Wanyamwézi porters, besides other personal attendants, and I had only one kilangózi. The post of kilangózi is considered an honourable one: he of course leads the way, and carries the heaviest load in the caravan, in order to make the pace, which, over fair ground, averages two and a half miles an hour. If those who carried the lighter loads were allowed to go first, they would walk faster than the rest, the caravan would get scattered over the country, the porters would fall a prey to the robbers or lose themselves in the trackless forests. The kilangózi, too, is often employed in negotiations with native chiefs about hongo, and he receives twice as much posho (food allowance) as the other porters. When a caravan is made up and the full number of porters engaged, the loads are distributed among them. The Wanyamwézi wapagazi invariably carry on the shoulder, and consequently prefer long narrow loads which can be easily shifted from one shoulder to another. Square boxes are much disliked, and it is often difficult to get men to carry them; and therefore all trunks for clothing and other personal property should be long and narrow—36 inches by 15, and a foot deep, is about the best size. The cloth for barter, hongo, and presents is always packed by the trader from whom it is purchased, in long sausage-shaped bales, which are covered with matting. Small heavy loads, such as nails, bolts, tools, and even books, should be made up into two equal weights and secured to each end of a pole, to be carried on the shoulder. Loads which require two men to carry them are also much disliked by the porters, and I have known a man choose to carry a shaft of 110 lbs. weight alone rather than share it with another man; the reason being that in going up or down steep hills and in crossing swamps a double load is extremely awkward, and if one man should stumble it throws a terrible strain on the other. The average load which a Mnyamwézi porter will carry is two frasila, or 70 lbs., the frasila being 35 lbs.; to this, however, they add their cooking pots, arms, ammunition, cloth, which they have received as hire, and any other property they may have with them, so that the total weight they carry is little short of 100 lbs. The Wang'uána porters however, who have been previously mentioned, will rarely carry more than 45 or 50 lbs.

The order of a day's march is generally as follows.

Early in the morning, i.e. about five o'clock, one gets up, the cook having risen earlier to prepare breakfast. While despatching this meal the servants are packing beds, bedding, and other things which may have been used; then the Europeans of the party go out and see that the porters are getting their loads, look after the saddling of the donkeys, pack up the scientific instruments, and despatch the sick, who should always start before the caravan, that they may not be left on the road. Meanwhile the servants have taken down and packed up the tents, and all being ready, the word is given to the kilangózi, who generally carries an antelope's horn, which he blows as a signal to start; he then shoulders his load, takes up the flag, and the caravan sets off in single file across the country. If there are two or more Europeans of the party, one should go in front of the main body to secure any game that may be seen before it is frightened away by the cries of the porters, who beguile the tedium of the way by songs and shouting. One or two of the Europeans should remain till the last, to see all safely out of camp and to make sure that nothing has been forgotten or left behind. If the march be a short one, no halt is made till the next camp is reached, but if it is a long one a rest is generally taken after three hours' journey, a large rock, a shady tree, or a stream of water being selected as the stopping-place. After a rest of an hour or two, which the Europeans of the party usually employ in getting a second breakfast, and the negroes in smoking, the march is resumed; and unless an unusually long one, no further halt is made till the camp is reached. Arrived at the place where it is intended to pass the night, a spot is chosen near the water supply, tents are pitched, the goods are piled under a tree or in the property tent, and, if in a district where wild beasts are common, a boma or ring fence of thorns is constructed round the camp. As soon as this is completed, the niampáras of the caravan collect round the tent with the cry of "Posho, Bwána" ("Rations, master"), a bale of calico is brought, and the quantities of cloth, or beads, if in a district where these are used, are measured out. A book is kept in which are entered the names of the niampáras of the caravan, with the number of men each has under him, and the cloth is issued accordingly. The cloth used for purchasing food is of three kinds, merikáni or unbleached calico sheeting; satíni, an inferior quality of the same material, and kaníki, a flimsy blue material made in India. The cloth is generally measured by the length of the forearm from the elbow to the tip of the middle finger; a rather unfair and arbitrary mode of measuring, as the length of the arm varies considerably in different people, and I have known natives when selling cattle and other things to bring some "big brother" with an abnormally long arm to measure their cloth for them. Each of these arms or cubits is called a mkóno; four mikóno make a shúka or upándo, and two shúka make a dóti, which is about four yards, and is the standard by which the value of cattle, slaves, and ivory is reckoned. The bolt or piece of thirty yards is called a júra. The average allowance of cloth for Wanyamwézi porters is one dóti per diem for sixteen men; the Wang'uána require rather more, or one dóti for twelve men. These figures also vary somewhat in different districts and at different times. Near the coast food is dearer, or rather cloth is of less value than in the interior, and in times of scarcity food is dearer than in times of plenty. Other kinds of cloth have to be taken as presents to chiefs or for hongo; e.g. Barasáti, Dubwáni, Sahári, Kikói, Joho, and Subáya, with prints, coloured pocket-handkerchiefs, etc.

Beads are used in some districts instead of cloth, the sorts most valued being merikáni and sámi-sámi: the former are small opaque white beads and the latter small transparent red beads with an opaque centre; but besides these, small blue, green, pink, black, and transparent white beads, large blue, amber, and opaque, white beads, and ringbeads of blue, green, amber, and transparent white are required. The beads are bought in large bundles or bunches: each string is called a tímba; two matímba make a kéte, and ten makéte a fúndo. The ordinary allowance is one kéte of the small sorts per man per diem. But beads are a very unsatisfactory medium of barter, as the fashion is always changing. and what is in the fashion one year may not be another; and negroes are as obstinate and unreasoning about their fashions as civilised nations. Brass wire of the thickness of a small goose-quill is also used for barter, chiefly in the countries round the Victoria Lake, while in Uganda and Unyoro, cowries, which are brought from Zanzibar, are extensively circulated.

But to resume our journey. Some of the sick men being better, we were able to proceed on September 13th, our course being now about west-south-west, following the bed of the stream, beside which we had encamped, for a mile or two; then we rapidly ascended a high ridge, from which a fine view was obtained of the mountains round us. The valley which we had just left was filled with mist, out of which the mountain-peaks rose like islands, red and gold with the rays of the rising sun. Leaving this ridge, we crossed a narrow valley or ravine, and began toiling up the steep mountain-side along a winding stony path which gave our donkeys a good deal of trouble, and on gaining the summit our aneroids showed that we had risen 1200 feet above our camp in the Kitángo valley. Instead, however, of finding ourselves on a ridge, we discovered that we were on the edge of a broad plateau which extended to the south-west as far as the eye could reach, broken only on the distant horizon by some low conical hills. Leaving the edge of the plateau, we gently descended and, finally encamped at the foot of a small grassy hill near a spring of beautiful clear water. We were now in an uninhabited district, consisting of a high table-land with short grass, and having a broad belt of forest on its most westerly side, where it again became mountainous, some of the peaks probably reaching a height of from 6000 to 7000 feet above the sea. We were here in a veritable hunter's paradise. Soon after reaching our camp a herd of wild donkeys was seen about a mile and a half distant, and the interpreter, who was a good shot, went after them, but could not get within range because of the open nature of the ground. As seen through a telescope, they appeared larger than our English donkeys, and of a reddish-brown colour. Early next morning we were on the move, as we had a long march before us, there being no water for six hours' journey; the wind was bitterly cold, and we set off at a brisk pace. We soon became aware of the quantities of game in this district; herds of antelopes of various species were seen, and the soil of the plain was full of the foot-prints of giraffes, rhinoceroses, buffaloes, and other large game. Later on in the day I saw three elephants, the first I had seen in Africa, and at night the roaring of lions, the sharp bark of foxes, and the melancholy howl of the hyæna formed a weird lullaby, quite in keeping with our other surroundings. Ostriches are numerous on this plain but we did not happen to see any. Five hours' march brought us to an open forest of mimosas, and near this we met some messengers from O'Neill, who with the first caravan had safely reached Mpwapwa, the first stage of the journey. Another hour brought us to a beautiful wooded valley with a clear stream flowing down it, the swampy ground along its edge being full of holes punched by the huge feet of the elephants, which were in the habit of coming here to drink, while bones and skulls of elephants and buffaloes lay bleaching in the grass. Here we halted for some time, and then another two hours' march through fine forest, among glorious mountain scenery, brought us to an open glade, where we pitched our tents close by a mountain torrent, and under the shade of some fine acacias. Next morning we were on the move again, and climbed a rocky path which wound along through the forest between well-timbered mountain-peaks. On emerging from the pass on the summit of a steep ridge, we saw before us the Tubúgwe valley, with corn-fields and red-walled villages scattered about. A steep winding path led us down into the valley, and we pitched our camp by the side of a stream which ran down its centre, under the shade of a magnificent mimosa. After my work was over I went for a bathe in the little stream, which presented a most fairylike spectacle. It had cut a deep channel for itself in the soft alluvial soil of the valley. This miniature ravine was completely arched over by a dense growth of reeds and bushes, and its sides were clothed with luxuriant masses of pale green maidenhair fern, relieved by the dark fronds of another species of Adiantum. We remained two days at Tubúgwe, and left on September 18th. The road, after leaving the camp, led past some villages and wound through an open jungle of stunted acacias to the top of a pass 800 feet above our camp. The summit of the pass was densely wooded, and we halted for a short time after our sharp climb, and, while resting, a hare ran through the caravan and was speedily knocked on the head; it was much like an English hare, only a good deal smaller. On resuming the march we followed the course of a long valley filled with magnificent forest, and at its lower end we got a glimpse of a small lake some distance below us. Then turning northwards, we crossed a very steep ridge and entered a valley with the dry sandy bed of a large stream winding down it, and soon after met some men sent by O'Neill to show us the way. Continuing our journey down the river-bed, where a small stream of water appeared and disappeared again at intervals, we at length emerged from the hills, and found ourselves on the edge of a broad plain stretching away to the westward, and dotted with villages, which are all included under the general name Mpwapwa. Then skirting the edge of this plain, we made our way to the village of Lukóle, one of the sub-chiefs of the district, where O'Neill was then staying.

CHAPTER III.

UGOGO AND IRAMBA TO NG'URU.

MPWAPWA is a district lying on the most westerly slopes of the Usagara Mountains and on the edge

MPWAPWA FROM THE MISSION HOUSE.

of the forest region which separates that country from the plateau of Ugogo. There are many témbes or small villages scattered about the plain, and these contain a tolerably large population, which is occupied in tilling the ground and rearing cattle. The principal crops are mtáma or millet (Arabic dhurra), mhíndi or Indian corn (Arabic esh er rif), mwére, a small grain growing on a head like a bulrush (Arabic dúchan), and pumpkins. The people live in témbes, which are houses made of a framework of poles plastered with clay, the walls being generally only about seven feet high; the roofs are flat, with a thick layer of clay to keep the water out, but in the wet season they generally leak terribly. These témbes are usually built in the form of a hollow square, enclosing a courtyard where the cattle are housed at night; as a rule there are only one or two openings in the outer wall to give access to the courtyard in the interior, and these are generally closed with strong wooden doors; the different rooms or houses open only into the court, in order to give greater security against the attacks of enemies and wild beasts, and in many districts the outer walls are pierced with holes for muskets. These témbes are horrible places, especially in wet weather, damp, close and foul; the goats and sheep too are often kept in the same parts as the family inhabit, and in the rains the floor is often ankle-deep in filth. The roofs of these témbes are frequently used as store places, and in harvest time heaps of ears of corn and rows of yellow pumpkins may be seen laid out to dry, or a huge box of bark called a "kalíndo," like a gigantic bandbox, and used to store grain in.

The district of Mpwapwa being a borderland, the people are of a somewhat mixed race, or rather representatives of a number of tribes, Wagogo, Wasagara, Makua, and others.

The people here eat a species of field-mouse, and the little boys may be seen coming home in the evening with numbers of them strung, like red herrings, on a stick.

The view from the spot where our tents were pitched was a very fine one. In the foreground the land sloped rapidly down to the river-bed, then for the most part dry; beyond, towards the west, for many miles stretched a broad plain, bounded on the horizon by a low range of hills, behind which the sun used to set in a sea of red and gold. The northern part of this plain was dotted with témbes, and, here and there, a huge baobab rose above the fields of waving corn; the southern half was covered with sombre forests of mimosa and acacia, where herds of buffalo, brindled gnu, and various species of antelopes roamed about. A mass of forest-clad hills formed the northern boundary of the plains, and was the home of numerous wild beasts, which paid nightly visits to the plain in hopes of picking up a stray lamb or kid; and far away in the south, the huge outline of the Rubcho Mountains towered into the sky, the summits being often lost in a veil of clouds.

Leopards were numerous here, and one evening, while sitting chatting and smoking in one of our tents, one of these creatures came to a témbe about fifty yards off, and getting its paw through a hole in the wall, seized a goat by the throat, and was attempting to drag it out when the approach of some men frightened it off. After this every one was on the *qui vive* for leopards, and one of my donkeys which had broken out of camp one fine night, and was indulging in the luxury of a roll in the sandy soil, nearly lost his life at the hands of one of my companions, who in the uncertain light mistook him for a leopard; he missed his mark, however, and the astonished donkey springing to his feet revealed his true character. Another donkey having broken loose on another occasion, came back with his flanks all torn and bleeding from the claws of a lion or leopard.

The local chief, Lukóle, was very civil to us, and used to send us fresh milk twice a day; he was, however, a dirty little fellow, and much addicted to "sitting on pombe" (i.e. getting drunk), of which there was a great brew once a week. We remained at Mpwapwa till October 9th, waiting for the native masons who were building a house for Clark, who was to be permanently stationed here. About a week after my arrival at Mpwapwa another of our caravans under a chief, Mganga by name, arrived, and on October 3rd Lieutenant Smith turned up unexpectedly. He had left the other two caravans, some distance from the coast, to follow him under the guidance of Dr. Smith and Mr. Mackay, and had come, with only a few attendants, by forced marches, in order to bring us the September mails. On October 7th the three first caravans, under O'Neill and myself, set off for the far west, Lieutenant Smith waiting for the remaining caravans. We camped on the night of the 7th at Chúnyo, about twelve miles from Mpwapwa, where were a few huts and the springs of bitter water which give their name, Marénga Mkáli (Bitter water), to the inhospitable forest tract which lies between that place and Ugogo. This Marénga Mkáli is a flat jungle-covered plain between thirty and forty miles wide, without a drop of water or a single human habitation; game however is tolerably abundant, and robbers are sometimes met who attack the stragglers from the caravans. On account of the scarcity of water the Marénga Mkáli is usually crossed in a single march. We began on the 8th with a "terekéza," or afternoon march, and kept on, with one or two halts, during the night, and at last reached the village of Debwe in Ugogo, a few miles beyond the jungle, in the afternoon of the 9th. Here we rested two days, and went on to Mvúmi on the 12th. Mvúmi is the largest district in this part of Ugogo, and here we had our first experience of that irritating system of robbery known as hongo. This hongo or blackmail is levied by the various local chiefs on all caravans passing through their country, and forms one of the largest items in the cost of an expedition to this part of Africa. This abominable practice has entirely arisen through the folly of the Arabs, who have no idea of combining together for trade purposes, and who submitted to this imposition rather than run the slightest risk of having their property seized by the natives. And from small beginnings this tax has so enormously increased, as, in some cases, to amount in the course of a few days' journey to from twenty to twenty-five per cent. of the total property of a caravan. The various chiefs are supposed to levy the tax at so much for every bale of barter goods, but there is no check upon them, and they can demand what they like, and as, in case of any conflict with the natives, the porters, who naturally prefer to keep a whole skin, would desert, one has no resource after one has exhausted all that diplomacy can do but to grin and bear it. The mode of settling the hongo is as follows: the day after a caravan arrives at the place where the hongo has to be paid, two or three niampáras, accompanied by some one who can speak Kigogo, go to the chief's témbe, taking some cloths, considerably fewer in number than the quantity he is likely to demand. The chief takes these and then demands a good many more, whereupon ensues a vast amount of talk, which may take two or three days, and which is rarely, if ever, concluded in less than one day. When the envoy has reduced the chief's demands as low as he can, he comes back and says the chief "is sitting on pombe and won't hear reason," or "his head has got big since the white man came," or "the white man is a great sultan in his own country, and must pay a big hongo," and "he must have twenty or thirty or forty cloths," as the case may be; so one measures out the cloth, only too thankful that another of the vexatious delays is over. The hongo having been paid, the big drum of the village is beaten as a sign that the caravan is at liberty to proceed, and generally a return present of a goat or bullock is made by the chief.

At Mvúmi an instance occurred of the wanton rascality of the Arab traders in trying to injure European travellers. An Arab on his way from Unyanyembe to the coast pitched his camp near us, and having called on us, was treated with great civility; and after our hongo was settled we wrote a letter to Lieutenant Smith telling him what we had paid, that it might be a guide to him, and sent it up to the Sultan of Mvúmi, requesting him kindly to give it to our "brother" whom we expected shortly to follow us; he agreed to do so, and took the letter. Just then in came our Arab friend, and on hearing what the Sultan had done, told him our story was all a lie, and that the letter was "medicine" to kill him; which so frightened the Sultan that he refused to keep it.

The first two marches in Ugogo were through open level country with huge masses of igneous rock scattered about, and many adansonias (baobabs) growing among the corn, with here and there a little scanty thorny jungle. The land was furrowed by watercourses, which, though now dry, showed that an immense volume of water must find its way from here to the Indian Ocean during the rainy season. At Matambúru, the second place where we had to pay hongo, we experienced our first thunderstorm, the forerunner of the Masíka or rainy season. From here to Bihawána, a march of twelve miles, the country was covered with forest. At some distance from our camp at the latter place was a fine baobab, the trunk of which was eighty feet in circumference about two feet from the ground. The chief of this district, which consisted of but three villages, was a very old man, rejoicing in the euphonious name of Minyítangáru. I went to see him at his particular request, and he professed himself so much pleased with me that he wished us to become brothers for ever after, and as a pledge of this relationship we were to exchange names, he henceforth passing by the name of Wilson, and I by that of Minyítangáru. Our next march was a short one to a wretched little village, Kididímo, where we left the Unyanyembe road, striking in a W.N.W. direction through a dense jungle of small shrubs, now for the most part bare and leafless; tracks of buffalo, rhinoceros, and elephant were numerous, and we saw many pitfalls dug for the latter. We encamped at night near a picturesque group of metamorphic rocks, with some pools of clear cold water close at hand. Four hours' march the following morning (October 21st) brought us to the district of Kitararu, and we pitched our tents in a picturesque grove of fan-palms (*Borassus flabelliformis*) near the chief's témbe. Crowds of natives came to stare at us, probably the first white man they had ever seen. We were now on the edge of the great salt-plain from which the Wagogo get the salt which forms with them an important article of trade. This plain, over which we travelled for several days, has very much the appearance of having formerly been the bed of a shallow lake, and I more than once detected on the sides of some low hills what looked like the remains of an old beach. The water on this plain is procured from deep wells, and is very brackish. At the time when we crossed it, viz., the end of October, it was as bare and dreary-looking as the desert, but judging from the enormous herds of cattle which were seen on every march, and from the large tracts of land under cultivation, it must be covered with an emerald mantle of vegetation in the rainy season, though then the only green things to be seen were the olive-coloured leaves of the fan-palms, and it was difficult to see how the cattle could possibly pick up enough to sustain life. The heat, too, was intense, the thermometer standing at 110° Fahr. in the shade for several hours in the day, while the fierce glare from the bare soil, and the phantom waters of the mirage, sparkling in the sunlight and looking, only looking, so refreshing and cool, increased one's discomfort. This plain is evidently flooded during the rainy season, as all the témbes were built on artificial mounds or had banks round them to protect them from the water. At a village called Mbahi, about the middle of this plain, we got some fresh fish of the silurus genus, and on inquiring where they came from were informed that they were caught in a large piece of water at no great distance, but the natives would not tell us the exact locality of this lake. About Mbahi and the district of Unyamguira, two marches west of Mbahi, were a few dry watercourses, but they were so winding, and the altitudes of the different villages as shown by our aneriods varied so little, that it was impossible to say in which direction the country was drained.

On November 1st we crossed the bed of the Unyamgogo, and were not sorry to leave behind the yelling hordes of Wagogo adorned with red paint and redolent of rancid castor-oil. But before bidding a long farewell to this irritating people it may be well to give a list of the places where our caravan paid hongo, and the amounts. Mvúmi, 27 cloths, 2 coils of brass wire, 2 bunches of amber beads = about $50; Matambúru, 16 cloths, 2 coils of wire = about $30; Bihawána, 6 cloths = $6; Kididímo, 6 cloths = $6; Kitararu, 10 cloths = $12; Mbahi, 15 cloths = $20; Puna, 15 cloths = $20; Unyamguira, 15 cloths = $20; total $164.

On November 3rd we were again on the move, and quitting our camp by the side of the Unyamgogo, we soon entered jungle, through which we travelled by a winding path for several hours, till we reached the foot of some precipitous cliffs, up which we slowly climbed by a zigzag path between huge boulders, over fallen trees and through dense masses of underwood. When we reached the summit of the cliffs the view amply repaid us for the climb: just beneath us, hundreds of feet below, was an undulating sea of foliage of every possible tint of green; farther on was the winding bed of the Unyamgogo, its serpentine course marked out by the detached pools of water which sparkled in the sunlight; along its banks here and there were the familiar tembes; still farther away, till lost in the blue haze which obscured the distant horizon, stretched the bare burning plain of Ugogo, the brown barren expanse being relieved only by an occasional palm grove. Leaving the edge of the plateau, which we had just gained, we kept on through the forest, gradually rising, and finally halted for the night, at a height of 1100 feet above our camp in the plains. The next day we reached Gange, a large village on the edge of the forest region, which lies between Ugogo and Unyamwezi; and here we found two or three small caravans waiting for us. They had heard of us on the road, and, knowing that we were well armed, were anxious to travel with us through the jungle, and thus be safer from the attacks of the Watuturu and Ruga Ruga. Early on the morning of the 6th we started for our eight days' march through an unbroken forest. We soon reached the bottom of a cliff similar to, though not so high as that which we had scaled on leaving Ugogo, and on reaching the top at once plunged into the forest in a W.N.W. direction. The forest continued during the whole day's march, with the exception of a small plain about a mile wide, where we came upon some of the nomadic Wataturu, a small warlike tribe who inhabit this jungle; they have no villages, but wander about from place to place with their cattle. For the first two days water was met with pretty frequently in shallow pools and pits. At one of the former, near the end of the second day's march, a dead elephant was found, and the porters at once threw down their loads and set to work to cut off the flesh. Our caravan was the leading one, and it was our men who found the elephant, but on the arrival of the other caravans, their porters also flew upon the carcase, and a furious row ensued. A quarrel took place between Mgánga, the chief niampára of my caravan, and Terekéza (lit. the cook), the leader of another party, as to who should have the elephant's tusks; swords were drawn, guns loaded, and a free fight ensued, the bullets whistling through the bushes in all directions: happily, however, no one was hit, and the fray subsided as quickly as it had begun. On the morning of the third day we were told that there would be no water, after leaving our camp, for a distance equal to two days' journey, and that we must accomplish the march, if possible, before next morning. We set off about 8.30 A.M., the road being, as before, through open jungle of small trees, or rather bushes, which were for the most part leafless, and gave little or no shelter from the blazing sun; here and there were tracts of dried mud, swamps during the rains, seamed with gaping cracks, and full of holes made by the elephants, which abound in this forest region. We continued our march, with one or two halts for cooking and rest, till 8.30 P.M., when O'Neill was seized with fever, and we had to stop. He and I with a few attendants were some distance behind the main body, so we lighted fires and lay down to rest. About half-past two in the morning, O'Neill being better, we were off again, and plodded silently on in the darkness, till at length dawn appeared, when we found that we had entered denser jungle, with larger trees and more of them in leaf, all signs that we were approaching water; and about eight o'clock we reached the banks of a dried-up river, called the Mvumbu, and pitched our tents in a fine grove of fan-palms, the huge round fruit of which, with its sweet orange-coloured pulp, was very refreshing to us, who had been for many weeks without fresh fruit of any kind. We obtained a plentiful supply of good water from holes dug in the sandy bed of the Mvumbu. The following march was a long and trying one; the jungle was very scanty except near a river-bed, which we crossed, where was a large grove of the Mahama palms (Borassus). Our kilangózi told us that we should reach a pool of water at night; so when at length, about eight o'clock, we arrived at the camp, I sent my servant for some water, but he soon returned with the dismal news that there was none; the pool had dried up. The two next marches were shorter than any of the previous ones, and each night we had thunderstorms with heavy rain. Near our last camp in the jungle were three remarkable detached rocks, which looked as though they had formerly been one, the softer strata having weathered away. At length on November 13th we emerged from the forest and pitched our camp near the village of Usuri in the district of Iramba; the journey though the forest region having thus taken eight days. After leaving Gange the country rose steadily till near the end of the second day's journey, when the aneroids showed a height of 4880 feet above the sea-level; from this point the land gradually sloped towards the west. The whole country was more or less covered with forest, the open spaces being few and far between. Elephants, buffaloes, rhinoceroses and giraffes were apparently numerous, with various species of antelopes, and large flocks of guinea-fowl and partridges were frequently met with, and at night lions, leopards, and hyænas used to prowl round the camp.

From Usuri (the Mgongo Tembo of Stanley) we went to Ushuri. Here lived Mgánga, the head niampára of our caravan, and as we approached the village the women came rushing out to meet us, uttering shrill cries of welcome similar to those known as zaggareet in Egypt. At the gate of the village, which was fortified by a strong palisade of poles ornamented with human and other skulls, Mgánga's father, a white-haired venerable-looking old man, met us, and greeted us most affectionately; then he and another member of the family took a live fowl and held it over the threshold of the gate, and all were asked to step over it, after which it was killed; the ceremony being supposed to bring "good luck."

The next four or five days' march would be, we were told, through a similar jungle to that which we had just left, and a halt of two or three days was required to lay in provisions for the journey. We reached Ushuri on November 15th, and hoped to be off in two or three days; but day after day passed and the men would not stir, the reason being that Mgánga was doing a little business on his own account, and would not start till it was finished, and the other niampáras would not move without him. On the morning of the 29th a man arrived with a letter from Lieut. Smith, saying that he and Dr. Smith, with the remaining caravan, were in the great pori, or jungle, several days' march from Iramba, and that their food was nearly exhausted, and they begged us to send them 300 rations at once. The note further said that Mackay had returned to Mpwapwa sick. No time was to be lost, so leaving O'Neill with the caravan, I set off at once for the jungle, taking a guide and two or three Wang'uána with me. We reached Mgongo Tembo about half-past twelve, having travelled very fast, and there spent three hours in buying grain and engaging men to carry it. The sun was low in the western sky when we again set off, and except for a five minutes' halt at Ulala, on the very verge of the jungle, in order to fill up our water bottles, we did not stop till we were far away in the depths of the forest, having travelled nearly thirty miles. We lighted huge fires, for fear of the lions, and stretching ourselves out beside them, were soon fast asleep. Early next morning we were off again, and tramped on for more than three hours, when a halt was called at the head of a gully to look for water, and just then the van of Smith's caravan was seen appearing through the forest. The food was distributed among the hungry porters as soon as all had arrived; the two Smiths came up with the last of the men, so we took advantage of the delay to get breakfast, to hear and tell the news, and to discuss our plans. Breakfast over, we started again, and camped that night at Ulala, on the edge of the forest. Some thieves attempted to get at our goods in the property tent, under cover of the darkness, but were discovered by one of the Wang'uána, who fired at them, and severely wounded one of their number, who however contrived to make his escape. The next day we went to Usuri, and there learnt that on the previous day (Nov. 30th) O'Neill had left for Ng'uru with his caravan. The chief of the district, Penzwa by name, called on us, and as it had now been discovered that the thieves who had entered our camp that previous night belonged to his territory, he sent us a present of a bullock, and begged us to say nothing about the attempted robbery, as it would deter travellers from using that route. On the 4th we went to Ushuri, and stayed a day there to lay in provisions for the long jungle. This district of Iramba was a very fertile one, and corn seemed to be plentiful, and was certainly cheap. Cattle were dear, but goats, fowls, and eggs could easily be obtained; the country was well watered, and the population a large one. There were two or three steep ranges of forest-clad hills where large flocks of guinea-fowl were found, and troops of monkeys. The villages were many of them very prettily situated by running streams, and all were strongly fortified with high fences, or palisades, of stout poles. Near most of the villages were groves of the mahama palms, as their fruit is much prized by the natives.

We left Ushuri on the 6th, as the Masika, or wet season, was fast approaching, and we had received several warnings already, in the shape of thunder-storms, during the fortnight we were there; and we were anxious to get as far north as possible before we were stopped by the rains. The first day's journey took us past numerous villages, for about two hours' march, and then we entered fine forest in which were numbers of adansonias. Then crossing a sort of pass, we entered a well-wooded valley, which gradually widened as we proceeded down it. Early in the second day's march the valley opened out into a wide plain with a low range of hills on either side, the forest rapidly disappeared, and at last we found ourselves in a flat plain stretching in a N.N.W. direction as far as the eye could reach; the soil was a rich black loam, with a dense growth, in most places, of strong coarse grass, which had been burnt over large areas, leaving nothing but blackened stubble. Trees were few and far between, except along the course of some streams, where there were often dense forests. The whole plain bore evident marks of being one vast swamp during the rainy season. The drainage was undoubtedly in a northerly direction, as we found from the marks on the banks of the river-beds, which we crossed, though in a distance of thirty miles the aneroids showed such a slight difference in altitude, that it would have been impossible to ascertain from that alone in what direction the country sloped, and I am inclined to think that this is the Nyakun swamp of Cameron, or at least is connected with it, and that it has been connected with the Nyanza; it may be the bed of a lake which has silted up, or has been drained owing to some gradual alteration in the level of the country. The second day's march was marked by a most terrific squall. We had halted as usual in the middle of the day, and had allowed the caravan to get a good start of us before proceeding. Distant thunder had been heard all the morning, but as it seemed to get no nearer, we paid little attention to it; soon, however, after resuming the march, dark clouds were seen gathering rapidly over the eastern range of hills, bright flashes of lightning were visible, the thunder grew louder and louder, the sky became dark, and there was an ominous calm all around; flocks of green parrots flew screaming past as if to escape the coming tempest, and nature seemed to be holding her breath in expectation of the blast. Nearer and nearer came the storm, its approach being marked by clouds of sand, grass, leaves, and twigs which were whirled along by the gale; darker and darker grew the sky, while, strangest sight of all, a beautiful rainbow spanned the gloomy storm-clouds from which the lightning flashed vividly and the thunder pealed incessantly. We hurried on, hoping to find some shelter, but not a tree was to be seen for miles, and scarcely a bush which could afford the smallest hope of protection from the storm. At last the tempest burst upon us a furious blast of wind, a blinding cloud of sand, a few heavy drops of rain, and then a torrent as if the flood-gates of heaven had been opened. The wind was so tremendous that the rain came almost horizontally, and it was with difficulty that we could keep our feet. We were wet through almost instantly, being quite unprepared for such a deluge. The face of the plain, which had been as dry as the desert, in a few minutes became a gigantic swamp, and we struggled on ankle-deep in mud and water, drenched by the rain, blinded by the lightning, and almost carried off our feet by the wind, till we reached a solitary bush which somewhat broke the force of the tempest; here we stood shivering till the storm abated a little, and then we set off again, and came up with the caravan, halting by the side of a small ravine, the porters looking as miserable as only negroes can look when they have to endure, what is to them the acme of discomfort, a thorough wetting. It was useless to think of proceeding any farther that day; so tents were pitched, and, after many vain attempts, a fire was at length lighted, and we were able to partially dry our saturated clothes.

The next morning rose fair and bright, and we were off at an early hour, the only trace of yesterday's storm being the muddiness of the plain for a short distance (for our camp was near the edge of the track of the storm) and the freshness in the air. The greater part of this day's journey was over a flat, almost treeless tract, covered with short fresh green grass and with large masses of a bulbous plant with a spike of white blossoms (*Chlorophytum affine*). Large herds of buffaloes, zebra, wild donkeys and various species of antelopes were seen at intervals during the day, but the march was much too long a one to allow us to go after any of them. Early in the day we crossed the channel of a considerable stream, and in the evening came to open swampy jungle, where many wading birds were seen, and we camped in a grove of baobab trees, which had a strange, weird look at night when their giant forms were lighted up with the ruddy glow of the camp fires. The next day (December 9th) we had a very long march. About two hours brought us to a low range of hills, and crossing these, we found ourselves in hilly wooded country through which the road wound for many miles; then we entered another plain, crossing late in the day the River Nange, a stream about eighty yards wide, with a uniform depth of three feet, and camped on its western bank. December 10th was our last day in the jungle. We were on the move before daylight, and for the first three hours made very slow progress. There had been heavy rains the previous day, and the soil, which was a tenacious loam, had become a soft sticky mass into which we sank ankle-deep at every step. After a time, however, the ground got harder, and we marched on more briskly; soon the jungle began to get less, and the trees disappeared, only underwood being left, a sure sign of the proximity of man: and at last we emerged on the site of a ruined village, of which no trace remained except a gigantic hedge of a species of euphorbia (*E. antiquorum*), which had once surrounded the village. Two or three miles more brought us to a small collection of témbes called Hambu. Here our whole caravan of Wanyamwézi porters took leave of us, this being the point to which they had engaged to come. They arrayed themselves in their best, coloured pocket-handkerchiefs, large-patterned prints and scarlet blankets, and having bid us most affectionate adieux, left us.

On inquiring for O'Neill we found that he was at another village some three miles from there, called Ng'uru, and we sent off a man with a note to tell him of our arrival. The news, however, had already reached him, and a man soon appeared with a note from him and some clothes for me, which O'Neill had thoughtfully sent over, for all my property being of course with the first caravan, I had not so much as a change of clothes with me. The first thing to be done was to get all our property together and overhaul it, and for that purpose we went over to Ng'uru and took up our abode there, and then transported all the goods of the second caravan in relays by means of our Wang'uána servants and the donkeys.

CHAPTER IV.

NG'URU TO KAGEI AND UKEREWE.

AFTER looking through some of our stores, we found that we had only a small supply left of the cloths most used for barter, and Lieutenant Smith decided to go to Unyanyembe, or Tabora, the well-known Arab trading depôt, which was distant about 100 miles, and purchase a fresh stock, and on December 12th he set off with a few Wang'uána, hoping to be back in ten days or a fortnight.

The work of hiring porters for the next stage of our journey had now to be undertaken, but at present it was useless to attempt it, for, the first rains having fallen, the whole population was employed in preparing the ground for sowing, and until all the seed was sown no men would engage as porters. Lieutenant Smith hoped to bring back a hundred men with him from Unyanyembe. Meantime we were busily engaged in repacking the loads, taking stock of all our property, cleaning tools and machinery, mending tents, saddles, etc., and getting all ready for the journey, as soon as we should get men.

We heard no news of Lieutenant Smith till the 24th, Christmas Eve, when a man arrived bringing a letter from him, and two baskets of mangoes and bananas, which formed a pleasant addition to our Christmas dinner; the letter said that Smith had been much hindered by sickness and other delays, and did not expect to be able to reach Ng'uru for another week at least; so, as the sowing was nearly over and several gangs of men had offered themselves as porters, it was decided that O'Neill and I should make up a small caravan and go on to the Lake, to select a suitable spot for a permanent encampment, and build huts if necessary.

Christmas Day was passed quietly, the only events to break the monotony of the day being an attack on the village by Ruga Ruga, or highwaymen, and a good dinner, the former of which ended in an ignominious flight on the part of the Ruga Ruga without any more mischief being done than a little corn stolen; the latter was prepared by the Doctor, who superintended the commissariat department. We tried hard the previous day to procure a bullock, that we might have the traditional roast beef, but none was to be found, and we fell back on some tinned beef brought out from England; we had also a famous plum-pudding given us in England to take out to Africa, with cheese, fruit, and coffee to conclude.

The next few days were busily employed in preparing for the journey, and after one or two delays we got off on December 30th, having a caravan of between forty and fifty men and twelve donkeys. Two or three miles from Ng'uru brought us to the top of some rising ground from which we had a magnificent view of a fine bold rugged range of hills to the N.N.W., reminding me much of the Sierra Nevada Mountains in Southern Spain. The first day's march, which, as is always the case, was a short one, brought us to a prettily situated group of villages called Masimbo, or "The Springs." There was a great deal of land here under cultivation, and round the villages were quantities of cotton bushes, which looked extremely pretty with their snowy masses of seed and large bright yellow blossoms. Leaving Masimbo, we crossed a steep ridge and plunged at once into a dense jungle, where thick creepers climbed from tree to tree, and the boughs, meeting overhead, shut out the burning rays of the sun, making it deliciously cool, and rendering travelling very pleasant. This jungle swarms with wild animals; elephants, giraffes, rhinoceroses, buffaloes, zebras, various species of antelopes, baboons, monkeys, lions, leopards, &c., were either seen or heard.

After some hours we emerged on to an open plain, and here we met a caravan of grain going to the south; several of the porters were men who had come with O'Neill and myself from the coast, and they stopped and shook hands with us, and seemed much pleased to see us. The northern side of this plain was bounded by a range of wooded hills, and, crossing the western end of them, we proceeded along their base for some distance. Here, not far from the road, we saw a number of baboons, great hairy creatures which walked on all fours, but on noticing us sat up on their haunches and barked like dogs. Another hour brought us to the Monungu, a stream about thirty yards wide, fifteen feet deep in its banks, and with about two feet of water in it. We crossed this river without any difficulty, and encamped in the jungle on the opposite bank. Next day we reached Semía or Semwi, a populous district lying at the foot of the Usanda range of hills; those which we had first seen on leaving Ng'uru. We had made the acquaintance of the chief of the village at which we stayed, on our way up, and he now welcomed us cordially. He had a common wooden chair which he displayed to us with great glee, and a few tin mugs brought with the chair from Zanzibar. The country here is thickly dotted with large adansonias, from the bark of which the natives make a very strong soft rope, which we afterwards found very useful for running rigging. Two days from Semwi brought us to the Livúmbu or Liwúmbu, a considerable stream flowing in an easterly direction, as indeed all the streams did in this part of the country. The people about here were very primitive; all the younger portion of the community dispensed with clothing altogether, and the married women contented themselves with a kilt of skin. After crossing the Livúmbu we entered a forest district, well watered, and with a few villages scattered about in clearings in the jungle. Three marches through this region brought us into the district of Usmao, a flat open table-land, well cultivated, and possessing large herds of cattle. The people seemed very warlike, and they need to be so, for they lived in constant dread of attacks by the Ruga Ruga of Mirambo, this renowned warrior and freebooter, whose capital was some 300 miles distant, having occasionally made raids into this country and carried off the cattle as spoil. Every one here went about well armed, the cattle were sent out to graze under a strong escort, the husbandman hoed up his fields with his spear stuck in the ground beside him, and even the women went in parties to draw water accompanied by armed warriors. Here is the northern limit in this part of Africa of the baobab (*Adansonia digitata*), and I did not meet with it again till north of the Bahr-el-Ghazal, in lat. 12° N.

From this point the character of the country changed; the forest disappeared, and it became more open, with broad grassy plains or valleys, separated from one another by low ridges, crowned with fantastic masses of igneous rocks, looking at a distance like the grey ruins of ancient castles. Stunted jungle or scrub of a species of thorny acacia was sometimes met with, and there large herds of brindled gnu, zebras, and antelopes were found. On Jan. 17th we came to the River Wami (not the Wami of Usagara), a tolerably large stream, which we crossed twice more, and which, after winding about in every possible direction, as many African rivers do, seems to find its way to Jordan's Nullah. We spent three days, the 19th, 20th, and 21st, at a large village called Wama, which was governed by a woman, a very rare occurrence in Africa, as the women are, as a rule, much looked down upon. Here, too, we found that the natives grow rice, a grain which is rarely found south of the Equator, except where Arab or half-breed settlers have introduced it, as the natives of the interior will hardly ever eat it. Leaving this village, we crossed the Wami for the third and last time, and the country soon became more hilly, or rather the rocky ridges became hills, the plains between still being extensive, and over them roamed flocks of bustards and a few ostriches. On January 26th, soon after starting, we saw a number of men coming to meet us, who turned out to be a deputation sent by Kadúma, chief of Kagei (or as Stanley spells it, Kagehyi), to invite us to settle at his village on the shores of the lake; he had heard of our coming, and fearing lest we should go to Mwanza, another village not far from Kagei, and with which he was at war, he had sent these men to secure us. We were delighted to see them, as for several days past our guide had kept saying "To-morrow, Inshallah! we should see the Nyanza." But the farther we went the farther off the Nyanza seemed to be. That evening we stopped at a large village called Wambwa, and were taken to the enclosure belonging to the chief of the place, and, he being away, we pitched our tent near a large tree under which were some old pots. Soon after the chief arrived, and when he saw where our tent was placed, got into a terrible state of excitement, as these pots proved to be his "medicine," for making rain, and he feared that the close proximity of the "white devils" would spoil his medicine. The chiefs in this part of Africa are always the rain-makers of the tribe, and keep up their authority by their supposed skill in this matter, and if they lose that skill they lose their position, and consequently are very jealous about anything that, as they think, will injure or lessen their supposed power. Some time afterwards, when living at Kagei, I put out my rain-gauge at the commencement of the rains, and the chief Kadúma came and entreated me to take it in again, as white man's medicine was stronger than black men's, and he was afraid I should stop the rain.

On Saturday, Jan. 27th, we got our first glimpse

of the great lake; after the march was over and the tent pitched, we walked out to some rising ground from which, we were told, the Nyanza could be seen, and there, far away on the dim horizon, was the shadowy outline of a large mountain, and at its foot a grey line, which was the long-looked-for Victoria Nyanza. The next day's march led through swampy valleys, between rocky barren ridges, and past large villages, whose dusky inhabitants poured out in crowds to see the strange white men, and we camped out at night under the shade of an enormous fig tree. Before daylight next morning all were astir, in a state of great excitement, for to-day our long six months' journey was to end, and before another sun set we should stand on the shores of that great inland sea and bathe in its cool waters. Our men arrayed themselves in their best clothes, and loaded their guns ready for a salute when we should see the great lake. We trudged merrily on through a long swampy valley, and climbed a steep hill from which we were to see the village of Kagei All were on the tiptoe of expectation, when on turning a corner in the road a glorious view burst upon us. There, 300 or 400 feet below us, stretched the wide expanse of deep blue water sparkling in the rays of the morning sun; far away on the horizon was the graceful outline of the island of Ukeréwe, and on the east the bold mass of the Majita mountain; two or three small islands with some large white rocks broke the monotony of its azure surface; from our feet the ground sloped rapidly down to the shore, clothed with a brilliant emerald carpet of young corn; fringing the lake was a belt of banana plants, and large fig trees, from which the conical roofs of houses peeped out, and their wreaths of blue smoke curling up into the calm air showed the

KAGEI FROM BEHIND THE VILLAGE.

presence of man; the murmur of the waves on the strand stole softly to our ears, and over all was a sky, the deep rich blue of which Italy could scarcely equal. Our approach was soon made known to the villagers by firing, blowing of horns, and all manner of unearthly noises, and they turned out in crowds to meet us. On nearing the village the chief Kadúma, a tall and rather good-looking man, though clad in most filthy clothes, came to greet us, and bade us welcome to his village, followed by Songoro, a negro trader who had an establishment here, and who was dressed in a clean white robe, looking cool and comfortable. After the usual compliments had been exchanged and flowery speeches made, Kadúma took us to one end of the village which he had set apart for our use, and showed us a large roomy hut which he had destined for the Wazungu; however O'Neill and I preferred to remain in our tent, which we pitched beside it, and stored most of our goods in the hut. Then we strolled down to the beach and had a most refreshing bathe in the cool waters of the Nyanza, and at night we lay down to rest with hearts full of thankfulness to Almighty God who had brought us thus far on our journey, and were soon soothed to sleep by the lullaby of the waves breaking on the rocky shore.

I had thus been exactly six months from Bagamoyo to Kagei, including all the various delays on the road. The actual number of marches was seventy-four, and the whole distance travelled about eight hundred miles, thus giving an average of nearly eleven miles a day.

The first thing we did, after getting matters a little settled, was to write letters to England, telling our friends of our arrival, and to the Smiths, whom we expected to follow us very soon, to in-form them where we had settled, and these were despatched on February 1st. On the 6th two canoes arrived from Lukonge, king of Ukeréwe, bringing us a present of goats and sheep, and a request that we would go over and see him; so on the 8th I returned with the messengers, O'Neill remaining behind to take care of the stores, and to receive the Smiths if they came. The canoes in which we crossed to the island were clumsy dug-outs, which were old and cracked and leaked terribly. The canoemen, who had no idea of keeping time, but paddled each on his own account, beguiled the time with songs, one of which was thus translated to me: "Many men are dead, for them we are sorry, for they never saw the white man; we have seen the white man and are glad." They also stopped at frequent intervals to refresh themselves with water snuff; this is prepared by filling a small bottle gourd with tobacco, two twigs are placed crosswise below the neck to keep the tobacco in, the gourd is then filled up with water and allowed to stand some time; this water snuff is then drawn up into the nostrils and retained there for several minutes, and as those who use it are thus obliged to speak only through the mouth, they all seem as if they had bad colds in the head. The first day we only got as far as the island of Vezi, a small rocky island abounding in waterfowl; there was one wretched little village on it, the inhabitants of which subsist mainly by fishing, as only a small quantity of grain could be grown there. The natives also eat a small fly like a gnat, but with green wings; these flies travel about in vast swarms which must contain countless millions, looking at a distance like clouds of brown smoke; they are borne along by the wind for considerable distances, and I have often encountered them on the Nyanza far out of sight of land. The islanders catch these flies, as they alight on bushes and shrubs, in a conical basket which is whirled rapidly round by means of a handle fixed radially to the rim.

There was a storm during the night, which delayed us for some hours, and when at last we did set off the sea was still somewhat rough, and our clumsy craft kept shipping water, so that I and my bedding got thoroughly soaked. By four o'clock we had reached the island of Ukeréwe and kept close to the shore. The island here terminated in a fine bold rocky coast, there being deep water close in shore, with some picturesque rocky islets at no great distance. A few natives were fishing, with rod and line, from the rocks, and stared curiously at me. We kept along the shore for some distance. till we reached a spot where the cliffs receded from the water's edge, and guiding the canoe through a fringe of ambatch bushes, we disembarked close to a large village. We went up to the village, and a hut having been cleared for my use, I soon had an admiring crowd round me, criticising every movement I made, and every feature and article of my dress. At night a violent storm came on, and the roof of the hut being anything but watertight, the rain came through upon me, and this combined with the presence of a colony of rats, which kept racing over me as I lay in bed, completely drove away sleep. The next day I went over to Bukindo, the capital of the island, which is a large straggling village with a number of irregular streets. Each hut stands in a small plot of ground where maize, millet, pumpkins, tobacco and other plants are grown. The town has a ring-fence all round it, access being had through gates, which are closed by ponderous slabs of wood suspended from a bar, and which are so heavy that it requires two men to open them; and for this reason they are usually propped up during the day, but let down at night, when they are further secured by a transverse bar passed through holes in the gate-posts. In the centre of the town is a large enclosure (formed by a high palisade of whole trees) where the king lives: it contains the huts of his wives, who number about thirty, the hut where the royal drums are kept, and a large number of storehouses for grain: these latter consist of large cylindrical baskets plastered with clay and raised above the ground on poles, and covered with a thatched roof. The king's enclosure has a gateway similar to those which give access to the town, and just outside is the court-house, a large circular building with open walls and a conical thatched roof supported on a forest of poles, where the king holds councils and conducts trials and receives his visitors. On these occasions he brings his throne with him, a large stool of native manufacture, ornamented with crocodile's teeth, lion's claws, and hippopotamus' tusks. Lukonge, the king of Ukeréwe, was young, and, for a negro, rather a handsome-looking man, and showed great intelligence, though his knowledge of the outside world was limited in the extreme; and on a subsequent occasion, when Lieut. Smith, O'Neill and I paid him a visit, he wished to know if there were any more white men in the world besides our three selves. He expressed a wish that white men should settle in his country and teach his people, and asked me if I would stay with him. Near Bukindo, the capital, the trader Songoro had an establishment where he grew rice, onions, tomatoes, and other vegetables foreign to the country, and near here, too, he was building a dhow or native craft to enable him to carry on better his trade in slaves. The greater part of the island of Ukeréwe is covered with forest, and it is connected with the mainland by a narrow swampy strip of land, through which are one or two narrow channels, known as Rugeshi. Nearly the whole of the island is under Lukonge's dominion; there is however a small part at the north-west of it, called Ilangara, which is governed by another chief, who was constantly at war with Lukonge; but since I last visited the island the people of Ilangara have been completely exterminated by the Waganda. I remained three days with Lukonge, and left him on February 12th; that night I spent at a village near the lake on the eastern side of the island. Here I found some hippopotamus hunters, who showed me the spear they used for killing these animals; it was a huge unwieldy weapon with a handle of heavy wood fourteen or fifteen feet long, the blade being about fifteen inches long, with only one barb, and just below the head a strong rope was securely tied to the handle. I was delayed another day on the island, leaving early on the morning of the 14th, and accomplished the return voyage in one day. I found O'Neill well and jolly, but there was no news of the Smiths. On February 19th two men arrived bringing, to our great delight, a packet of letters from England, for we had received no news since leaving Mpwapwa, more than four months previously. At the time that the men left Ng'uru both the Smiths were still there. Two or three weeks passed without any news, though we were expecting every day to hear of the approach of the second caravan. Our time was spent mainly in writing, and working at Swahili and the language of Kagei, Kisukuma. We had intended, on arriving at the southern end of the lake, to make preparations for building a boat, by cutting timber and erecting workshops; but on arriving at

Kagei we found that there was not a stick of timber to be had, suitable for boat-building, within many miles; so that we could do nothing. At length on March 4th a messenger arrived from Lieut. Smith saying that he and Dr. Smith had both been very ill, and that many of their men had deserted; so O'Neill and I sent off some men and donkeys to meet them and assist them. On March 29th Dr. Smith arrived, having been carried in a hammock, for he was so weak he could not stand. Up to Ng'uru he had not had an hour's illness, though the rest of us had been down with fever repeatedly; but soon after O'Neill and I started he had his first attack of ague, followed by rheumatism, which had terribly reduced him, and he looked a mere shadow of what he had been. Lieut. Smith arrived on April the 1st with a detachment of the caravan, the first having come with Dr. Smith, and the third being behind under the charge of an interpreter. As soon as all the goods had arrived, we set to work overhauling the whole of our stores, and housing and cleaning tools and machinery. We had brought with us a small cedar boat in sections; she was built by Messenger of Teddington, and was intended to be used on the Wami or Kingani in keeping up communication between Zanzibar and Mpwapwa. But those rivers proving unnavigable, Lieut. Smith decided to take her up country: she had been built in sections in order that she might be easily carried by men if there were occasion; these sections, however, proved to be much too heavy to be carried, even by four men, and had to be further subdivided. This boat, the *Daisy*, was intended for a steam-launch, and was fitted with twin screws, but her boiler was too heavy to transport, with the limited number of men at our disposal, and so it was left at Bagamoyo.

As might be expected after an overland journey of eight hundred miles, the sections of the *Daisy* arrived at Kagei in a somewhat battered condition, and when we first came to examine her it seemed an almost hopeless task to make her seaworthy; however there was no alternative except to build a new boat altogether, so the native carpenters were set to work under O'Neill's direction, and in a few weeks the little craft seemed in a fair way to become a sound, useful boat. As originally built, she was forty-three feet long over all, six feet wide, and four feet deep, and had three sections, but we cut six feet out of the middle section, for, as sent out, she was too long and narrow to encounter the stormy seas of the Nyanza; we also added another six inches of height to her gunwale, and fitted her with three lug-sails. It soon, however, became clear that, however well the *Daisy* might do for light work, she would never be strong enough to carry cargo of any weight; so it was proposed that we should buy the dhow which Songoro was building at Ukeréwe, and which he was willing to sell, as it would answer our purpose and save us the trouble of building another boat. Accordingly, Lieutenant Smith went over to Ukeréwe to inspect the dhow, and on his return on May 3rd decided to buy her. That same day, Dr. Smith was seized with dysentery; he had been rapidly improving since he reached Kagei, and though still far from strong, yet was beginning to look more like himself. But this terrible disease took a firm hold of him, and spite of all efforts he gradually sank. On the morning of May 11th he seemed decidedly better, and when breakfast was ready we left him quietly sleeping; after breakfast, Lieutenant Smith went into the hut to see how he was, and immediately after called O'Neill and me. "I am afraid he is going," he whispered, but it needed no one to tell us so, death was plainly written on his face; and in a few minutes more he passed away, calmly, peacefully, like a child hushed to sleep in its mother's arms: a death strangely in contrast to that which, ere that year closed, was to overtake two of those standing round his bed. We laid him to rest that evening close by the shore of the lake, while the dusky forms of those for whose sake he gave up all, stood reverently by and wondered not to see the white men weep. We turned our steps homewards, sorrowful and silent. Few words were spoken that night, and the thought uppermost in our minds was "Who will next be called?"

We raised a mound of stones over the grave, and cut a short inscription on a block of granite, which we placed above all. And there he sleeps within sound of the waves of that glorious inland sea, another of that noble band of Christian heroes who have died for Africa.

The *Daisy* progressed slowly, and it was not till the beginning of June that she was ready to be launched. Before our expedition left England letters had been sent to Mtesa, king of Uganda, and to Rumanika, king of Karagwe, telling them of our wish to settle in their country, and asking them to send word to us if they were willing to receive us, but up to this time we had received no answer from either of these monarchs, and thinking it best to wait a little longer for news, we settled to go over to Ukerewe and complete the dhow which we had bought. Accordingly, on June 15th, we left Kagei with a large cargo of goods and a number of passengers; some of the Wang'uána remained at Kagei to take care of the stores, of which the greater part was left there. We weighed anchor at half-past six, and having a strong breeze, made a rapid run, reaching the entrance to the Rugeshi straits in three and a half hours. The water channel through the straits was choked with grass, papyrus, water-lilies, and other aquatic plants, and it took us a long time to get the *Daisy* through, for, being heavily loaded, she

DR. SMITH'S GRAVE AT KAGEL.

was rather deep in the water. At length, about half-past two, we reached Bukindo, and pitched our tent on a sandy strip of ground on the borders of the jungle, and near the place where the dhow was being built. The next few days were occupied in making a camp, while Lieutenant Smith returned to Kagei for another cargo of stores. At last, on June 22nd, news came from Uganda. I had been away in the forest all day with the carpenters, cutting timber for the dhow, and as I was returning in the evening O'Neill met me with the good news that canoes had arrived from Uganda, bringing letters of invitation from Mtesa. So, after reading the letters and talking over the matter, it was finally settled that Smith and I should go on in a few days to Uganda and see how the land lay, and whether Mtesa was really anxious for us to settle in his country; and if this were so, that I should remain in Uganda, and that Smith should return to Ukerewe to O'Neill, who, meantime, was to stay on the island and complete the dhow. Next day some more canoes arrived from Uganda, bringing another letter from Mtesa, begging us to come at once; so it was arranged that Smith and I should leave on the 25th, and all hands were set to work preparing the *Daisy* for the voyage, and collecting provisions, for we expected to be several days at sea. Songoro, who had been to Uganda several times, prophesied that we should be a fortnight on the way.

CHAPTER V.

LIFE IN UGANDA.

THE morning of the 25th of June rose bright and sunny, with a strong breeze blowing from the south-east. A good supply of fresh meat, fowls, sweet potatoes and flour was put on board the *Daisy*, and a perfect stack of firewood. All were on board, including two of the Waganda sent by Mtesa to act as pilots, and, by half-past nine, the boat was pushed off, the sails hoisted, the flag unfurled, and we had started on our voyage across the unknown waters. The breeze blew fresh, and, with all sail set, we flew through the water, past villages, banana groves, hills and capes. The island of Ukeréwe was soon passed, and in less than an hour we were off the strait that separates it from Ukára. Smith wished to land on this island to take bearings in order to fix its position, and we ran along within a short distance of the shore to look for a suitable landing-place. The general appearance of the island was bleak and barren; there were large tracts of dry brown grass, through which wandered a few wretched-looking cattle; two conical hills rose to a height of 200 or 300 feet above the lake, in the centre of the island, but they were rugged and stony, with only a few stunted bushes scattered thinly over their sides; nearer the shore, however, the land seemed more fertile, as villages of grass huts were visible, surrounded by gardens and groves of bananas. The coast-line was irregular, narrow bays alternating with bold rocky promontories, where some of the natives were fishing, and we were much struck by their diminutive size as they sat perched up on the rocks, looking more like monkeys than men. We coasted along the whole of the eastern side of the island before finding a landing-place; but at the extreme north-east corner we discovered a deep narrow inlet, with high rocky shores and a sandy beach at the farther end, where a number of canoes were drawn up. There were two villages of small grass huts on the rocks, and crowds of natives assembled to watch us, all of them being armed with bows and arrows, spears or slings. We were able now to judge better of their size, which was decidedly small, and I should think that the average height of the 200 or 300 natives gathered there was under five feet; they seemed about the same size as the Akkas or Tikitikis, of whom I afterwards saw a specimen at Rumbek in the Bahr-el-Ghazal province. As we went up the bay the crowd raised a loud musical shout, which proved to be their war-cry, though we did not take it to be such, so different was it to any war-cry we had hitherto heard. We went up the creek at a great rate, intending to run the boat on the beach, but in order to do this we had to make two tacks across the creek, and this happily checked her speed. As we neared the beach the order was given to lower the sails, and at this instant the man on the look-out called "Rocks on the port bow," so the boat was brought sharply round and ran broadside on to the beach. As the keel grounded on the sand we were greeted with a volley of arrows, stones, and spears, and the whole of the crew, who were stowing the main and mizen sails, threw themselves down in the boat, with the exception of one man, who seized an oar and pushed her bows out. Not a moment was to be lost if we were to escape with our lives, for the natives were running up, and would have speared the crew as they lay in the bottom of the boat; so I snatched up an oar, jumped up on the stern sheets, and with a vigorous push sent the *Daisy* out into the water. Just at that moment, a man standing about thirty yards off fired an arrow at me, which struck me on the upper part of the left arm, and remained in the wound. I threw down the oar and pulled out the arrow, which proved to be a poisoned one. I turned round to tell Smith, and for the first time saw that he had been wounded too, for the blood was pouring down his face from a wound over the eye, caused by a sling stone. We had a medicine chest handy, and our wounds were speedily dressed, Smith himself, though in great pain, sucking the wound in my arm. Two of the crew were hurt; one had a scratched finger and the other a slight wound on the arm, and both were crying like babies. The fore sail had never been lowered, so the boat was soon carried out of reach of missiles; when the crew discovered this they got up, suddenly becoming very brave, and expressed great anxiety to return and fight the natives, but were not allowed to put their valour to the test, and were much astonished that we would not let them fire on our assailants. Our forbearance, however, bore good fruit, for the Wakara were so much surprised that we did not retaliate, that they subsequently visited our camp at Ukeréwe, and apologised for having attacked us; they had taken us for slave-traders! As soon as we found ourselves in the open sea, we shaped our course for Uganda. Contrary to our expectation, the breeze kept up the whole day and during the night also, so that we attained an average speed of between five and six knots an hour. Lieutenant Smith was in such pain that he was disabled, and I had consequently to take the management of the boat.

About seven o'clock the next morning (26th), we came in sight of land, which our pilots declared to be the coast of Uganda, but it proved to be only some rocky uninhabited islands. In about two hours more we entered what looked like the mouth of a large river, but which we found to be only a narrow channel between some islands. Our two pilots were quite at a loss to know where they were, so, seeing some people who had come to the beach to stare at the strange craft, we put them ashore to make inquiries. The scenery here was superb, as most of the land was lofty, with steep banks or precipitous cliffs, clothed with a wealth of vegetation for which I was quite unprepared. Indeed, no traveller in Africa can form any just estimate of the fertility and luxuriance of the vegetation within the rainy belt, unless he has actually visited it, for the forests outside this zone, even in the river valleys, are poor when compared with those within the region of perpetual rain. When our guides returned, having obtained some idea of our position, we resumed our voyage, and during the rest of the day we were occupied in threading our way through the winding channels between groups of lovely islands. Night fell, and found us still some way from the mainland; at last, however, about eight o'clock, we cast anchor off a large village, and our guides, who told us we had now really reached Uganda, left us to convey the intelligence to Mtesa.

Next day we were visited by the chiefs of the neighbouring villages, who brought us presents of milk, fruit, meat, and vegetables, and our Wang'uána brought wonderful accounts of the beauty of the land and the marvellous abundance of provisions. On the 28th a chief named Simbuzi arrived with a present of goats and cattle from Mtesa, and a request that we would come on at once; so we disembarked, and having discharged all the cargo, had the *Daisy* dragged up high and dry out of the reach of the waves. The following day we started for the capital with a large escort and a number of men carrying our property. The village at which we had landed, by name Ntebbi, was just at the entrance to Murchison Bay, and, on leaving this place, we got a fine view of the greater part of it. Our road led past several large hamlets surrounded by extensive groves of plantains, and with stately mpafu trees casting a deep cool shadow. We skirted along the shores of the bay in a northerly direction, passing through magnificent forest glades, dim and cool, with a luxuriant undergrowth of ferns. In the middle of the day we halted at a small village, and, on resuming the march, turned in an easterly direction, the road leading along a high ridge from which magnificent views of the lake were obtained, and a glorious panorama of hill and dale, diversified with splendid forest. We spent that night at a large village, and the following day went on to Rubaga, Mtesa's capital, which we reached on June 30th. We were taken to a group of huts set apart for our use, in sight of the palace.

July 2nd was the day fixed for our first interview with Mtesa. From an early hour numbers of natives, dressed in the picturesque costume of the country, had been seen hurrying past our compound towards the palace. About eight o'clock Simbuzi and another chief, Serúte by name, attended by a few soldiers, came to fetch us, and we set off dressed in our best, accompanied by some of our servants bearing the presents for the king. About 150 yards through a narrow lane with gardens on either side, brought us into a magnificent road some eighty yards wide, leading straight up to the palace, which stood on the top of a hill about three-quarters of a mile distant. At the farther end of this road, outside the palace gates, was a vast crowd of natives, as noisy and inquisitive as any London mob, but much better behaved. As we drew near the palace enclosure, a sliding door was thrown open and a file of soldiers, dressed in white uniforms and armed with guns, came out to meet us, and then, turning round, marched before us. The palace itself is approached through a number of courts, separated from each other by high fences with sliding doors between, and, in each of these courts, two files of soldiers were drawn up, who presented arms as we approached. On entering the last court a number of drummers beat a most deafening salute, and a bugle rang out the call to dinner. Hat in hand, we entered the hall of the palace, a fine room about seventy feet long. All the great chiefs of the country were here seated along the walls on wooden stools; they were dressed in Arab chogas of various colours, and presented a brilliant spectacle. All rose as we entered, and we made our way up to the farther end, where stood Mtesa, dressed in Turkish costume and wearing a handsome sword; he shook hands with us and motioned us to two seats, and we had time, while the drums were beating, to survey the scene and make mental observations on the king and his court. Mtesa at that time was a very fine-looking man, tall and slender, with a Coptic type of features, delicate hands, and large expressive eyes. Silence having been ordered, our guide was called, and narrated his adventures, his finding us at Ukeréwe and the return journey to Uganda; then our letters of introduction were read and our presents produced. Smith apologised for the small number of the latter, some having been stolen on the road, and Mtesa remarked " Great rivers swallow up small ones, and now that I have seen your faces I do not think of anything else." Soon after our interview terminated, and we returned to our house favourably impressed with all that we had seen. In the afternoon we had another interview with Mtesa, and explained fully to him the object of our coming to his country; we also asked him to give us land to build on, permission to hold services in his palace on Sundays, and to teach his people. He gave us land at once, and promised to send men to help in building a house. We wished to build a brick house with two storeys, but he would not consent to that; so we agreed that he should build us a house in native fashion, but according to our plans, with doors and windows, and this was at once begun.

The next Sunday, according to our agreement, I held a service at the palace, about 100 persons being present, including Mtesa himself. The service was conducted in Swahili, for Mtesa understood that language perfectly, and many of the chiefs spoke it more or less.

The new house, which was situated in a large garden or plantation of about two and a half or three acres in extent, progressed but slowly, and it was three weeks before the roof was on. Meantime one or other of us was constantly up at the palace, talking with Mtesa or speaking to his people. At first Smith was unable to get out much, as he suffered terrible pain in his wounded eye; for, as we afterwards discovered, a piece of glass from his spectacles, which he was wearing at the time of the attack, had been driven right into the eye, completely destroying the sight.

Smith remained with me in Uganda till July 30th, when he left to return to Ukeréwe. His intention was to help O'Neill to finish the dhow, and then to explore the Shimiyu and Ruana rivers, which both flow into Speke Gulf, to ascertain if they were of any value as a means of approaching the Nyanza, and to survey the southern part of the lake (a work for which, being a naval officer, he was well fitted). This having been accomplished, he hoped to return to Uganda with O'Neill and any other who might by that time have reached the Lake. I walked some distance on the road towards Ntebbi with him, and, on parting, he promised to return as soon as possible. Poor fellow! I little thought it was the last shake of the hand I should receive from him in this world. I walked slowly home, realising for the first time that I was alone. Alone as far as all human fellowship and sympathy were concerned, but still not alone, for God was watching over me.

About a week after Smith's departure, I moved into the new house, which had a fine view of the palace from the verandah, and at once began getting the garden into order. I had a number of seeds which I had brought from England, a good many choice vegetables and useful plant seeds having been kindly given me by the authorities at Kew, through Professor Thiselton Dyer; only a few, however, of these came up, and among them the *Eucalyptus globulus,* which for a time did well and grew rapidly, then suddenly all the young plants died in a few days, probably from my ignorance of how to treat them or to regulate the amount of moisture. I also sowed a quantity of wheat and onions, which both did very well, and planted cassava and sugarcane; and later on, when the rains began, I cleared a piece of swamp at the bottom of my garden, and sowed it with rice, which throve astonishingly. Near the house I sowed a few flower seeds, and when the plants came into blossom, they made the place look quite bright. These flowers were a great puzzle to the natives; when they began to blossom, they were much struck by them, and wanted to know what they were. "Were they food?" "No." "Were they medicine?" "No." "What were they, then?" "Oh, only to look at." But *that* they would not believe; that a man should be such a fool as to take the trouble of cultivating plants only to look at was more than they could credit, and so at last some one who had seen me out sketching with my colour-box came to the sagacious conclusion that they must be "paint."

Meantime I was busy working at Kiganda and forming a vocabulary by the help of Mufta (the young negro left here in 1875 by Stanley), and of Simbuzi, the chief already mentioned, and who used to come and see me nearly every day. I was constantly up at the palace, and had frequent interviews with Mtesa, generally at his luchiko, a council which was held almost daily, and which was attended by the principal chiefs of the country. Frequent opportunities presented themselves for religious discussions, in which Mtesa showed an immense amount of shrewdness. Things went on thus quietly for some time, there being but few incidents to break the monotony of the weeks. One somewhat alarming event happened, however, and that was the discovery of a huge python or boa constrictor in my garden. I had a few goats which had been given me as presents by Mtesa and his chiefs, and these were allowed to graze in a waste piece of ground at the bottom of my garden. Two or three of these goats had disappeared since I came to the new house in a most mysterious manner; they could not well have been stolen, for they disappeared during the day while my men were with them, and at night they were kept in a hut where one of the servants slept. I was greatly puzzled to know what had become of them, till one afternoon, when I was sitting in my verandah reading, one of my servants came rushing up to the house exclaiming that they had found a python; so I fetched a rifle, and, slipping in a couple of cartridges, went to look for it. At the bottom of the garden I found all my men standing round a clump of bushes in which they said the reptile was lying, and they pointed to an opening where they said I could see it. I looked and looked again, but could perceive nothing but what I thought to be some withered leaves; at last, however, I saw that these brown and yellow leaves were the markings of the head of an immense snake, and taking careful aim at it, I fired. The smoke hung so thick about the ground for some seconds that we could see nothing, and when it cleared away, the reptile was gone. This was alarming; I must have missed it, and the creature, roused from its torpor by the report, might any minute fasten on one of us. My men however declared that it was hit, and began searching carefully in the rank grass, which was about five feet high, and soon we saw some reeds a few yards off moving. The men at once began beating these down, and one of them catching sight of the python, threw a spear at it and wounded it; this brought it struggling and writhing out of the grass, and getting a good view of it, I put a bullet into the thickest part of its body, and broke its spine, thus rendering it perfectly helpless. A rope was then fetched and tied round it, and it was dragged up to the house for examination. On measurement it proved to be about fourteen feet three inches long, and thirty inches in circumference at the thickest part of the body. We then found that my first bullet had passed right through the head, but without touching the brain. These reptiles are very common in Uganda, and just about the time that I had killed this one, one of Mtesa's numerous wives was swallowed by one.

For some time after Smith's departure, Mtesa was extremely friendly, and supplied me pretty liberally with food, but afterwards he became very remiss in this respect, and left me for weeks at a time without any. Smith also, thinking that the supplies from the palace would be kept up with the same liberality as at first, had left me comparatively few cloths and beads, and I was often very much puzzled how to get a meal. Mtesa, too, began to bully me, to try and get me to promise him arms and ammunition; when we first came he broached this subject, and seemed much disappointed at our refusal to have anything to do with the matter, and for a long time he never referred to it again. But after Smith left, hoping, I suppose, to find me more compliant now that I was alone, he was perpetually bringing up the subject and laying traps for me, to try and get me to promise to make him guns, or at least to assist him in procuring arms. Both these things, of course, I persistently refused to do, and in consequence I was in his black books for some time. One of the ways in which he showed his displeasure was by turning me out of the house he had given us. As I afterwards found, this was at the suggestion of one Hamis, an Arab employé of Said bin Salim, governor of Unyanyembe, and Burton's and Speke's former Ras Kafilah. Mtesa wanted at first to send me into some wretched little huts as bad as could be, but I absolutely refused to stir till he built me a decent house, and this he at last consented to do. I had tried hard to buy land when we first settled in Uganda, and had begged Mtesa to

let me give him something for that on which the
house was built, as that would have given us a right
to it, which the natives would have respected, but
Mtesa could never be induced to sell in any way.

When Smith left Uganda, he said he hoped to
be back there by the end of October, but I heard
nothing about him till November the 11th, when I
received a budget of letters from England, which
Smith had sent on by an Arab. I had not had a line
from England since February, and it may well be
imagined what a delight it was to get these letters
and papers, though they were most of them fifteen
months old. A letter from Smith said that the
mail had been brought with a caravan of stores by
an Englishman named Morton, who had left again
for the coast, that the dhow was nearly finished, and
that when that was done and he had explored the
Shimiyu, he and O'Neill hoped to come on to Uganda.
Another month had passed away, I had moved into
my new house, and matters were going on much as
before, when one morning, as I was walking up to
the palace, I was overtaken by a negro trader
named Sungura, or the Rabbit, who lived in Uganda,
and he told me that a white man had arrived in
Uganda from the North, that his name was Abdul
Amíni, and that he was sent by Colonel Gordon to
see Mtesa. Of course I was anxious to see this
" Mzungu," but he was ill for some time after he got
to the capital, and Mtesa, who did not wish me to

see him, put all possible obstacles in my way. At last, however, on December 27th, I met him at Mtesa's court, and he proved to be Dr. Emin Effendi (now Bey), who had been sent by Colonel Gordon on a diplomatic errand to Mtesa. Dr. Emin seemed much surprised to see me, and asked if I had just arrived in Uganda, and was immensely astonished when I told him that I had been there six months. He had known of our mission, and had expected to have heard of our arrival, and on entering Uganda had repeatedly inquired if there were any news of us, but was always told that there was none; and when he asked Mtesa himself, he received the same answer, that nothing had been heard of us. The Doctor, who spoke good English, gave me all the latest European news, which was some nine months more recent than any I had, and kindly offered to do anything for me that he could. On leaving the palace we walked together down the hill, followed by a large crowd, and on reaching the turning down to my house, I invited Dr. Emin to return home with me, and we both proceeded towards it, but had not got far when three or four chiefs came rushing after us, and insisted on the Doctor returning to his own quarters.

The next day I went up to the palace again, hoping either to see Dr. Emin or to get permission to visit him, but without success. Mtesa, however, told me that he had heard that O'Neill had reached

Ntebbi, and would be at Rubaga in a day or two; of Smith he said there was no news, but I concluded that O'Neill had had charge of the *Daisy*, that she, being the better sailer, had arrived first, and that Smith would shortly follow in the dhow. So I returned home with a glad heart to prepare to receive them. I heard nothing more, however, that week, and on the morning of Sunday, 30th, I went up to the palace to hold the usual service. There was an unusually large attendance, and during the service a man came and told me that Hassáni, our interpreter, who had been with Smith and O'Neill, had come, and wished to speak to me, and I told him to wait till service was over. After service I was preparing to leave, when Hassáni suddenly appeared with two or three other men, and kneeling down before Mtesa, said in Swahili, "Seyidi, bwana Smith bwana O'Neilli na Wang'uána wao wote pia wamekufa; Lukonge wamewaua." ("Your majesty, Mr. Smith and Mr. O'Neill and all their Wang'uána are dead; Lukonge has killed them.")

I could hardly believe my ears; the blow was so sudden and so severe, that it almost took away my breath. So, after putting a few questions to Hassáni, I told Mtesa that I must go home and think about it. When I got home I cross-questioned Hassáni, but could not get much out of him beyond the fact that the dhow had been wrecked, and that, some dispute having arisen about her, between Lukonge and Smith, the Wakerewe had attacked and murdered Smith, O'Neill, and their men, and also Songoro the trader, from whom the dhow was purchased, and who happened to be with them at the time. I thought over the matter, and decided that at all risks I must go down to Kagei, or if necessary to Ukeréwe, to inquire into it. In the evening I went up to speak to Mtesa about it, and on my way met one of the principal chiefs, Chambalango by name, who said Mtesa was very angry Lukeréwe had killed his "guests," and that he talked about sending a thousand canoes to punish him. I told Mtesa that I had made up my mind to go to Kagei and find out all I could about the murder of Smith and O'Neill, and asked him to do nothing till we returned. He quite approved of my going, and said he did not think Lukonge would have dared to kill white men, and his (Mtesa's) guests too, and might be only detaining them as prisoners in order to extort a heavy ransom. He offered also to send two or three men with me, and to this I agreed.

Before leaving, however, I was anxious to see Dr. Emin, and get him to forward letters for me to England: so, the following morning, I went up to the palace, and asked Mtesa to let me go to see the Doctor; after some hesitation he consented, but said I must go at once; and selected several men to go with me. I suspected that Mtesa's objection to my visiting Dr. Emin was the fear that I should send letters through him to Colonel Gordon, and this I afterwards found was the case, and the reason of hurrying me off in this way was to prevent me returning home to get any letters which I might have written. However, I was prepared for this, and having written my letters the previous evening, had brought them with me. I found Dr. Emin living in a nice hut on the road to Nabulagalla, Mtesa's other capital, and about two miles from Rubaga. He welcomed me very warmly, and I spent the greater part of the day with him, exchanging notes with him and receiving much valuable information. On leaving, Dr. Emin gave me a number of medicines of which I was in great need, for the small stock which I had brought with me from Kagei had long been exhausted under the frequent demands made upon it by the natives; he also gave me a quantity of tea, soup, spices and other good things, and last, but not least, a bundle of English newspapers. I in return gave him some objects of natural history and a copy of my meteorological observations during the six months I had been in Uganda. I also entrusted a packet of letters to the Doctor, choosing a moment when all Mtesa's men had left the hut to slip them into a box. I had made it a rule always to have two or three letters begun, so that should an opportunity of sending a mail occur, I might have something ready to send at a moment's notice.

The following day was spent in waiting for Mtesa's men who were to accompany me, but who did not turn up till evening. I left Rubaga on January 2nd, 1878, and reached Ntebbi at noon the following day, the remainder of that day being spent in getting the *Daisy* ready for sea, and collecting provisions. We got off early in the morning of the 4th, with a light breeze from the N.E., and kept among the islands all day. At night the wind died completely away, so we anchored near an island, intending to wait for daylight to go on; but, about midnight, a violent storm broke on us, and the men, fearing that the *Daisy* would drag her anchor (as the bottom was a bad one), begged me to go farther out, which I did, but in the darkness got on the top of a sandbank with only a few feet of water on it, and where there was a terrific swell: fearing, however, that we should get on the rocks, I anchored there, and spent the rest of the night tossing about in a most violent manner.

The storm left a good breeze behind it, and as soon as the east was grey, we weighed anchor and ran rapidly on for three or four hours. About noon we got clear of the islands, and then the breeze died suddenly away, a dead calm ensuing, relieved only by occasional puffs of wind; and this continued all night, so that when we woke up on the morning of the 6th, we found that we had only made about four miles since the previous evening. There was not a breath of wind the whole day, the sea being as smooth as glass, without a ripple to break the calm surface, and our boat lay like

> A painted ship upon a painted ocean,

with a scorching sun overhead and a fierce glare from the water. At night I got the men to row for some hours by promising them a bullock when we reached Kagei, and we made pretty good progress, so that in the morning an island was just visible on the southern horizon. A breeze sprang up too, and we made about three knots an hour. Before long, however, storm-clouds began to gather in the S.E. and N.W., and about ten o'clock the wind shifted to the S.E.; we tried tacking, but did not make much progress. It soon became clear that we were between two storms, and that if possible we must get out of their track, so, having noticed what I thought to be a low barren island to the west at no great distance, I turned the *Daisy's* head in that direction. This supposed island proved afterwards to be the hilly coast of Uzongora, distant some thirty miles. The wind had begun to freshen now, the lightning gleamed more brightly, and the thunder rolled nearer. With every stitch of canvas spread, we raced over the waters; there was a man at every rope and sheet, and not a word was spoken. The wind grew stronger, and the waves began to be crested with foam; the crew were getting nervous, but we kept on with all sail spread, till at last the water began to come in over the lee rail; then the order was given to shorten sail, and as the gale increased, the sails were furled, till we were running with only a double-reefed foresail and jib. At last, with a blinding flash of lightning and a terrific crash of thunder, the storm was on us, and there was nothing left for us to do but turn the boat's head round and run before the gale to meet the other storm. We soon met it, and the sea which was raised by the conflicting forces was terrific; the *Daisy* was tossed about by the waves like a cork, and every minute I thought she must be swamped. The crew were perfectly panic-stricken; some cried like children, others began saying their prayers, the only occasion, during the whole time they were with me, on which I ever knew them to pray, though they professed to be strict Moslems. Only one of them retained his senses, and with his aid, I got the boat's head round, and we flew along with the gale, which carried us in a southerly direction. When at length the storm cleared off, we found ourselves close to the island which we had sighted in the morning, and which proved to be Stanley's Alice Island. We made for this place, and anchored for the night in a fine, almost land-locked bay on the N.E. side. We had more rough weather after leaving Alice Island, and on one occasion I was rather alarmed by seeing three waterspouts at the same time, all within a short distance of the *Daisy*. On the 10th we sighted land again, and in the afternoon passed the island of Kome, and ran along the coast of Uzinja, finally reaching Kagei about noon on January 12th, having thus been nine days at sea.

On going up to our quarters in the village, almost the first person to greet me was one of our carpenters, a man of the name of Sisamáni, who had been with Smith, and was supposed to have been killed. As soon as I saw him I thought there was some chance of the report of the murders being false, and I at once demanded his story, but it only confirmed the news which Hassáni had brought, and proved beyond a doubt that both my poor comrades had indeed fallen. I began at once to collect all the information I could get about the massacre from the Wang'uána and others, and also from a young Msukuma chief called Nunda, who had been over to Ukeréwe with Smith, and had escaped from the fight.

It was very difficult indeed to get anything approaching to a connected account of the sad affair, and there are many details of it which are still obscure, and which probably will never be cleared up in this world; but the following is the story which I think is nearest the truth.

After the purchase of the dhow (which, it must be understood, we were told was free of all claims on the part of Lukonge) and Smith's and my departure for Uganda, things went on very smoothly for a time, till O'Neill caught a negro, Hamis by name, a slave of Songoro's, trying to cheat him in some oil which he had agreed to buy, and O'Neill refused to deal with him. This greatly enraged Hamis, and in order to revenge himself he told Lukonge not to let the dhow go, and assured him that Smith had never paid for her. So when the dhow was launched the king, one fine morning, made a raid upon our building-yard, and carried off the dhow's mast, rudder, and anchor. Smith, who had now returned to Ukeréwe, of course expostulated, and then it turned out that Songoro, contrary to his representations, had never paid Lukonge a farthing for the timber of the dhow, and had besides appropriated twenty-five dollars' worth of property which Smith had sent by him as a present for that monarch. Songoro at first denied this, but it having been conclusively proved after a three days' discussion in Lukonge's presence, the latter professed himself thoroughly satisfied that Smith had acted fairly by him, and returned the mast, &c., saying, however, that Songoro must pay him three frasila (105 lbs.) of ivory for the wood which he had cut. To this Songoro was obliged to agree, and left some slaves and other property as a pledge with Lukonge. The dhow was then rigged and departed, with everything on board, for Kagei: but on nearing that place a storm came on, and the bottom being bad, she dragged her anchor, drifted on to the rocks and became a total wreck. Some time was lost in fishing up the cargo of the dhow and breaking her up, and then Smith and O'Neill started for Uganda in the *Daisy*, towing a small dingy behind. But the wind was fresh, and the strain of the dingy proving too great for the *Daisy* to stand safely, they were obliged to put back. Meantime Songoro had collected the requisite amount of ivory, and Smith said

UKEREWE AND THE ISLAND OF VEZI FROM MY TENT AT KAGEI.

he would go over to Ukeréwe, and see fair play between him and Lukonge. He and O'Neill accordingly went over in the *Daisy* with several servants, independently of the boat's crew. All went round in the *Daisy* to Bukindo, and stayed at Songoro's establishment. The ivory was paid and the pledges restored. Then it seems that Lukonge meditated treachery against Smith, O'Neill and Songoro, and

Songoro suspecting this, asked Smith to allow him to send some of his wives and children over to Kagei in the *Daisy*. Smith seems to have expected an attack, and begged O'Neill to go round in the *Daisy*, so that he at least might be safe; but O'Neill refused, saying, if there was any danger he would share it with Smith. Smith consented to Songoro's proposal, and ordered Hassáni to take the boat round through the Rugeshi Strait to Nasso, a large village on the southern side of the island of Ukeréwe, and there to wait for orders. Some of Songoro's wives and children were sent off at once overland to Nasso, and arrived there about the same time as the *Daisy*. Hassáni, who had been privately warned about Lukonge's intentions, got the women on board, and saying that he was not going to stop and be killed, set sail for Kagei. They had not got far from land when the party arrived at Nasso, and at once made signals to Hassáni to return, but he refused, although implored to do so by the women on board. Smith and O'Neill, with their servants, the chief Nunda, two Waganda, Songoro and his party stayed at Nasso, hoping no doubt that the *Daisy* would ere long return; but, either that same evening (December 13th, probably) or the next morning, they were attacked by Lukonge's men, and after a brave resistance were nearly all massacred, only two or three saving themselves by flight. O'Neill shot thirty of his assailants dead, and wounded many more, before he fell from an arrow which struck him in the head; Smith was almost the last who fell, and was said by some to have been writing in a book nearly the whole time of the fight. Some of the Wang'uána tried to escape by swimming, but were hunted down by the Wakerewe in canoes, and speared in the water. Among those who were killed was Hamis, Songoro's slave, and the originator of all the trouble. After all was over, Lukonge cut off the heads of Smith, O'Neill, and Songoro, and hung them up in his principal hut; the bodies he threw into the Lake. Sisamáni, the carpenter, was taken prisoner, and after being kept in captivity eight days was released and sent back to Kagei.

The news of the fight and massacre was soon brought over to Kagei by the runaways, and Hassáni sent men down to Unyanyembe to meet Mackay, who was supposed to be on his way to the Lake, to tell him what had happened, and then, after waiting some days longer, came over in the *Daisy* to Uganda to tell me. The immediate cause of my companions' death was Hassáni's desertion; for, had he obeyed orders and waited at Nasso, it would have been possible to have transported the whole party by relays to one of the nearer islands in a very short time, and as the Wakerewe are badly provided with canoes, they would have been safe there. Besides that, had the *Daisy* been at hand, they would have been able to hold their own against the natives, as nearly all the ammunition was on board, and it was not until all the cartridges were expended that the Wakerewe were able to close with them.

It was not till months after my visit to Kagei, and subsequent to Hassáni's dismissal, that I found all this out. This further evidence was obtained chiefly from the accounts of the two Waganda who were with Smith, and who were the most trustworthy witnesses of all, as they had no special bias in favour either of Lukonge or the Wang'uána and Hassáni which would influence their evidence. Had I known this earlier, Hassáni would certainly not have escaped scot-free as he did.

CHAPTER VI.

KAGEI TO TABORA AND BACK.

AFTER collecting all the information about Smith and O'Neill's death, I began overhauling all the stores and taking stock of what was left. I soon found that there was very little cloth, and that I could not go on much longer without supplies. On January 16th men arrived from the coast bringing a batch of letters, which contained, amongst other news, the pleasant intelligence that two more men had been sent out with orders to join Mackay, who had recruited his health, and was intending to come on to the Lake. He had constructed a road from Sadaani to Mpwapwa, and at the time the mail runners left the coast had formed a caravan of bullock waggons, and was about to start with his two companions. As it was extremely doubtful when this caravan would arrive at the Lake, I decided to go myself, with a few men, to Unyanyembe, and buy a sufficient quantity of cloth to last me for some time. I engaged twelve men of Kadúma's, the chief of Kagei, to go with me and bring back my supplies, and with these men, three servants, and the two mail runners, I left Kagei on January 19th. I followed pretty much the same route as that which O'Neill and I took on our journey up the previous year. The caravan was small, and the men lightly laden, so we travelled rapidly, spite of very wet weather, and reached Semwi on the 28th, thus doing in nine days a distance which occupied twenty-five days on my previous journey. I rested one day at Semwi, being delayed by the flooded state of the river Monungu. When I arrived at the village the chief was making up a caravan to go down to the coast, and I was witness to the ceremony of "doctoring" it, to make it "lucky." The intending travellers having been collected in the open square of the village to the sound of a drum, were inspected by a haggard old mganga, or sorcerer, who had been making "medicine" for them. This medicine was a dirty white liquid contained in a calabash, and of which he took a good mouthful and squirted it over each of the party; whereupon the women of the place, who had assembled to watch the operation, set up a loud yell, and then began marching about the village singing and howling, a performance which they kept up, to my great discomfort, for several hours. Next morning there was an exciting leopard hunt close by. During the night a leopard had got into a neighbouring village, and all the people had turned out to try and kill it. The village consisted of a group of témbes with a tall hedge of euphorbiæ round it, and having a considerable space, between the hedge and the huts, covered with high grass, in which the leopard had taken refuge. On hearing about it, I took my rifle and went over to the place with some of my men. A large crowd was collected outside the boma, or fence, armed with guns, spears, and clubs. All were afraid to venture near the spot where the creature was said to be concealed, and contented themselves by firing random shots into the bushes, at far greater risk to the villagers than to the leopard. On the arrival of my men they plucked up courage, and two of my servants with some others began beating the grass, and soon made the leopard show himself; he tried to bolt, but finding himself surrounded, sprang right on the top of two of my men, knocking them down and scratching them badly; so I took them back to the village to dress their wounds, and handing my rifle to one of the mail men, told him to be more careful; but I had not been back long, and had scarcely finished dressing the others' wounds, when he came in, his face streaming with blood and one ear completely torn off. It seems they had driven the leopard into a corner of the hedge, and this man was peeping in to see where it was, when the beast sprang out on top of him and tore the ear away. Ultimately the creature was killed, but not before it had badly wounded six more men. Next day, the 30th, we continued our journey. An hour's march brought us to the valley of the Monungu, which was flooded: we entered the water about a mile from the river, and it got gradually deeper, till, near the northern bank, it was up to my armpits. On reaching the actual banks of the river, which were a little higher and had only about three feet of water above them, we found that the bridge was completely washed away. Men were sent into the jungle to cut creepers, and with these we formed a handrail which was fastened to trees on either side, and then we crossed by holding on to the rail and feeling for the logs, which had formed the bridge, with our feet. This was such a long operation that it was far on in the afternoon before we were all across, and we had to encamp in the jungle on the opposite side on the first dry spot we could find. At night, some lions, attracted by two or three cows we had with us, kept up a concert round our camp. The following day we reached Masimbo, the point at which O'Neill and I had struck the Unyanyembe route when on our way to the Nyanza the previous year. We left Masimbo on February 2nd, our road lying through cultivated country during the whole march. I went on in advance of the caravan, and, while halting under a tree for the men to come up, saw a man rushing along the road after us with a red blanket on his shoulders streaming in the wind; he came up to two of my servants and greeted them most affectionately, and then rushing up to me, almost embraced me in his eagerness. I was the man who had acted as O'Neill's and my kilangózi from Mpwapwa to Ng'uru; he was chief of a village near, and hearing that I was passing, came out to meet me. He expressed great sorrow that we had not camped the previous night at his village, as he "would have given us something to eat," and begged me to pay him a visit when I returned from Unyanyembe. Soon after parting from our demonstrative friend we narrowly escaped a fight. As we were passing through a field, an old woman who was hoeing corn took fright, and, thinking us Ruga Ruga (highwaymen), rushed off to the village screaming, and soon a crowd of men, armed with guns, bows, and spears, came rushing down towards us. I walked slowly to meet them, and as they got near shouted their ordinary salutations. They stopped, evidently astonished at hearing a white man address them in their own language; we entered into conversation with them, and the affair ended in a hearty laugh at the fright they had received, and in plentiful abuse of the old woman who had raised the alarm. From there we went on to the village of a chief called Mtinginya, a man of great authority in this part of the country as he had made blood brotherhood with Mirambo, the renowned African Buonaparte, also because he possessed a large number of guns. He had the character of being well-disposed towards Englishmen, and my men were looking forward to a good feast. As soon as we were seen from the village a number of men came rushing out to meet us, yelling and brandishing their arms, and a stranger to African modes of welcome would have thought that we were all going to be murdered on the spot. Mtinginya received me very courteously, and I was soon surrounded by a curious throng watching my every movement. They were much exercised about a swinging lamp that I had, and could not for a long time make out what it was, but finally came to the conclusion that it must be a hat. At this village I saw the first attempt at carving which I had ever observed among negroes, viz., the figure of a woman, life-size, on the gate of the village. The idea could scarcely have been copied from the Arabs, as Mohammedans consider it a sin to make any figure or image of human beings.

Just as we were starting, the following morning, two men, sent by Said bin Salim, the Governor of Unyanyembe, to make inquiries about the massacre at Ukeréwe, arrived; and, among other news, told me that Mackay and his party had reached Ugogo some three weeks previously, and would soon be at Unyanyembe. The two succeeding marches took us through jungle with clearings at intervals and large well-fortified tembes. On emerging from the jungle on February 4th we entered a plain with numerous tembes scattered about it; to our surprise we heard heavy firing at no great distance, and on turning a corner came in full view of a brisk fight which was taking place between 300 or 400 of Mirambo's Ruga Ruga and the people of a large village about half a mile from the road. We quickened our steps on seeing this, as we were not anxious to be drawn into the row. At every village sentries were stationed, and challenged us as we passed; and once a fine-looking chief came running out and advised us not to stop in that district, but told us of a village where we might safely stay the night. On February 7th I reached Uyui, a large village in a district of the same name, about twenty-five miles N.E. of Tabora. I had not been many minutes in the village when I was informed that a white man was encamped not far off, and wanted to see me. I wondered who it could be, as it was hardly possible for Mackay's party to have arrived so soon; so I at once set off, and soon reached the camp, when I found the "Mzungu" to be an Englishman, Morton by name, who has been already mentioned as having brought up some stores for us to the Lake. He had been paying a visit to Mirambo, and was now on his way to the coast. He told me that there had been a rebellion at Unyanyembe, headed by an Arab, Abdullah bin Nasibe, surnamed by the Wanyamwézi, Kisésa, or the Valiant, from the courage which he had displayed in the wars between Mirambo and the Arabs. Said bin Salim the governor had been driven out and Kisésa had usurped his post. This rather upset my plans, as Morton said it would not be safe for me to go to Tabora just yet, and there was no news of Mackay, the story told by Said bin Salim's men being an utter falsehood; so I decided to wait a few days here to see how matters turned out, and to write home accounts of the events of the last few weeks. On February 11th, news having come that Tabora was quiet again, I went over there, and was hospitably received by Kisésa and his brother, Sheik bin Nasib, at their comfortable house in Kwihara, where I remained until the 15th. I may mention here that the name Kazeh, given by Speke and Grant to Tabora, and which has puzzled some travellers, was the name of Musa Mzuri's house; most of the Arab houses having distinctive names. Sheik bin Nasib had been a long time at Unyanyembe, and I had several conversations with him about Livingstone, Burton (Haji Abdullah, as he is called), and other travellers, more especially Speke, who is undoubtedly the most popular of all the European explorers in this part of Africa. Sheik bin Nasib had also, in his younger days, been to Karagwe and Uganda, and told me long stories about Dagera and Súna, the fathers of Rumanika and Mtesa. Súna he represented as an intensely nervous man, who was in constant dread of assassination, and who would, on that account, never sleep in his own house, but waited till it was quite dark, and then used to sneak out to the house of one of his favourites and spend the night there. I found that the Arabs here had a curious idea that the rocks, of which there are many round Tabora, produce fever. On asking Sheik bin Nasib how it was there was so much ague at Tabora, "Don't you see those?" he said, pointing to the rocks; "those are the cause of it." I believe Humboldt speaks of a similar idea being entertained by the South Americans.

On the evening previous to my departure, Kisésa had asked me if I should be willing to conduct to Uyui some of Said bin Salim's wives and children, who had been left behind when the ex-governor had to flee, and of course I consented. So in the morning I went out to a small village on the edge of the forest, which lies between Unyanyembe and Uyui, and there I found the women and children with a number of servants. The women were not in a condition to ride, and wished to make the long march at night, to avoid the heat of the day, and accordingly we started about six o'clock P.M. and marched on slowly for several hours, but finally were compelled by a violent thunderstorm to halt. We reached Uyui about half-past nine the following morning, receiving a most enthusiastic welcome from Said bin Salim's people, who had thoughtfully prepared for us an excellent breakfast. The king of Uyui, Majémba Gána, gave me a good témbe inside the Kwikuru, or capital, and supplied me liberally with food during my stay. Said bin Salim also frequently sent me presents of fowls, curry and rice, so that I lived in clover.

Uyui is a large town for Africa, and consists of a collection of well-built témbes closely packed together, with winding streets shaded by large fig trees. It is strongly fortified with a palisade of high poles and a deep ditch, and, if provided with a good stock of water and provisions, could hold its own for a long time against a besieging enemy. There is a dense population in and around the capital, so that it offers a good field for missionary operations, and the Church Missionary Society has now (1881) a prosperous station there. The king, whose real name I never heard, goes by the pseudonym of Majémba Gána, or "The hundred hoes," the origin of which is said to be the following circumstance. Some years ago, when Mirambo was less powerful than he is now, he had made a raid to the east of Uyui, and had obtained a large amount of booty; being anxious to return home by the shortest route, which lay through Majémba Gána's territory, and not knowing how the latter was disposed towards him, Mirambo sent a deputation to him with a hundred hoes and a hundred bullets, with the following message, "If you desire peace take the hoes to till your fields; if you desire war take the bullets, for you will need them all."

Majémba Gána took the hoes, and has ever since been on friendly terms with Mirambo.

I remained a few days more at Uyui, hoping to get news of reinforcements, but none came; so, after having sent letters after Morton, who had left for the coast during my absence at Tabora, I started for the north on February 21st. The rainy season was now at its height, and large tracts of country were under water, making marching very unpleasant. However, we pushed on fast, for, as the porters were going home, they needed no other inducement to travel well, and after spending a day with Mtinginya reached the Monungu again on March 4th. We found this river even fuller than it had been on the journey down, six weeks previously, and it was only crossed after many hours' work, up to our waists in water the whole time. We stayed a day at Semwi to rest, and here I found that Said bin Salim's two men, whom I had met at Mtinginya's, had played me a mean trick. Some of Songoro's people who had been at Kagei at the time of the Ukeréwe massacre had left for Unyanyembe, on hearing of their master's death, with a quantity of property which had been advanced to Songoro by Said bin Salim to trade with. This property they had left at Semwi in the chief's care, promising him a present if he would look after it. On the governor's men arriving here, they heard about this property, and, having ascertained that the chief was a friend of mine, represented to him that it was my property and that I wanted it in a great hurry, and would give him a good present when I returned; whereupon the chief foolishly gave up the goods, and on my arrival came and asked for his present. Of course I knew nothing about it, but it took nearly a whole day to convince the chief that it was no concern of mine.

After leaving Semwi we made very rapid marches, the weather being finer and the country generally drier. On March 8th, as we were passing through some jungle, and when approaching the district of Usmao, I was much surprised by the appearance of Hassáni, and about a dozen of the Wang'uána whom I had left at Kagei. On seeing me they fired off their guns, an insane custom, which they observe on all possible occasions. I asked what they meant by disobeying my orders and leaving Kagei, and learnt that they had all run away in a panic upon hearing some absurd story about the intention of Lukonge to come and attack our depôt. This was a most improbable tale, as, though Smith and O'Neill had been killed, yet the Wakerewe had been far too severely punished in the fight to willingly face firearms again. These gallant fellows (the same who lay down in the boat when we were attacked at Ukara) hoped to frighten me, by this means, into returning to Zanzibar. However I kept on, and on emerging from the jungle we saw a number of men

coming to meet us, decked out in their war costume.
A party of natives from this district had attached
themselves to my caravan, and I thought this demonstration must be to welcome them home; but, as
we advanced, I saw armed men rushing towards us
from every direction, and noticed some cattle being
driven off in hot haste towards the villages: this
and the total absence of women (always a bad sign)
showed me that a fight was imminent. Still I
marched on steadily, telling the Wang'uána to keep
together and be quiet. I tried to get into conversation with one or two niampáras, but they only
answered my "Wanga ruka?" (How are you?) and
"Shiza" (Good morning) with surly grunts. Matters
grew worse, the crowd around us thickened every
moment, and at last a great burly fellow knocked
the kilangózi down and snatched the flag from him;
one of the Wang'uána flew upon him and recovered
the flag. I thought a fight must ensue then, for,
though the Kagei men behaved admirably, and were
as cool as possible, the Wang'uána were beside themselves with fear, and it was all I could do to restrain
them, for I was determined, if there *must* be a battle,
I would not begin it. I had, however, no doubt that we
should have overpowered them, as, though far outnumbered by the crowd, we were much better armed,
and I had with me several Waganda who were on
their way from Zanzibar with 80 lbs. of gunpowder
for Mtesa. Just at this moment an old niampára

who had travelled with me before, and with whom I had been on friendly terms, elbowed his way through the crowd, and sending them to the right-about with a big stick, came up to me and greeted me very affectionately. He then walked at the head of the caravan to the chief's village, while another niampára walked behind and kept guard in the rear. On making inquiries, I found that the report of the Wang'uána's guns had been heard, and they concluded that it must be Mirambo and his Ruga Ruga about to make a raid on the district.

Next morning, when preparing to start, a number of the Wang'uána came and said, if I persisted in returning to Kagei they must leave me. So I told them they were a lot of cowards, that I was not going to turn back for their tales, that they were welcome to go, as not one of them was worth his salt, and reminded them that by thus breaking their contracts they would forfeit every farthing of pay. Well, they said, they must go, but begged that I would give them a letter to the English Consul at Zanzibar. "Oh, with pleasure," I said, "and you will all be put in prison when you get there," and with that I gave the order to march. That same evening, about an hour after I reached the next camp, they all arrived, the imaginary dangers of Kagei having vanished before the prospect of imprisonment. On March 15th our eyes were gladdened once more by the sight of the Nyanza, and that same evening we reached Kagei, having made about seventy miles in the last three days.

Having now safely arrived at Kagei, I made preparations for returning to Uganda. I first set the carpenters to work overhauling the *Daisy* and getting her ready for sea. Then I looked through all the stores and repacked them, as I wished to take with me as large a cargo of goods as possible, especially of those things which the Wang'uána were most likely to steal. I then intended that the *Daisy* should return and bring a second cargo to Uganda, leaving at Kagei only the heavy tools and machinery, which would have to wait for an engineer to be turned to account. The *Daisy* was more out of repair than I had supposed, and I did not get off till March 22nd. We had a good run across the Lake, reaching Ntebbi early in the morning of the 25th. Here I met an Mganda chief, who was just starting for Kagei to meet me, bearing a letter from Mtesa, in which he begged me to return as speedily as possible; so I sent word to the king of my arrival, and requested that men might be sent to transport my goods up to the capital. On the 28th I sent the *Daisy* back to Kagei for a second cargo. One of the crew, Baraka bin Asman (who was precisely the reverse of what his first name signified, viz., "a blessing"), wanted to stay in Uganda, but as the *Daisy* was short of hands I refused, and on his persisting, I told him if he did not obey orders I should punish him, whereupon he burst into tears and wept like a child. This man was an inveterate opium-eater, and when he could get his darling drug was in a chronic state of maudlin stupor. I reached Rubaga on March 31st, and the following day had an interview with Mtesa, who seemed much pleased to have me back again; and I heard an amusing story of the discomfiture of a mandwa, or sorcerer, who, one day, just after Mtesa had sent to meet me, appeared at court and assured him that I should never return to Uganda. Next day came the news that I had arrived at Ntebbi; so Mtesa sent for the mandwa, and asked him if he had heard that this prophecy had been nullified. "Oh," was his reply, "the Mzungu has reached Ntebbi, but he will never reach Rubaga." "Do you mean that I am to kill my guest?" said Mtesa. "No, you are a liar, and your prophecies are untrue: you shall go to prison;" and the man was put in the stocks there and then. I found, on inquiring, that Dr. Emin had been nearly three months in Uganda and had left only a short time before my return.

On April 30th two mail runners arrived from Ntebbi, bringing a large batch of letters, newspapers, and periodicals. They had come over in the *Daisy*, which was then lying at Ntebbi. Among other letters was one from Mackay, in which he said he was then (January 11th) about to despatch a caravan under the care of an Arab, to Kagei, and he himself hoped to follow later on. On May 5th the Wang'uána arrived from Ntebbi with most of the goods which they had brought over, and for the next three or four days I was very busy writing letters for England and making out discharge notes for the Wang'uána; for I had decided to dismiss them all, as I was thoroughly disgusted with them, for they were, as a lot, lazy, dishonest, and insubordinate, besides being a considerable expense. The Wang'uána all left on the 12th of May, and I got two Waganda boys for servants.

CHAPTER VII.

UGANDA AND THE WAGANDA.

THE country of Uganda is situated on the north, north-west, and west of the Nyanza or Victoria Lake. Its boundaries are, approximately, the Kagera, or Kitangule, river on the south, the thirty-first parallel of east longitude on the west, the first parallel of north latitude on the north, and the Nile on the east. The western frontier of the country is very ill-defined, and may be found to extend considerably beyond the limit here assigned to it. The Equator, as will be seen from a glance at the map, divides the country into two tolerably equal parts.

Three provinces are included under the general name Uganda : viz. Uddu in the south between the Kagera and Katonga rivers, Singo in the west, and Chagwe in the east. To these must be added the group of islands (probably about 400 in number) known as Sesse.

The physical features of the country vary considerably in different districts, and for the purpose of description may, roughly speaking, be divided into the coast portion and the interior portion. Along the shore of the Nyanza, and for some distance inland, the country is mountainous, especially at the extreme north-west corner of the Lake, where ranges of flat-topped hills occur, intersected by deep swampy valleys. Down these valleys sluggish streams make their way to the Nyanza, their beds choked by dense masses of reeds, papyrus, and grass; while their sides are clothed with magnificent forest and a rich undergrowth of ferns, of which I collected some fifty species; long rope-like creepers hang from every tree; troops of grey monkeys swing from bough to bough, and make the woods ring with their discordant shrieks; flocks of large grey parrots fly screaming about; delicate little honey-birds, their plumage glowing in the sun like living rubies or emeralds, hover over the bright-coloured flowers on the forest's edge, and in the open glades countless butterflies, of all the hues of the rainbow, flit about. As the traveller gets farther from the Lake the valleys widen, the hills lessen, the forest trees are gradually supplanted by the wild date palm, and rank grasses take the place of the ferns. Near the northern boundary the hills, with one or two exceptions, disappear, and the country becomes a plain intersected at long intervals by huge rush drains, and covered with open forest or jungle, where the eland and other antelopes, herds of elephants, buffaloes, zebras, rhinoceroses, and wild boar find a home.

The eastern part of Uganda, between Rubaga and the Nile, consists of undulating country, the ridges running in a N.N.E.—S.S.W. direction, and intersected by deep, narrow valleys. The steep sides of these ravines are dotted with splendid forest trees, whose foliage is so dense as to create a perpetual twilight, even at noon, while festoons of graceful creepers and feathery ferns overhang rapidly flowing streams whose clear cold waters reach to the knees, the whole scene being one of weird beauty, and an almost perfect realisation of one's childish dreams of fairyland.

The coast region of Uganda is the most fertile district that I have seen in Africa. There, as everywhere through the Equatorial belt, the banana flourishes; every village and every hut is surrounded by vast groves of this plant, and on climbing some mountain in the more densely populated districts the traveller sees all round him these broad tracts of pale green, reaching far up the sides of the hills, and extending in every direction as far as the eye can penetrate. The extreme fertility of the country is owing to the abundant supply of moisture; for, lying, as it does, within the belt of perpetual rain, there are showers during every month in the year. The two periods of maximum rainfall are March, April and May, and September, October and

November. During these months rain falls nearly every day, usually accompanying thunderstorms which recur at almost the same hour each day with remarkable regularity. The mean annual rainfall is not however very great, and will probably be found to be about 50 inches. The climate of Uganda is a remarkably mild one, and the temperature is very uniform all the year round, owing, doubtless, to the great elevation of the country (viz. from 5000 to 6000 feet) and the proximity of the vast bodies of water in the Victoria and Albert lakes. During the whole of my residence there the temperature never rose above 90 degrees Fahrenheit in the shade, and rarely fell below 50 degrees at night, while during the middle of the day there was generally a pleasant breeze. There is however a good deal of ague, especially in the swampy districts near the capital, though this will doubtless become much rarer among Europeans as better houses are built.

There being two periods of maximum rainfall in the year, there are two crops of cereals in the twelve months, consequently the natives of Uganda reckon each period of six months as a year. The year and the month being their only divisions of time. The first month of each of these years is called "the month of sowing food," and the other months those " of eating food."

One feature which strikes the traveller in this

country, and which shows the superiority of the Waganda over the surrounding nations, is the wonderful roads which connect the principal villages with one another and with the capital. These roads often lead straight as an arrow over hill and dale, through forests and across swamps, and, even in the more thinly peopled districts, are kept wonderfully clean and free from weeds. Across the larger swamps causeways are carried, with bridges, formed of trunks of trees, at intervals to give free passage to the streams which filter through them. One very large morass between Rubaga and Murchison Bay had a regular corduroy road formed across it by trunks of the wild date palm, which were laid side by side on the treacherous surface of the floating vegetation, and formed a secure and permanent road.

The mineral products of the country so far seem to be of little value. The geological formation of most of the rocks is igneous or metamorphic. The surface soil for a depth of a few feet is a rich black alluvium: under this is a bed of red sandy clay averaging probably about thirty feet in thickness, while under this again there is in many places a deposit of tolerably pure china clay of unknown thickness; a large quantity of talc is found in some places, and at the outcrop of the metamorphic rocks on the hillsides, moderately good specimens of rock crystal are procured. There is a considerable quantity of ironstone in some districts, but it is impossible to say to what depth it extends. As far as can be ascertained, there are no sedimentary rocks in Uganda, and no metal except iron is known to exist.

Several tribes are to be found in Uganda, living in different districts or scattered through the country.

The most important tribe, in every respect, is that of the Waganda, with whom may be classed the islanders (Basesse) who inhabit the islands along the coast of Uganda, as they come of the same stock, and speak a dialect of the same language. They are pure Negroes, with dark chocolate-coloured skins, and short woolly hair. The men are rather above the average height, well made and powerful, and the women when young are often good-looking, with small neat hands and feet.

The Wahuma, who come next in importance, are a singular race; under the names of Watusi and Wahuma, they are found scattered throughout Eastern Central Africa, from the equator to the seventh parallel of south latitude. As Speke has shown, they are probably descended from the original inhabitants of Abyssinia. They are a tall, fine race, with handsome oval faces, thin lips, and straight noses. Their women are particularly handsome-looking, and are highly valued as wives by the Waganda chiefs. Wherever met with, the Wahuma are the herdsmen of the country, living chiefly on milk and flesh, and but rarely cultivating the ground, and consequently in Uganda, where they are despised, it is almost impossible to induce a Mganda to tend cattle. These Wahuma are a very exclusive race; they have a distinct language of their own, live in out-of-the-way villages, generally on the borders of the jungle, and rarely intermarry with the surrounding tribes.

There are a few Wanyambo, or natives of the south of Uddu and Karagwe, to be found in Uganda. They are inferior in physique to both the tribes already mentioned (though probably they have an admixture of Wahuma blood in their veins), and speak a different language. They are generally cowherds.

The last tribe which claims our attention is that of the Wasoga, who come from the country of Usoga to the east of Uganda. They are a brave, warlike race; but have been gradually subdued by the Waganda, a large part of Usoga being under Mtesa's sway. They are a good deal darker than the Waganda, and generally wear their hair long. They are considered good musicians, and there are many of them in Mtesa's bands; and also a number of Wasoga women are scattered about the country in the harems of the various chiefs; these are mostly prisoners taken in war and given as presents by Mtesa to his officers.

Albinos are often met with in Uganda, being apparently commoner there than among any other tribe I have seen. They are looked upon as curiosities, and are kept in the establishments of the king and great chiefs. Their hair is straw-coloured, their skin, which is rough and coarse, is of a pinkish-white colour, and their eyes are very sensitive to light. No clue can be got from the natives about the origin of these monstrosities. The assertion which has been made that they are the offspring of the union of brothers and sisters, all, even Mtesa himself, absolutely deny. They say that the parents sometimes have one or two normal children, then an albino, and then another normal child; and they further assert that albinos have been known to intermarry, and to have perfectly normal children.

There are a few dwarfs to be seen about the court, where they are privileged nuisances, like the jesters of the Middle Ages, and like them, they are petted and indulged, and often become possessed of large herds of cattle, goats and sheep.

The total population of Uganda, after very careful calculations, I estimate at five millions. Of course this estimate can only be an approximation, but I believe it will be found to be in the main correct.

The female population is largely in excess of the male, the proportion being about three and a half to one. This excessive preponderance of the females over the males is due to three causes.

1. Careful observation has established the fact that there are a good many more female births than male, and on taking the groups of children playing by the

roadside there will always be found to be more girls than boys.

2. The Waganda are constantly at war with one or other of the nations round them, and their battles, being hand-to-hand encounters, are fearfully destructive. In one engagement which came under my immediate notice, fifty per cent. of the Waganda warriors were killed, and, as they gained the day, the loss of their opponents must have been even greater.

3. The rule with the Waganda, when they have taken a town or district, is to put all the full-grown men to death, and to take the children and women prisoners, and as the Waganda are almost always at war, there is a constant influx of women, who are distributed among the chiefs and successful warriors.

The above estimate, if correct, would show the total male population of Uganda to be about 1,400,000, and as every man who can handle a spear and shield is a soldier, the total military strength of the country would be probably from 500,000 to 600,000 men. It is not likely, however, that (at the most) more than a third of this number would ever be available at one time for war.

The Waganda are distinguished from all the neighbouring nations by their dress, as with the exception of the Wanyoro they are (as far as is known) the only tribe in Central Africa who clothe themselves from head to foot. The laws about dress are very strict, and it is death for a man or woman to be found in the public roads without proper clothing. When in their houses they are not so particular, and the younger women often dispense with it altogether. When going into battle, too, the men divest themselves of all their garments, with the exception of a loin-cloth, in order to give greater freedom to their limbs. The national costume is the mbugu, or bark cloth, which is worn by the men as a loose flowing robe tied in a knot over the shoulder, leaving both arms bare, and coming down to the feet; while the women fasten it tightly round the body, just under the armpits. Sandals made out of buffalo hide are often worn, and fantastic head-dresses or turbans of calico or coloured pocket-handkerchiefs. Over the mbugu a robe of beautifully dressed skin is sometimes worn by the chiefs. These robes are made either of a whole bullock-skin with the hair on, or of two or three goat-skins sewn together; but the one which is most highly prized consists of from twenty to forty skins of the "ntalaganya," a diminutive antelope, about the size of a hare, which has a beautifully glossy coat of a rich dark brown colour.

Foreign dress, however, is gradually making its way among the people, and Mtesa himself has quite discarded the native mbugu in favour of Arab and Turkish costume. The commonest article of foreign dress is the kanzu, or shirt of calico, which reaches down to the heels, and is secured round the waist by a sash or girdle. Kuftans or chogas, embroidered gowns of woollen stuff, and of various colours, are worn by the king and richer chiefs, while trousers, stockings, red shoes, and fezes have been introduced, and are gradually spreading through the country.

The arms of the Waganda are spears, which are generally very well made; the head is about fifteen inches long, the blade being about two-thirds of that length; the shaft is ordinarily about seven feet long, and beautifully turned. They also carry a large oval shield which covers the greater part of their bodies. These shields are made of a light wood, and slope backwards at a slight angle, and are covered with open basket-work made of thin strips from the stem of a creeper. There is a boss in the centre, and the inside is hollowed out to reduce the weight; a wicker handle, frequently made in the shape of a lizard or some other creature, is fastened inside. The Wahuma use bows and arrows in addition to spears. The bows, which are rather large, are unusually stiff; the arrows are about three feet long, and often hideously barbed, and sometimes poisoned; but owing to the extreme stiffness of the bows they seem unable to discharge an arrow effectively to a greater distance than forty yards.

The Waganda, besides their native weapons, possess a tolerable number of guns, the total number in the country being probably about 2000. These include almost every kind of fire-arm, from the primitive matchlock up to modern breach-loading and repeating rifles. The commonest kinds are flint-locks and smooth-bore percussion guns, which are mostly cheap and inferior weapons manufactured in Belgium, and their bursting causes numerous accidents. Owing, however, to the scarcity of ammunition, they are not much used in war, though some of the Waganda are excellent marksmen.

Mtesa has also four small cannon, such as are used on board ships for signalling; of these he is very proud, and thinks they are capable of performing wonders if used in the field.

These weapons are all imported from Zanzibar, as the Egyptian government absolutely forbids trade in arms and ammunition with negro tribes.

The Waganda, in common with many negro tribes, are a decidedly musical race, and have a tolerable variety of musical instruments. The most important of these is the nanga or harp. It consists of a stout hemispherical framework of wood, over which the skin of some animal is tightly fastened to form a sounding-box, the skin of a large species of water-lizard (*Varanus niloticus?*) being the one usually employed. From six to eight strings, made of the twisted intestines of the goat or sheep, are secured to a rib which runs along the centre of this box, and are then stretched to pegs inserted in holes bored in a curved bow which rises from the box. By these pegs the strings can be tightened or relaxed as in our violins, the bow being bound tightly round, between the pegs, to prevent its splitting. The strings are struck with the fingers as in the European harp. Drums, ng'oma, are largely used by the Waganda, and are of various shapes and sizes. The larger drums are conical in shape, and are formed of a block of hard sonorous wood, carefully hollowed out. The head is made of a large ox-hide, which is carefully fitted to the shape of the drum, and secured by numerous strips of skin to another hide fastened round the bottom, and can be tightened, if required, by twisting the connecting bands. These drums are generally placed on the ground, or suspended round the neck of the performer, and beaten, on the upper side only, with two drumsticks. There are also long narrow cylindrical drums, of which the head only is covered with skin, generally that of the water-lizard or a large snake, the bottom being left open. These are usually carried under the arm and beaten with the palm of the hand.

There are several large drums, of unusually fine tone, which belong to Mtesa, some of them having been made by former kings. They have each a distinctive name, and are kept carefully guarded, being only used on grand occasions.

The harmonicon, "madinda," has the greatest compass of any of the musical instruments of the Waganda. It consists of a number of pieces of a hard resonant wood, thick at the two ends, and scooped out in the middle, which are laid side by side across two logs, and struck at either end by two drumsticks. There are from twelve to twenty of these pieces, and they are often played on by two performers at once, one on each side, so that a chord of four notes can be struck.

None of these musical instruments have sharps or flats, but only whole tones; though this does not arise from the inability of the native ear to appreciate semitones, for when taught European music. they can distinguish them readily enough.

The Waganda have two sorts of wind instruments, flutes and horns. The former, "ndelle," are made of a large reed or the hollow stalks of an umbelliferous plant, and have from two to four holes which can be closed with the fingers. They are blown from the top like a clarionet.

The horns, ng'ombe, are the horns of cattle and antelopes, and are blown at the side. Some of them have the tip cut off, leaving both ends open, the smaller aperture being closed with the finger at pleasure, and so producing two notes. These are used both as musical instruments and to convey orders from the chiefs on the march and in battle. Besides these instruments, they have small iron bells which are tied to the wrists and ankles, and are used to keep time with to the music. They make also rattles, which consist of bottle-gourds, filled with dried peas, the necks being then stopped up. They are used for the same purpose as the bells, and generally form part of the stock-in-trade of the medicine-men, who employ them in their incantations. The Waganda have a considerable variety of tunes, and those to which they dance are quite distinct in style from the songs. It need hardly be said that they have no written music, all tunes being played by ear.

The tools used by the natives of Uganda are comparatively few and simple. The hoe, nkumbe, which is the universal implement for tilling the ground, is heart-shaped, with a long tang or projection, from the broad end, which is firmly tied to a hook-shaped wooden handle about three feet long. They have two forms of axe, the one a rude wedge-shaped piece of iron, which is inserted in a heavy wooden handle, and is used for felling trees and splitting up firewood; the other is a much more elegant instrument, with a broad thin blade almost crescent-shaped, and is fastened like a knife in the end of a long well-balanced handle of wood.

The knives are always curved, the blade being about nine inches long, and very thin. The iron, which is all obtained from native ore, is hard, of fairly good quality, and takes a tolerably keen edge. The flat part of the blades, both of the knives and axes, is covered with a thin film of black oxide of iron (except just along the cutting edge), which prevents them from rusting. They are also sometimes painted with red oxide of iron, procured from an ore resembling hæmatite.

The tools used by the blacksmiths in making these implements are generally of the rudest possible description; oblong stones serve as hammers, and large flat ones as anvils, the tongs being often merely pieces of green wood with a cleft in them. However a few iron hammers and tongs have been imported from Zanzibar, and some of the native smiths are skilful in the use of the file, which has also been introduced. The bellows which supply the blast for their charcoal fires consist of two earthen pots firmly bedded in the ground; over the mouths of these a pliable skin is fastened, while to the centre of this sticks are tied, which a boy, holding one in each hand, works rapidly up and down alternately, thus giving a constant blast. There is a hole near the bottom of each pot, on the side facing the fire, and through this the blast passes to a clay tube which conducts it to the hearth.

The food of the Waganda, especially of the lower classes, is chiefly vegetable; the principal article being the banana. As already mentioned, this grows everywhere in Uganda, and requires little or no cultivation. There are several varieties of this plant, which shows that its introduction, assuming that it is not indigenous, dates back a considerable period. These varieties are used for different purposes, some being boiled, others roasted, and others again made into wine, and each has a distinctive name. The usual mode of preparing the banana is to cut it from the plant while green, to peel and then boil it, when it closely resembles mashed potatoes in appearance. It is also cut in slices and dried in the sun, in which state it can be kept for an indefinite period against times of scarcity or for use on a journey; as so prepared it is pounded to a coarse flour in a wooden mortar, and either boiled to a pudding or made into cakes.

The sweet potato forms, next to the banana, the main article of food, and is the chief vegetable cultivated by the natives.

In addition to these plants, the Waganda also grow *Colocasia antiquorum, Helmia bulbifera,* yams, several species of beans, two or three kinds of pumpkins, a species of solanum, sugarcane, a kind of red spinach, cassava, maize, millet, tullaboon, and sesamum. The coffee-tree is extensively cultivated, but the berry is very small. The wild edible fruits are not very numerous, the principal being the matungru, mpafu, nsale, mzabibu, and a fruit like a custard-apple. The matungru is a species of amomum. The mpafu is a fruit like a damson, with an intensely hard stone and a sweet nut-like kernel. The tree which produces it is the finest in Uganda, attaining a height of from 100 to 200 feet, with huge branching arms, and a trunk often five feet in diameter. It has pinnate leaves, and the bark when wounded yields a white, opaque, sweet-scented gum resin which is highly prized by the natives. Uzongora, on the west of the Victoria Lake, is the only other country where I have seen it, but Cameron mentions a tree of the same name as having been met with by him near the Tanganyika Lake.

Besides these native fruits and vegetables, the Arab traders from Zanzibar grow wheat and rice; onions, tomatoes, guavas, pomegranates and papaws have also been introduced by them, and are gradually spreading through the country; while from Egypt have come radishes, and the *Hibiscus esculentus* (Arabic baumian). Meat is eaten by all who can obtain it, but with most it is a luxury rarely indulged in. The beef is tough and insipid, and usually utterly devoid of fat. Sheep are comparatively scarce, and the best meat is goat's flesh, which when young is tender and well-flavoured. Fowls and eggs are but seldom eaten. Near the Nyanza and on the islands fish is largely consumed, there being a great variety in the Lake, from the diminutive "mukéni," about the size of whitebait, up to the huge "kambári," which often weighs 100 lbs. and upwards. Some kinds of fish are dried and sent inland, being exchanged for coffee and other products.

The modes of cooking in vogue among the Waganda are comparatively few, but some of them show a considerable amount of ingenuity. The pots used for most culinary operations are large globular earthen vessels holding about two gallons. For the purpose of boiling bananas a large leaf of the same plant is laid carefully in the pot, and the peeled fruit having been placed in it, water is poured into the pot, underneath the leaf, so as not to touch the bananas, which are thus *steamed only*. If meat or fish have to be boiled, a young banana-leaf is taken and the greater part of the mid rib removed, it is then held for a few seconds over the fire, thus rendering it tough, so that it will bend without breaking; the meat, etc. is then tightly tied up in it and placed on the top of the bananas, and the whole cooked together. By this means the meat is rendered tender, while all the gravy is retained in the leaf, and can be served up with it. Meat is also baked in these pots, two or three sticks being placed across the bottom to prevent the meat touching it and getting burnt. Smaller pieces are skewered on sticks and roasted over the hot ashes. Some kinds of bananas and the ears of maize are roasted in the ashes.

The chiefs and upper classes of people generally eat with their families and head slaves. The meals are served up in a large hut, the floor in the middle of the room being covered with a layer of banana-leaves; on these the food is placed, and every one gathers round in a circle. The hands are first washed, either with water or with circular napkins, the size of small plates, cut out of the succulent stem of the banana; these napkins contain so much sap that no water is required. Then all fall to with their fingers, a slave cutting pieces of meat off the joints for the party, with a knife or sharp splinter from a reed. If the host wishes to show particular attention to a guest he pulls off pieces of fat or other choice morsels and hands them to him, or he may produce a little salt. Good salt is a great rarity in Uganda, most of what is commonly used being of a dirty grey colour, and intensely bitter. The best is said to be brought through Unyoro, from the west of the Luta Nzige or Albert Lake. The meal over, the hands are again washed, coffee is handed round, and pipes produced. The coffee is invariably chewed by the Waganda, and never made into a beverage. The berries are gathered before they are ripe, boiled, and then dried in the sun. When chewed they have a pleasant aromatic taste, and tinge the saliva green. Every one in Uganda with any pretensions to being called a gentleman carries some of these berries with him, which he offers to his acquaintances when he meets them. The Waganda never drink during meals, but at the conclusion take huge draughts of water or plantain-wine.

The plantain-wine, or "mwengi," is made from the ripe fruit; this is peeled and mashed up in a trough with fine grass, water is added, and the liquor thus obtained is squeezed through a strainer into large bottle-gourds. When first prepared it is sweet and non-intoxicating, and is then called "mubisi"; but when allowed to stand it ferments, and becomes sour and intoxicating, and is then called "mwengi." Boiled millet is sometimes added, and it is then called "málwa." Mlamba is a weaker beer prepared in a similar manner. The Arabs have introduced the manufacture of spirits from this mwengi, and distil a most intoxicating liquor from it, containing a high percentage of alcohol.

Milk is used to a considerable extent by the Waganda, though some of them will never touch it. It is almost always used in the curdled state, for the majority of the cattle are in the hands of the Wahuma, near the great forests, often two or three days' journey from the capital, so that it is impossible for the milk to arrive in its normal condition.

The domestic animals of Uganda are cattle, sheep, goats, dogs, and cats. As already mentioned, the Wahuma are the principal owners of the cattle, which are large-made animals, either altogether hornless, or having only very short horns, the prevailing colour being brown or iron-grey, though cattle of all the ordinary colours are to be seen. They are bad milkers, giving only from half a pint to a pint and a half at each meal; for they will not give any milk unless the calf is sucking at the same time, and should the calf die they become dry altogether. A curious custom prevails with regard to milking the cattle. Men only are allowed to perform this operation, women being absolutely forbidden to touch the cows' udders. The sheep belong to the Somali breed, and are wretched-looking creatures; but comparatively few are kept by the natives. The goats are in many respects the most useful of the domestic animals, as they will eat almost anything, fatten quickly, and are very prolific; but they are very mischievous, and if they get into a garden soon make dire havoc among the trees and plants. Dogs are kept, but not nearly to the same extent as in Speke's time, those now found in the country being mostly used for hunting antelopes. They more nearly resemble a smooth English terrier than any other dog, and are generally of a tan-colour. As a rule they are miserable curs, and seem to be in a chronic state of alarm, with their tails always between their legs. A few cats are to be found, but they are useless for rat or mouse-catching, and are very noisy at night.

Fowls are kept by the Waganda, but they are very lean, as they are never fed, but live on what they can find. They are rather a nuisance about a house, as they bring foxes and leopards to the place.

Mtesa has a menagerie at Nebulagalla, where he has a lion, and one or two other animals, but though his hunters frequently bring young buffaloes, antelopes, leopards, and other animals, they never live long, and his menagerie never seems to increase. He had a young elephant when I first went to Uganda, but it did not live many months. He had also a tame tiger-cat for two years, which used to roam about the palace at pleasure.

The Waganda are great hunters, and have a regular system of catching the smaller antelopes. Elephant-hunting is a regular occupation with many of them, and they display great coolness and courage in boldly attacking this animal with their spears. For this purpose they always go in parties, three or four of them attacking an elephant simultaneously, dividing the creature's attention, and thus lessening the risk, but spite of all precautions many fall victims in this perilous pursuit. The elephant is also caught in pitfalls, which are dug near the ponds which it frequents, or in its accustomed haunts; they are about seven feet deep, and taper to a point at the bottom, so that the unfortunate animal which steps on one of these artfully concealed traps gets its feet jammed in the narrow hole, and is completely at the mercy of the hunters, who quickly despatch it with their spears.

Buffaloes are caught by a wreath composed of the branches of a thorny bush, so contrived that the thorns all point inwards; this is secured by a rope to a heavy log of wood, and placed in spots which the buffaloes frequent. When the animal steps on the ring its foot goes through it, and the thorns acting like the barb of a hook prevent its being shaken off, and the heavy log which is attached so impedes the creature's movements, that it is powerless to escape from the hunters.

The smaller antelopes are captured by means of nets. These nets are made of thick cord, and are about four feet high; they are supported on stout stakes, and placed in the open runs in the forest. A whole village often joins in the sport, each family contributing one or two nets; watchers are concealed near to turn the animals towards them and to kill them when entangled in the meshes, while the rest of the party, accompanied by their dogs, drive the game into the trap.

Lions and leopards are caught in traps made of heavy logs of wood; the animal in entering to get at the bait displaces the logs, which falling on him crush him to death.

On the shores of the Nyanza, the wild geese are often snared by a thin cord which is fastened to the bent bough of a tree, or a wand planted in the ground, on the gravelly or shingly beach where the geese come to search for worms and insects; a noose is formed at the free end of the cord and lightly secured to a peg or stone. The bird while searching for its food puts its head through the noose, and setting the cord free, the bough springs back and draws it tight, the struggles of the captive only serving to tighten it.

Fishing is largely carried on by the islanders, and the Waganda living near the shores of the Lake. The ordinary mode of fishing is with the rod and line. The hooks are generally small, and without barbs, and are made of native iron. The lines, which are very fine and strong, are manufactured from the fibres of a species of aloe. A light reed or cane about ten feet long forms the rod, and fish of from one to four pounds are easily landed with this tackle. The bait used is earth-worms and fresh-water shrimps. Night lines are also employed, the main cord being from 200 to 400 feet in length, with short lines at intervals of about ten feet; the hooks used for these lines are much larger than those used in rod-fishing, and are curved outwards. Large stones are fastened to the main cord to sink it, and floats of ambatch-wood are attached for the purpose of recovering it. These lines are set from canoes at some distance from shore. Two kinds of fish-traps are employed by the Waganda; the first consists of large conical wicker baskets about four feet high, and containing near the bottom a ring of twigs radiating inwards, so as to allow the fish to pass in without difficulty, but closing up tight with pressure from within. These baskets, to the number of eight or ten, are tied side by side, and taken out to sea and sunk with stones so placed that the baskets lie on their sides, their mouths facing the shore. After a time they are hauled to land by long ropes, to which boughs are fastened for a little distance from the baskets to prevent the fish escaping as they feel the water shoaling. Large quantities of fish are caught in this manner. The Waganda also employ fish-baskets exactly like our lobster-traps, and in the same manner.

Nearly all the wild animals which are peculiar to Africa are found in Uganda, and many parts of that country are a veritable hunter's paradise. The elephant frequents the vast forests on the northern frontier, and herds of them occasionally make raids on the banana-groves, among which they commit terrible havoc. Buffaloes abound in some districts, and are much dreaded by the natives, who rarely attack them. Like the elephants, they sometimes make dreadful ravages among the banana plantations. Rhinoceros and zebra are fairly common, the skins of the latter being highly prized. There is a great variety of antelopes to be met with in the forests, from the huge striped eland (*Oreas Livingstonii*) down to the diminutive ntallaganya, about the size of a hare; there being in all about a dozen species. There are a good many lions, although they are rarely seen. Leopards are numerous, and often come into the villages, attracted by the fowls. Chimpanzees and several species of monkeys are found in the forests, as are jackals, foxes and hyænas, but hares are rarely met with. In the Nyanza great numbers of hippopotami are found, while a large otter, much valued on account of its beautiful fur, frequents its shores. Rats abound, and crocodiles are numerous in the Lake, and much dreaded by the natives, but they have an inveterate foe in the shape of a large water-lizard, which digs up and destroys their eggs. Snakes are very abundant in Uganda, many of them being venomous; a harmless species, of a bright green, gives its name to that colour. Boa constrictors are not unfrequently met with, and in my garden at Rubaga I shot one fourteen feet long.

Among birds the most noticeable are the parrots, vultures, kites, and fish-eagles. There are two species of the former; one being the grey parrot, famed for its powers of talking, the other a small yellow and green bird. The first of these parrots is very common among the forests on the shores of the Lake, and is often seen in flocks of two or three hundred. The vultures are the scavengers of the towns and large villages, and there are always great numbers of them about the capital, where they feed on the victims of the executioners. Kites abound everywhere, and are very destructive to the chickens. The finest bird in Uganda is undoubtedly the white-headed fish-eagle (*Maliaetus vocifer*), which is found on the Nyanza, and the various streams where fish exist. Guinea-fowl are numerous in the jungle, and afford good sport, in addition to which their flesh is excellent eating, but they require heavy shot to bring them down; No. 2 is best. On the Lake vast quantities of water-fowl are met with — ducks, geese, storks, cranes, the sacred and glossy ibis, darters, herons, gulls, and the gorgeous scarlet flamingo.

Mosquitoes swarm in Uganda, and constitute at times a veritable plague. White ants are numerous, and very destructive, and quickly destroy the poles used to support the native huts. Some kinds of timber, however, they do not touch, notably the stems of the wild date palm, which are consequently largely used in house-building. In the months of August and September they emerge in the perfect or winged state from their nests, and are then caught by the natives in vast numbers for food; they usually come out in the evening, and the Waganda erect small huts over their nests to catch them, as at first they are very feeble on the wing and are easily caught. At this season groups of children may often be seen seated by the roadside, round one of these nests, picking up the insects as fast as they appear, and putting them into their mouths. They are generally fried, and when properly cooked are by no means to be despised.

Locusts are also eaten by the Waganda, and resemble fried shrimps when cooked.

The driver ant comes occasionally in swarms into the houses, and drives out everything, taking possession of the whole place. Their bite is like the prick of a red-hot needle, and no one who has ever been attacked by them will willingly run the risk of another visitation.

The occupations of the Waganda, generally speaking, may be said to be husbandry, house-building, and fighting. The cultivation of the ground is chiefly carried on by the women, house-building and fighting being the only occupations which are considered worthy of men. The gardens of the Waganda are as a rule extremely neat, and are separated from one another and from the road by high fences of the tiger-grass, or by hedges of euphorbia and other bushes. The hoe is universally used both for turning up the earth and for removing weeds. The different plants, sweet potatoes, beans, sesamum, etc., are sown in separate plots, divided by paths, and kept carefully free of weeds. In making fresh beds for any plant the soil is generally turned up to a depth of about nine inches. The principal objects of cultivation, beyond those already enumerated under the articles of food, are tobacco and the bottle-gourd. The tobacco is usually sown pretty thickly in small beds, and when the seedlings are sufficiently large they are planted out in rows. The bottle-gourds are generally grown over a framework of sticks, or are trained over the huts, the object of this being to allow the fruit to grow suspended in the air, that it may preserve its shape, for if it is allowed to rest on the ground the lower side becomes flattened. The banana or plantain is generally grown alone, as where they are tolerably thickly planted the shade they cast is too deep to allow other plants to thrive under it. These groves are well kept, the dead leaves and rubbish being periodically removed, and sometimes, together with the weeds from the other parts of the garden, piled round the roots of the bananas, this being the only attempt made by the Waganda to manure the ground. Immediately round their houses the Waganda have small gardens, divided from one another by high grass fences, and in which a few large banana-plants and a variety of vegetables are grown.

In house-building the natives of Uganda are superior to any of the negro tribes of Africa that I have seen, the houses of the upper classes being neat, clean, and roomy. The establishments of the principal chiefs are very large, sometimes covering several acres, and comprising a large number of huts. The whole area is surrounded by a high fence of grass, the supporting poles being generally trees, a species of Ficus, which furnishes the mbugu or bark cloth, being the most common; these trees throw out a large crown of branches, which afford a pleasant shade. There is usually only one gateway, which gives access from the highroad into a small courtyard enclosed by high fences, and in this yard is a small hut or porter's lodge. The whole area is subdivided by fences into a number of courts or gardens, shady with bananas and fig-trees. In each of these courts one or more houses are built, those in the inner courts being occupied by the owner and his harem, while those in the outer ones are tenanted by the slaves. All the chiefs of high rank have such establishments in the country as well as their town house at the capital. The houses of the bakopi, or peasants, in the villages have generally only one court in front of the house, and many have no courts at all, but stand singly here and there among the vast banana-groves which surround each village. The houses are usually circular or dome-shaped in form, and being thatched down to the ground, look like huge bee-hives. The material employed is the stout stems of the tall tiger-grass, which attains a height of from fifteen to twenty feet. A ring of fine grass, closely bound round with the fibrous outer part of the banana stem, is laid on the ground, and a number of the tiger-grass stems securely tied to it with strips of papyrus; then a second and third ring are added at intervals of about fifteen inches. The framework so formed is now raised on poles on the site of the intended house, and more rings are added, fresh tiger-grass ribs being worked in as the structure widens. At length, when the curvature of the rings becomes sufficiently slight to allow of these same stems being bent without breaking, the rings are formed of them instead of the fine grass employed at first, the whole umbrella-shaped frame being gradually raised as the work proceeds, till the required height is attained. Then sufficient poles are left inside to support the whole, the ends of the ribs are trimmed off, and the doorway is cut out. A bank of earth is afterwards made all round, and consolidated by wetting and stamping it, in order to prevent the water soaking into the house during the heavy rains. Bundles of long grass are now tied on to the ribs to form the thatch, beginning of course from the bottom, and finally a peak formed of a large sheaf of grass very tightly bound together is added, the edges of the thatch over the doorway are trimmed, and the house is complete outside. Porches are generally added, and the floor having been levelled and the partitions, of the same ubiquitous tiger-grass, having been erected, the building is finished. When newly built these houses are remarkably clean and neat-looking, but as there are no windows, and no outlet for the smoke except the doorway, they are very dark, and soon get discoloured with soot.

In making the holes for the supporting pillars, should the ground be hard, water is poured over it, or else the watery tissue of the banana is squeezed on it, to soften it so that the soil can be readily loosened with the spear or pointed stick which is usually employed for this work.

In the houses of the poorer classes a partition is generally made across the centre of the hut, facing the door, the front part being the living-room, and the back the kitchen, for, owing to the rainy climate of Uganda, cooking operations are not carried on so much in the open air as they are in many parts of Africa. The sides of the hut are often separated from the body of it by curtains of mbugu, behind which are the sleeping-places of the family. But in the establishments of the chiefs separate huts are assigned for these different purposes.

The floors of the huts are strewn with soft, fine grass, which is carefully laid down; first a small bundle of even length is placed on the ground, and then another at right angles to that, and partially overlapping it, then a third at right angles to the second, and so on, forming a series of squares, till the whole floor is covered. A few houses may be seen occasionally with gable roofs and vertical walls, but they have probably been copied from foreigners, and do not need description; Mtesa's palace at Rubaga being the only one which merits any notice. This was a lofty building, some ninety feet long and supported on huge pillars, each being formed of a large tree. A fine hall occupied about two-thirds of the total length of the building, and on either side were two long, narrow rooms where the court or baraza was occasionally held. At the back were a number of smaller square rooms, through which access was gained to the interior of the palace grounds.

Mtesa has several times changed the site of his palace, and consequently of his capital, for the houses of the katikiro or lord chancellor and principal chiefs are always built round that of the king, and consequently, when a fresh spot is chosen for the palace, a small town of houses springs up round it, and the old ones are deserted and soon fall to pieces or are pulled down. The old capital of Banda, where Speke and Grant saw Mtesa, has totally disappeared, and not a single house is to be seen on its site; and one or two other towns have shared the same fate. At present Mtesa has two capitals, Rubaga and Nabulagalla, and lives sometimes at one and sometimes at the other; but during the two years I was in Uganda he was living at Rubaga. Shortly before I left the country he changed the position of his palace, because he thought the place where it then stood was unhealthy: in this case he only moved a few hundred yards away, but even then the katikiro had to move his whole establishment, and to build new houses for himself within the orthodox distance from the palace.

The Waganda are very particular about their houses, and I have known a whole house pulled down and rebuilt for some trifling flaw or fault.

Cattle-breeding, which is the only other occupation to be noticed, is confined almost entirely, as already mentioned, to the Wahuma.

The manufactures of the Waganda are, for an

uncivilised race, rather varied, and may be classed under pottery, bark cloths, basketwork, mat-making, metal-work, woodwork, leather-making and dyeing.

The pottery of the Waganda is of two kinds, coarse and fine. The coarse kind comprises the large jars used for carrying water in and for cooking; the former are globular, with a narrow neck, and contain from one to two gallons, while the latter have very wide, shallow necks, or are open hemispherical vessels with no necks. The finer kinds of pottery are the black drinking-bowls and tobacco-pipes. These are made of a fine clay containing a large amount of mica, and which is procured from the beds of streams, and is probably formed from the detritus of igneous rocks. The pipes and bowls made of this clay are very thin, and beautifully finished and smoothed, but as no flux or glaze is employed, they are very brittle. When first burnt these articles are of a light grey colour, but after being suspended in the smoke of a wood-fire they become a permanent black. Two shapes of pipes are used, one with a round bowl, and containing a very small amount of tobacco, and the other with a conical bowl which will hold half an ounce or more; both kinds of pipes and the drinking-bowls are often tastefully ornamented with patterns, which are sometimes coloured with red oxide of iron and white clay.

The bark cloth, or mbugu, is procured from a

species of fig—*Ficus ludia*—which grows abundantly throughout Uganda. When at its full size, it is about sixty feet high, and four or five feet in girth, but it is from the younger trees that the bark is usually taken. Two incisions are made round the trunk, and a third vertically joining the other two. The cylinder of bark is then stripped off, the outer surface is carefully removed, and the bark is laid on a smooth square block of wood, and rapidly beaten with heavy wooden mallets. These mallets have circular grooved heads, which give to the bark a ribbed appearance like corduroy, and under their blows the bark quickly extends, like gold under the gold-beater's hammer, becoming, of course, at the same time thinner. When it has been beaten out to the requisite thinness, which is generally a day's work, the bark is hung up to dry, and afterwards any holes which may have been produced in the beating are neatly patched with the trimmings from the edges. These mbugu, when new, are of a yellow-brown tint, closely resembling freshly tanned leather; some of the finer sorts, however, are of a dull brick-red colour. They vary much in quality, some of the better kinds being beautifully soft, and these are procured chiefly from the Sesse group of islands. The principal fault of this cloth is that it soon decays if it gets wet, but owing to the extreme abundance of it in the country, this is of small consequence. When old and worn, it makes excellent tinder, and I have frequently seen it used by the Waganda (and have also used it myself) for this purpose. They twist it tightly into a rope, and carry it with them on a journey to light their pipes with, as in this state it will smoulder for hours. The tree from which the bark has been removed is not killed by the operation. The wound is covered with banana-leaves, which are bound closely round it, a sort of skin forms over it, and in process of time new bark grows.

In common with most negros, the Waganda are very skilful in basketwork. The materials generally employed are grass, and the leaflets of the wild date palm. Of the former they make large shallow, circular baskets, which are used as dishes to convey food in; to form these, a continuous ring of fine grass, bound closely round with plantain-fibre, is coiled on itself in a wide spiral, the individual rings being sewn strongly together with the same fibre; and so carefully and tightly are these baskets made, that they are perfectly watertight. Small baskets, with lids, are made of the leaflets of the date palm for carrying the indispensable coffee-berries. The fish-traps and basketwork on their shields have already been mentioned.

They make beautiful tubes for drinking their native beer through. A hollow curved stick is taken and covered with close-fitting basketwork of the date palm leaflets dyed various colours, while at the bottom is a strainer made of various coloured grasses, terminating in a "crown" knot.

The mats, which are an invariable article of furniture in every respectable family, are made of strips of the young leaflets of the wild date palm. These leaflets are dried and bleached in the sun, and then cut carefully into strips and plaited into large mats, elegant patterns being often made by working in blue, red, or black strips. These mats are very pliable, and will roll up without cracking or splitting.

In metal-work, the blacksmiths of Uganda are very superior to their neighbours. They obtain their iron from ore found in the country, and though rather short, it is of good quality. Steel, except as imported, is unknown to them. Their spears, knives, etc., have already been mentioned. They also make various articles, such as spears, bells, and rings, of the brass and copper imported from Zanzibar; and Mtesa once showed me some brass cartridge-cases made by his smiths, which, though only cast, were wonderfully true and smooth. The Waganda are very clever at imitating articles of European manufacture, and frequently convert flint-lock muskets into percussion guns.

The only noticeable articles of woodwork are their walking-sticks and milk-pots. Walking-sticks are carried by all the aristocracy of Uganda, and are made out of a hard white wood, and are beautifully turned and polished. The milk-bowls are made by the Wahuma out of a solid block of wood. They are pear-shaped, containing about a quart, and are very neatly formed and very true.

The work in which the Waganda most excel is the dressing of skins. The hides, after being dried in the sun, are stretched tightly in a frame, and the inner surface is carefully removed with a knife. Then they are rubbed over with a stone, which produces a fine grain, and butter or oil having been worked in, they are again exposed to the sun. This process makes the skins as soft and pliant as kid-leather, and preserves them perfectly. Sometimes the hair is also removed, but more commonly it is left on. Small skins of antelopes and other animals are often dressed in this way, and sewed together form robes which are highly prized by the Waganda.

Stout sandals, sometimes tastefully ornamented, are made of buffalo-hide. The Waganda also dye their mbugu in various patterns, the most common pattern being diamonds, which are printed or dyed in black. The black dye appears to be the soot of a sweet-scented wood. It is mixed with oil, and applied to the mbugu. They also obtain a yellowish orange dye from a tree called mulilila, resembling our lauristinus. It is a gum, and exudes from the bark in small drops or lumps.

A whole volume might be written on the customs of the Waganda, but the limits of this book will only allow of a slight sketch of their manners and customs.

The salutations of the Waganda are very varied; on meeting an equal, the ordinary salutation is Kulúngi to which the other responds with Kulúngi; Otía and Otiáno are also frequent salutations, to which the same word is given in reply; but often a much more elaborate performance is gone through, somewhat as follows:—Otia! otia; Otiano! otiano; Erádi! erádi; Nyogi! nyogi; Mam! mam. Then ensues a series of grunts, such as one might fancy a couple of pigs would greet each other with. When an inferior salutes a superior, he either kneels down or bends forward, leaning on his stick or spear, and says Otía sébbo or Kulungi sebbo (sir), to which the superior replies É. When two friends meet after a long separation they embrace one another, laying the head first on one shoulder and then on the other, uttering at the same time a series of grunts. The chiefs, on entering the baraza or court, salute the king by stooping or kneeling before him and touching his outstretched hand between the palms of both hands, and then raising their hands to their lips. The recipient of a favour from the king or chief expresses his gratitude by kneeling down and putting both hands together, moves them up and down several times, uttering the word Nyanzige, or shortly Nyanzig—I thank (you); the plural of which is Twanzig—we thank (you). Or he snatches up a couple of sticks or spears, and dancing about and charging towards the king or chief, declares his loyalty and fidelity, and boasts of what he will do in return for the favour shown him.

One thing which strikes the traveller on first seeing the Waganda is the utter absence of all tattoo marks, and of any disfigurement of their persons, such as the enormously distended lobes of the ear, so common among the Wagogo and other tribes south of the Nyanza; all such practices being absolutely forbidden by their laws. Nor do they extract or file any of their teeth, a custom almost universal among negros. Mutilations, except as a punishment, are prohibited, and are punishable by death.

The diseases to which the Waganda are subject make a formidable list, and include most of the principal diseases known to European physicians. Small-pox is one of the most fatal, coming at intervals in epidemics, and carrying off thousands of victims; it is of a very virulent type (confluent), consequently so few of those attacked by it ever recover, that it is rare to find a person, in Uganda, marked with it; which at first might lead a traveller to supppose that it was almost unknown. It is probably brought by traders and others from the East Coast, where it is chronic. Syphilis is extremely common, especially among the men, in all its forms, and is a frequent complication in other diseases. Dropsy, measles, rheumatism, ague, bronchitis, ophthalmia, cholera, and a form of leprosy, are all to be found: of the latter, leprosy, I never saw a case, but, judging from the descriptions given by the natives, it certainly is known in Uganda. Temporary madness is pretty common, and generally lasts for three or four days; but persons thus afflicted do not become very violent.

Many, especially women, suffer from epileptic fits, and girls who have this complaint are difficult to dispose of, and are often married without being paid for. No medicine is used in either of these illnesses.

Persons are often observed with white patches on their hands, faces, and legs; there is no disease in the skin, but merely an absence of pigment.

The Waganda are very clean in their habits, washing frequently, and never smearing their persons with fat, which is such a common practice among negros; the fact of their being entirely clothed obviates the necessity of this.

The Waganda are not so particular about their hair as many tribes, as they rarely dress it in any way, and generally shave the head bare. A larger number of them, however, have beards than any negro race I have seen except the Wanyamwézi.

They are a drunken race, though happily it cannot be said in their case that it has been acquired from their intercourse with Europeans. Owing to the extreme ease with which the banana-wine, "mwengi," can be obtained, even the poorest can indulge in it, and when not at work they sit sucking it through straws or the ornamented tubes already mentioned, consequently in the evening a considerable percentage of the men, of what may be called the upper classes, are in a state of semi-intoxication. It is, however, rare to see them helplessly drunk; nor does the mwengi seem to produce headache and sickness as most European liquors do, and as is the case with the grain-produced pombe of Usukuma and Unyamwezi, and the merissa of the Soudan. This I attribute to the absence of the higher alcohols, known commonly as fusel-oil, consequent on the alcohol of the mwengi being derived from sugar, and not from starch, as is the case where grain is employed.

Gluttony is also a common vice with the Waganda, and I have had men pointed out to me, who were said to have eaten a whole goat at one sitting. They sometimes gorge themselves to such an extent that they are unable to move, and appear just as if intoxicated.

They are also great smokers, the women being as much addicted to smoking as the men, but they never use tobacco in the shape of snuff, nor do they chew it. The tobacco of Uganda is of very good quality, and is always used pure, without any mixture of foreign substances; it varies very much in strength, some being comparatively mild, but most of it is very strong; it is not made up into cakes, but used in the whole leaf. Most of the tobacco plants are not allowed to seed, the flower-buds being picked off before they open.

The servants in Uganda are all slaves, the majority being born in slavery, and a tolerable percentage are prisoners, children mostly, taken in war. They are, as a rule, fairly well off, and are not often badly treated; but of course they are liable to be sold to the Arab and half-breed traders for guns, ammunition, cloth, etc. They often live on terms of familiar intercourse with their masters, and are treated as part of the family. Their condition more closely resembles that of the Russian serfs before their emancipation than that of the slaves at Zanzibar and on the East Coast. One of the principal evils resulting from slavery in Uganda is that it causes all manual labour to be looked upon as derogatory to the dignity of a free man, and this is one of the most formidable obstacles which the missionary and philanthropist encounter on trying to elevate the people and introduce legitimate trade and commerce.

Polygamy is universal in Uganda, from Mtesa, who is said to have seven thousand so-called wives, down to the poorest mkópi, or peasant, who can scrape together enough to buy a couple. As a natural result immorality is frightfully common, and all the more so owing to the vast harems of the king and chiefs absorbing a large part of the female population, so that many of the lower orders cannot get wives. The marriage bond is a very loose one, and is a purely business arrangement. The ordinary price of a wife is either three or four bullocks, six sewing needles, or a small box of percussion caps, and I have often been offered one in exchange for a coat or a pair of shoes. There are no laws forbidding the marriage of near relations, and they frequently do marry; indeed on the death of any man the eldest son inherits all his father's wives, with the exception of his own mother. The women rarely have more than two or three children, and the law is that when a woman has borne a child she must live apart from her husband for two years, at which age the children are weaned; and the king and principal chiefs have establishments in the country where their wives are sent for that period. In the case of the birth of twins great rejoicings take place. On the fifth or sixth day after the birth all the villagers assemble outside the hut where the mother and children are living; the women dress themselves with a girdle of banana-leaves, and dance, or rather sidle, in a circle round a couple of drums (which are vigorously beaten for several hours by relays of men) singing a monotonous sort of chant; the men squat about and watch the dancing, or amuse themselves by wrestling, which is one of their favourite amusements. The happy father, dressed in all his finery, meantime wanders about from group to group, receiving the congratulations of his friends. The navel cord is preserved, and in the case of chiefs is covered with beads and other ornaments and attached to a stand, the whole looking like a huge horse-shoe magnet with its keeper attached. In the case of the king's there is a chief of high rank whose duty is to take care of it, and bring it to court on certain occasions.

When a chief dies he is buried in a wooden coffin. Slaves are not buried, but their bodies are thrown into the jungle. Criminals who have been executed are generally left just where they fell, sometimes even in the highway, no one daring to remove them, and are devoured by the hyænas and vultures.

When a man dies possessed of property it is divided amongst his sons, the wives, as already mentioned, going to the eldest son, though he may, if he likes, share them with the other children.

The Waganda have a great variety of names, but as a rule each person has only one, though the kings and some of the chiefs have more. Some names are special favourites with them, *e.g.* Mukassa, the name of the lubari of the Nyanza, for they see nothing improper in assuming the names of their gods; names of animals and insects are also given to people. Many names have definite meanings; thus, Mtesa means one who tries or decides causes; Mkavia or Mukavia, another of Mtesa's names, means "he who makes to weep," being derived, by a process very common in the Bantu languages, from the verb "kavia," "to make to cry," which again is the causative form of the verb "kava" or "kawa," "to cry, howl, or bark." This name was taken by Mtesa on the occasion of a great victory gained by his troops over the Wasoga.

There are no special days in the year, as far as can be ascertained, and no special seasons of rejoicing or festivals, with the exception of the day on which the new moon is first seen; then guns are fired and drums beaten; but this is probably a custom introduced by the Arabs, as it is only observed at the capital.

The only trade of any importance carried on with Uganda is entirely in the hands of the Arab and half-breed merchants from Zanzibar. These men bring guns, ammunition, cloth, beads, and a few other articles, which they barter for slaves and ivory. Uganda is the most northerly station of the Zanzibar traders, for though they penetrate to Unyoro, yet their depôt is at Rubaga and there they collect their goods and form their caravans to go south to Unyanyembe. A pretty brisk trade in slaves is still carried on from and through Uganda, and I met on one occasion as many as 200 going down the Lake, in canoes furnished by Mtesa, to Kagei in Usukuma; and old Kadúma, the monungwa or chief of Kagei, asserts that at least a thousand slaves from Uganda come down every year to that port, and many more go by the Karagwe route. The Waganda have advanced far enough on the road towards civilisation for a number of wants to be created by the introduction of articles of foreign manufacture which can only be supplied from external sources. They require cloth, beads, guns, powder, shot, brass wire, etc., which can only be procured from the Arab traders, and the only two things with which they can purchase them are ivory and slaves: the supply of ivory is limited, and is steadily on the decrease, as the elephants are killed off, and so they sell their slaves. These causes will also operate to increase the slave traffic unless some external check is put upon it, for the wants of the people increase year by year, and the Arabs are always glad to take slaves, as they are more profitable than other kinds of merchandise. Consequently there is a continual drain on the slave population, which is already beginning to make itself felt. And if the bad policy of the traffic is represented to the Waganda in this light, they acknowledge it at once, but reply "We must have guns and gunpowder and cloth, and we have no ivory to buy with, so we must sell our slaves." The only hope of really checking this nefarious trade is by introducing legitimate commerce, and as in this the Arabs cannot successfully compete with Europeans they would soon be starved out of the country. The principal of these Arab traders is one Mohammed bin Ibrahim, who has been some twenty years in Uganda. Said bin Salem, the governor of Unyanyembe—Speke and Burton's old Ras Kafilah—used to send some of his head slaves up to Uganda to trade, and the 200 slaves which I have just mentioned belonged to him.

The bulk of the ivory taken in Uganda comes into Mtesa's hands, and also a good deal from Usoga, chiefly as tribute; this is all sold to the Arab traders for cloth and guns, and ultimately finds its way to Zanzibar. There was formerly a small trade with the Soudan, coffee, tobacco, mbugu, and cattle being exchanged for fezes, calico, and red slippers. But since the evacuation of Mruli by the Egyptian troops all communication with the North is at an end.

There exists a small amount of internal trade in salt, mbugu, dried fish, and the various articles of native manufacture, but it is of very slight importance, and does not of course add in any way to the wealth or prosperity of the country.

As will have been gathered from what has been already mentioned, trade is carried on by means of barter, and money, strictly speaking, is never used; still there is a recognised standard of value to which everything is referred, and that is the dóti, four yards or eight cubits, of unbleached calico. Two dóti are the price of a cow, and a shúka, or half a dóti, of a goat or sheep. Cowries, which are brought from the East Coast, are the small change of Uganda. They are used in strings of one hundred each, ten strings, or one thousand cowries, being equal to one dóti. Beads of various kinds and brass wire are also employed as money, but not nearly to the same extent as cloth and cowries. The cheapest way of buying food, especially for a small party, is to purchase a bullock, and having killed it exchange small portions of the meat for bananas, sweet potatoes, fowls, eggs, and other provisions which will keep. For meat being a rarity among the bakópi (peasants) they are glad to get it, and a much larger quantity of food can be obtained in this manner than by buying it directly for cloth or cowries.

CHAPTER VIII.

GOVERNMENT AND LANGUAGE OF THE WAGANDA.

THE government of Uganda is a very perfect form of the feudal system. The king is theoretically owner of all the land, but this has become, to a great extent, a legal fiction, and the three leading chiefs of the country are practically the owners. The Waganda may be roughly divided into four great classes, viz.: slaves; bakópi, or peasants, who form the bulk of the population; batóngoli, or chiefs of the second rank, and bakúngu, or chiefs of the first rank. The bakópi are in many respects the most important class, partly on account of their numbers, partly because they supply the soldiers who have made the name of the Waganda to be feared and hated in all the neighbouring countries. It is from their ranks also that the second order of chiefs, the batóngoli, is recruited, and the sons of batóngoli, their rank not being hereditary, become again bakópi. It is also, I believe, among these peasants that the efforts of the missionary will be most successful, and that here again, as in numberless instances, history will repeat itself, and that the earliest and sincerest converts will be drawn from among the poor of the country. The batóngoli, or second order of chiefs, govern districts under the bakúngu, and in time of war have to furnish a certain number of men as soldiers. Their position is frequently bestowed upon them as a reward for distinguished bravery in battle, and is tenable only for life, not being hereditary. The term batóngoli, however, is a vague one to a certain extent, and there is often a wide difference between the members of this class, some ranking very high at court, while others are but little removed from the bakópi. The bakúngu, or highest order of chiefs, like the batóngoli, vary a good deal in actual position. They form the bulk of the great council of the nation, and the three leading bakúngu are hereditary, the present representatives of the three families, in their order of precedence, being Mkwenda (or Gabunga), Sakibobo, and Kangao. The chief officer of the kingdom under the sovereign is the Katikiro, or lord chancellor; he is appointed by the king, and holds his office for life, or during the king's pleasure, and takes precedence of all other nobles, sitting next the king in council. He need not be of good birth, and may even be, as the present katikiro is, the son of a mkópi, or peasant. All these chiefs are, in virtue of their position, magistrates or judges, and decide civil and criminal causes which occur in their respective districts, though all the more serious cases have to come before the leading bakúngu, the katikiro, or even the king himself; and the accused has always the right of appeal from a lower to a higher authority. There is, of course, no written law by which cases are decided, but there are certain principles of equity, in accordance with which decisions are given. Both plaintiff and defendant plead their own cause, and call witnesses, but cross-examination of witnesses excepting by the judge is not allowed. The decisions given often display a vast amount of shrewdness and knowledge of character. Besides those already mentioned there are two persons of great importance about the court, and these are the chief brewer and head cook. They hold a high position at court, sit near the king, and take part in the great council.

The Luchíko, or council, is the real governing body of the nation. It consist of the king, katikíro, bakúngu, and leading batóngoli, together with the chief cook, brewer, and one or two other sycophants. Under ordinary circumstances this council meets every day, and spends some hours in discussing the affairs of the nation. It is usually summoned and dismissed at the king's pleasure, but on special occasions the chiefs have the right to demand that it be assembled if they think fit. In minor points the king can act as he pleases, but in all important affairs he is bound to consult the council, which is largely influenced by the three leading bakúngu already mentioned; and if they agree in requiring anything, no king would dare to oppose them, as they would undoubtedly depose him, and place another monarch on the throne. From this it will be seen that Mtesa is by no means the absolute monarch he has been represented by many travellers.

The katikiro, the three bakúngu, and one or two others, favourites of the king, form a sort of privy council, to which all matters of paramount importance are first referred. Sometimes during a general council these men are called aside by Mtesa to consult on important points; they gather closely round the king, talking in whispers, while one of the harp-players, who are always in attendance at court, plays and sings to drown the sound of their conversation. All the chiefs are expected to be in attendance on the king for three months consecutively, and then are allowed to be nine months at their country establishments. However, most of the bakúngu, and some of the leading bantóngoli live at the capital, unless absent at war.

The royal family of Uganda is of a different nationality to the Waganda, and belongs to the Wahuma tribe, to which reference has already been made. Mtesa, through the admixture of Negro blood, has lost the pure Mhuma features, but still retains enough of the peculiar characteristics of that tribe to stamp him as belonging to a distinct race from his subjects. He professes to trace back his descent, through an unbroken line of between thirty and forty kings, to Kintu or Ham, the founder of his dynasty. The following list of kings was given me by Mtesa himself, but whether the different sovereigns are distinct persons or not is a very doubtful matter; many of the names being probably those of the same person, for it is the custom of the kings of Uganda to take additional names on their accession or in remembrance of any great event. Thus Suna, Mtesa's father, had four names, and Mtesa himself has six. And this supposition is made more probable from the fact that the Waganda have mentioned to me other names of kings than those given in Mtesa's list. The kings, arranged chronologically are: Ham or Kintu, Chwa, Kalemela, Kimela, Rumaansi, Tembo, Kigala, Wampamba, Kaima, Nachibinge, Mrondo, Sekamanya, Jemba, Suna I., Chimbugwe, Kataréga, Mtébe, Juko, Kaémba, Tibandeke, Ndaula, Kagúra, Chikúrwe, Mawaánda, Msánje, Namgába, Chabagu, Junju, Wasaja, Kamanya, Suna II., Mtesa.

Besides these names I have had Semakokilo and Sematimba given me as kings of Uganda.

Mtesa, the present monarch of Uganda, is now about forty-five years of age, and when I first knew him was tall, slender, active, and graceful in his movements, but he has now aged a good deal, and become broken by long illness. He is shrewd and intelligent, having learnt to read and write

Arabic, and he can also speak several African languages besides his own. He has a keen eye for the main chance, and will never lose for want of begging. His great aim and object is self-aggrandisement. He wishes to make Uganda the greatest country in the world, and himself the mightiest monarch, and he thinks that the presence of Europeans at his court will add to his prestige and increase his wealth. He is always glad to welcome a traveller, because he is another pigeon to be plucked. He quite understands that Europeans are acquainted with many things of which he is ignorant, and he wishes to acquire as much of this knowledge as possible, and also to employ their skill in procuring arms and ammunition, believing that the secret of a nation's greatness consists in the amount of the munitions of war which it possesses: and with this view he bullies all European travellers, to try and induce them to give, make, or procure these objects of his desire for him. It is this also that has made him wish to have Europeans settle in the country. He is a thorough man of the world, and when he pleases can be as courteous and gentlemanly as any of our own aristocracy. He takes an intelligent interest in a wide range of subjects, and will discuss for hours abstruse points in theology, political economy, or philosophy. He is intensely fickle, and never knows his own mind for two days together, and like a spoilt child is always wanting a new toy. This trait of Mtesa's character accounts for his changes of religious profession. He is crafty, and knows well how to swim with the stream of popular opinion. He is very superstitious, and if he dreams of any of the gods of the country, he takes it as an omen of ill, and immediately offers human sacrifices, sometimes to the number of several hundreds, to appease the anger of the offended deity. He is, however, too shrewd and intelligent to believe in many of the grosser superstitions which find credit among his people.

He has great veneration for the memory of Capt. Speke, who left behind him a high character for manliness and integrity, of which subsequent travellers have enjoyed the benefits. Mtesa labours however, under the great disadvantage of being surrounded by a crowd of worthless sycophants, who pay him the most fulsome flattery, but who would depose him without the least compunction if they could gain anything by it. In his younger days he proved himself brave and warlike, and, spite of his many cruelties, seems to have a strong hold on the affections of the lower classes.

His treatment of individual Europeans depends very largely on their treatment of him; a firm yet courteous demeanour he always respects, and any traveller who will behave in this way to him, and who will not unnecessarily obtrude his differences of opinion, nor insist on them too strongly, and above all who is perfectly truthful and honest with him, will obtain a great amount of influence. For my own part, during my two years' stay in Uganda, I never had any serious personal difference with him, and the same can be said by more than one other European who has stayed at his court. Mr. Felkin in particular can bear me out in this remark.

The laws relating to the succession to the throne are peculiar. When a king dies, his successor is chosen from among the deceased monarch's children by the three hereditary bakúngu, with whom alone the choice rests. A child is always elected, and during his minority the boy's mother, if living, acts as queen regent, and with the aid of these three nobles, governs the country, the young king being meanwhile trained up in the traditions of his ancestors. Should, however, the three chiefs not agree in the choice of a successor, they go to war about it, and the victor places his nominee on the throne. The reason of this singular law is, no doubt, to prevent intrigues during the king's lifetime. The brothers of the king elect are kept in confinement during his minority, and when he comes of age all are burnt, with the exception of two or three who are preserved to keep up the succession, in case the young sovereign should die childless. The children of the king have no rank or status on account of their birth, and the princesses are not as a rule allowed to marry, only a few of Mtesa's numerous daughters having been given as wives to neighbouring kings or to the great nobles of Uganda.

The administration of justice has already been described. The punishments which are inflicted are imprisonment in the stocks, mutilation, and death. The stocks consist of a heavy block of wood with a hole in it through which the foot is placed, and a peg is driven in which prevents it being withdrawn. This is a punishment confined to small offences, such as petty thefts and insubordination on the part of wives or slaves. Theft is punished frequently by cutting off the hands, ears, or nose. Adultery is punished invariably by death, and murder occasionally, but more often only by a fine. The Waganda have a variety of modes of execution, some of them being horribly barbarous. Beheading and strangling are those commonly employed, and human sacrifices are always beheaded. For the worst offences the victim is bled slowly to death by gashing the body with sharp splinters of a reed, care being taken to avoid the larger arteries and veins. A small army of executioners is kept in Mtesa's employment, and some of them are always in attendance at court. They wear ropes round their heads, or a hideous fringe of grass, which adds to the ferocity of their looks.

The prestige of the Waganda as a nation rests mainly upon their warlike character, which tinges the whole of their life and government. As already mentioned, every man who can handle a spear and shield is a soldier, and the rapidity with which an army can be collected is astonishing. When the king and council have decided on a campaign, the great war-drum is beaten, and the following morning vast crowds of warriors assemble outside the palace attired as if for battle, their ordinary clothes being laid aside, and only a loin cloth being worn, their faces whitened with ashes to give them a ghastly appearance and strike terror into the hearts of the enemy. The king stands outside the palace gate holding a shield and two copper spears, which may be carried only by the king and the principal chiefs. Round him are his nobles, similarly armed. Every body of warriors as it approaches, dancing and yelling, comes up to the king, and, going through the motions of attacking, vows fidelity to Mtesa and vengeance on his enemies ; then they retire to the side, and a vast crowd gradually forms round the monarch, a lane being kept clear in the middle, up which fresh groups of warriors come to perform the ceremony of swearing fidelity. Meantime, the great drums of the palace boom out the war signal, which can be heard for miles around. When the greater number of the warriors in the immediate neighbourhood of the palace have collected, the king calls out the chiefs who are to have command of the forces, and gives them their commissions, and afterwards the vast assembly disperses. The commanders then send for the various batóngoli who are to furnish the men, the numbers each is to bring are settled, and the time and place of rendezvous agreed upon, and then gradually the army departs for the scene of conflict. In battle each man carries two or three spears; they advance in open order towards the enemy, dancing about and yelling; when they get within range they hurl one or two spears, and then close with the remaining one, the conflict then becoming a hand-to-hand engagement, and consequently fearfully fatal. Should the commanding chief be killed, the whole body take to flight.

The Waganda are nearly as successful in naval engagements as they are upon land, and possess a large fleet of war canoes. These are mostly distributed among the numerous islands off the coast of Uganda, the chief of each island having two or more canoes under his charge. Many of these war canoes will hold forty men, and are splendidly made vessels. A finer sight can scarcely be imagined than a fleet of two or three hundred of these graceful vessels threading their way among the wooded islands of the Nyanza, their paddles keeping time to the rhythmical beats of the war-drums. Each canoe carries a certain number of fighting men, the proportion of these to the paddlers being about two to one. The paddlers are protected by shields, and in case the enemy are pursued to shore, they remain in the canoes close at hand, lest the enemy should prove victorious and a retreat become necessary. The canoes are apportioned out to various chiefs, under whose command they fight, the whole being under the chief admiral of Uganda. The present admiral is called Gabunga, and has a magnificent establishment on the mainland between Murchison Bay and the Katonga river. The canoes are made in the

UGANDA CANOE AND FISH-TRAP.

following manner: A long straight trunk of a tree is taken and adzed to the shape of the bottom of the vessel, and then carefully hollowed out down the middle; it is tapered off at both ends, and at the bow a sort of horn is formed which projects some three or four feet beyond the cutwater when the canoe is finished, and a number of small holes are bored with a red-hot iron along each side. Then two long planks, hewn with the axe out of the solid trunks of trees, are taken, and a number of holes having been bored to correspond with those in the bottom log, the two are tied together with the root-fibres of various plants, curved boards being added at either end where the canoe narrows; then two other planks are added and secured in a similar manner: the first row of planks are sloped outwards at an angle of about 60 degrees, thus giving additional breadth to the canoe, the second row being vertical. Large holes are made along the lower edge of the second row of planks to receive the thwarts, and at the bow a large piece of wood is fastened, projecting like horns some three feet on either side of the gunwale, by which the canoe is drawn up on land. When completed thus far, the outside of the vessel is painted a light red, with iron oxide obtained by burning an ore resembling hæmatite, and then the seams are all caulked by thrusting in plantain-fibre, which has been steeped in water, from the outside. Then a curved prow called "nsanda" is added, the top being ornamented with a pair of antelope's horns, and from this to the bow a fringe of grass is fastened to give additional ornament. This prow is loose, and is usually removed when the canoe is drawn up on land. The canoes are steered by the two last paddlers in the stern, and, except in the largest ones, only one paddler sits on each thwart.

The religion of the Waganda is in some respects a more intelligent one than that of many Negro nations. Idolatry, properly so-called, is unknown; they have no images, nor any outward symbol of their gods. They believe in a Supreme Being who made the world and mankind, and whom they call Katonda, or the Creator, but they offer no worship to him, as they consider him too exalted to pay any regard to mankind. Their principal objects of worship are inferior gods or devils called lubari. These demons are supposed to inhabit certain places or localities, and to exercise special powers over various objects. The principal of these gods, and the most generally feared and worshipped by the Waganda, is Mukusa, the god or lubari of the Nyanza. This deity is a sort of Neptune, who is supposed to live in the Lake and to control its waters, and also to exercise a considerable influence over the whole country of Uganda. From time to time he enters into some person, either man or woman (at the present time it is a woman), who thenceforth becomes the oracle of the god, and who is supposed to possess, in consequence, supernatural powers, to be able to cure diseases, to withhold the rain, bring wars, famines, pestilences, etc., on the land, and to foretell events. This person who is the representative or personification of the god has an enormous influence over the minds of the people and chiefs, and thus indirectly exercises an important control over the government of the country. When about to make a voyage, the Waganda always make offerings to this spirit, to propitiate it. The canoes are gathered together some distance from shore, and the chief in charge of them, standing up, places some bananas or other food on a paddle, and, holding it over the water, prays to the god to give them a prosperous voyage and to bring them safely back to their homes; then he throws the fruit into the water, begging the god to come and take it.

Others of the demons are Chiwuka and Nenda; they are gods of war, and are supposed to inhabit certain trees in various parts of the country. At these trees the Waganda, before going to battle, pray and make offerings to the deities, the offerings consisting of live animals, goats, sheep, and cattle, which must invariably be black, which are given to the guardians of these trees, who receive them on behalf of the god. Another lubari is called Ndaula, and appears to be identical with one of the former kings of Uganda; he is supposed to reside on the summit of Mount Gambaragara (Mount Gordon Bennett of Stanley), and is said to bring small-pox, and is worshipped as the personification of that disease. Thunder is also worshipped, and on the spot where lightning is seen to strike the ground either an arch is erected, under which no foreigner is allowed to pass, or a small hut is built, covering the place; the hut is not repaired, but allowed gradually to fall to pieces, and when it has disappeared the ground is common again. There are also river gods in different parts of the country, to which human sacrifices are sometimes offered. The former kings of the country appear also to be regarded as demi-gods, and their graves are kept with religious care, and houses are erected over them, which are under the constant supervision of one of the principal chiefs of the country, and where human sacrifices are also occasionally offered. The Waganda are extremely superstitious, and have a great belief in charms which are manufactured by their medicine-men. These charms are made of curiously shaped pieces of wood, horns and similar rubbish, and are supposed to ward off disease and to protect the wearer from the bites of venomous snakes, which are very common in Uganda, and much dreaded by the natives. These medicine-men, mandwa, have immense influence over the people, and are consulted by them on all manner of subjects. They profess to be able to foretell events, recover lost or stolen property, and to make rain and wind. They also practise as regular doctors, using herbs and the roots and bark of various trees, and are tolerably successful. They have two or three remedies for ague, but whether these will be found to be of any real value in the hands of European practitioners remains to be proved.

Foreign religions have so far made but little impression upon the Waganda. Although the

Mohammedan traders have been settled in the country for at least sixty years, they have made no converts, for Mtesa's so-called conversion to Mohammedanism was merely nominal, and even the Arabs themselves do not claim him as a convert. He would never submit to circumcision, and one hundred boys and youths who had submitted to that rite believing that Islamism would become the national creed, were all burnt by Mtesa's orders. This rite, which is a *sine quâ non* with Mohammedans, seems to have been the great stumbling-block in the way of the acceptance of that creed by the Waganda, and that has been the chief objection which has always been alleged by them against Islamism whenever I have mentioned the subject.

With regard to Christianity, I believe that it will be readily accepted by the lower classes, but the majority of the chiefs, than whom would be difficult to find a prouder class of men, will, I fear, strenuously oppose its introduction into their country.

The visits of travellers to Uganda, and the presence of foreigners there, are beginning to produce a decided impression on the country and people, and though at present confined mainly to the court and neighbourhood of the capital, it is extending gradually through the land. All foreigners are supposed to be the king's guests, and during their stay in the country, to be lodged and fed at his expense. When a traveller reaches Uganda he must send word to the king of his arrival, and request permission to proceed to the capital; this is generally graciously accorded, and a chief, with a body of men to act as porters, is sent to escort the traveller and his goods. While on the journey this chief and his followers live on the people whose villages they pass through.

On arriving at the place where it is intended to spend the night, the party takes possession of the villagers' huts, eating their provisions and stealing their goats and fowls, and, as a rule, no resistance is offered to this abominable treatment. Occasionally, however, if the party is small and the village large, the people refuse the required accommodation, and a fight ensues.

On reaching the capital, the traveller will have a compound allotted to him, with huts for himself and servants, and there he is expected to live during his stay in the country; and permission has never been accorded to any European to live in any other part of the country than the capital. At first, after the arrival of a traveller in Uganda, he will be liberally supplied with food, especially if Mtesa thinks he will get a good present; but after a time it will rapidly diminish, and he will be obliged to purchase provisions.

The Arab and half-breed traders from Zanzibar live mostly in the villages near the town of Nabulagalla (Stanley's Ulagalla), where there is quite a little colony of them. They are either agents of large Arab traders in Unyanyembe, or men who have run away from their masters on account of debt, and who are afraid to return. There are also a few Soudanis and Dongolowis, deserters from the Egyptian troops at Mruli. They are chiefly in Mtesa's bodyguard, and have taught their comrades something of drill.

The Waganda have a high idea of what is due to strangers or guests, and it is said that no foreigner has ever been murdered there—which, in Central Africa, is saying a good deal. Many of the chiefs, however, are very jealous of foreign influence, and some of them once told me that if they had had their way neither Speke nor Grant, nor any other European, should ever have set foot on the soil of Uganda. They are especially jealous of Egypt, and look with great fear on any extension of its territory in the direction of their country.

Foreigners are allowed to be present at the luchiko or council, already mentioned, and are often appealed to for advice on various social and political questions, but they are rigidly excluded from taking any part in any matter connected with the succession to the throne; and indeed, under all circumstances, it is by far the best plan to keep out of all local politics; interference in these matters rarely does any good and frequently seriously compromises the traveller.

In case of a civil war occurring in connection with the succession, all foreigners are taken to one place, where they are placed under the care of a chief, who has to provide them with food and shelter, and who is responsible for their safety so long as they remain there; but if they go beyond the appointed limits, they do so at their own risk.

As already mentioned, foreigners are beginning to exercise a certain amount of influence over the people, and this increases year by year, and we are able to see a considerable advance in this respect since Speke's time. The Arabs, having been longest in the country, naturally have hitherto made the greatest impression on the people, though this has not been so great as might have been expected from the quickness with which the Waganda pick up and imitate anything new. The most marked change produced by foreign influence is in the matter of dress. In Speke's time mbugu were universally worn, and no person, except members of the royal family, was allowed to possess cloth; now all that is changed. Mtesa has quite abandoned the use of the native bark cloth, and the majority of the chiefs rarely wear it; and instead of its being considered a crime for a commoner to possess cloth, many even of the bakópi wear it. Fire-arms are yearly increasing in numbers, and will, no doubt, in time change the mode of warfare. Foreign fruits and vegetables have been introduced, and are being spread through the country. Since Speke's time chairs and stools have been introduced, and are used by many of the chiefs, whereas formerly all sat upon the ground. The few European tools, such as files and screw plates, which have found their way to Uganda have been adopted, and are skilfully used by the native workmen. And if good stone or brick houses were built, there is no doubt but that they would be imitated by the Waganda. We built a square house in the mission grounds at Rubaga, with vertical walls and a gable roof, dispensing with the forest of poles which the native huts require to support the roof, and very soon some of the chiefs began to build similar ones on a smaller scale.

In some respects, the most useful result of the intercourse of the traders from Zanzibar with the Waganda is the introduction of the Swahili language, for though the people generally do not understand it, yet in most large villages two or three natives will be found who can converse in it; while at court it is widely spoken. Mtesa knows it as well as his own language, and most of the leading chiefs understand something of it, so that the traveller who comes to Uganda from the East Coast will find himself able to communicate directly with the people.

The Waganda have a considerable variety of games and amusements, such as dancing, singing, and wrestling.

In dancing the men and women keep separate. There are two sorts of dances, one of which consists of a shuffle performed singly or in groups by boys. The feet are never raised off the ground, and the performer advances or recedes, shuffling along, the knees slightly bent and holding the arms stiffly by the sides, with the hands stretched out, the palms being held downwards, while the whole body is writhed about, every muscle being brought into action. It is a most disgusting performance, as the dancer looks exactly as if in an epileptic fit. It is excessively exhausting, and cannot be kept up for more than two or three minutes consecutively. The other manner of dancing is more like the European style, for although the performers dance singly, and not in couples, there are regular steps, and there is a musical accompaniment.

The Waganda are very fond of singing, which is generally accompanied on the nanga or harp. There are regular professional singers, like the minstrels of the Middle Ages, who are retained by the king and chiefs, and who are always in attendance at the court. When singing they frequently extemporise, their language being specially suitable for this purpose, bringing in allusions to passing events or to persons who may be present. Their songs are of several descriptions, some being in praise of the king or great chiefs, others war-songs, and others again dirges or laments for dead chiefs and warriors. I give two specimens, the first being in praise of Mtesa, and the second a lamentation over some dead chiefs:

I.

Thy feet are hammers,
Son of the forest.*
Great is the fear of thee;
Great is thy wrath;
Great is thy peace;
Great is thy power.

II.

Oh, separator !†
Oh, Sematimba!
They tied goats;
They tied goats for him in vain.
Son of a king,
He has no pride.
He freely gives plantain wine.

Lubinga! Lubinga!
Him of whom I speak,
He has no pride.
For he freely gives plantain wine.
Mkwenda! Mkwenda!
Whose home is Chikongi.‡
Him of whom I speak,
He has no pride,
For he freely gives plantain wine.

I have just referred to the fondness of the Waganda for music. They have regular bands, which belong mostly to the king, each band being under a leader, who performs the same functions as a European

---

* A synonym for the lion, which is the emblem of royalty.
† A synonym for death.
‡ Chikongi is the place where he is buried.

bandmaster. These bands are either string bands or composed of wind instruments and drums. In the case of the string bands, the performers are generally Wasoga, who are considered the best harpists in that part of Africa. Mtesa also possesses what may be called a military band, consisting of two or three brass bugles and some brass drums. The drums and one of the bugles have been made by the king's smiths. These instruments are played on by boys who have learnt one or two military calls and the roll on the drum from a coast negro, a Malagasy, Toli or Tori by name, who was formerly cabin-boy in a French vessel, and who has been in France, and seen something of European civilisation.

The young men of Uganda are very fond of wrestling, in which they show great skill. They commence each bout by taking hold with the right hand only, the left being held behind the back, but when they have got a good grip the left hand is brought into use. The throw generally employed seems to be that from the hip.

The boys also frequently engage in kicking matches, such as are in vogue, or used to be, in some parts of France. The only game, properly so called, which the Waganda know, is that called mweso, for which they use a board containing thirty-two holes, in four rows of eight each. It is played by two people; each player has a certain number of stones, which he places in his two rows of holes, and the game, which is a very complicated one, and requiring a considerable amount of calculation, consists in trying to get all the stones of the opposite player. They redistribute their stones in turn, and on stopping at a hole may, under certain conditions, take their opponent's stones out of the two holes opposite. It is a most fascinating game, and the Waganda will sit for hours over the mweso board. It is probably not a native game, but introduced from the East Coast, where a somewhat similar game, called " bao." is played by the Arabs and Waswahili.

The children in Uganda, as everywhere in the world, may be seen playing games in imitation of the doings of their elders, and making mud-pies by the roadside.

The language of Uganda, or Luganda, as it is called by the natives of the country, belongs to, what Dr. Bleek calls, the Zangian genus of the middle branch of the Bantu languages. By the term Bantu is meant that great family of African languages, extending from the Cape of Good Hope, where it is represented by the Kafir tongue and its dialects, through Eastern and Central Africa to the Equator and to the West Coast near Sierra Leone, where the Bullom and Timneh languages are allied to the Kafir. Next to the South African members of the great family, the best-studied language is the Kiswahili, spoken on the East Coast about Zanzibar from the Somali coast almost to Natal. This Kiswahili is the trade language of Zanzibar and Eastern Central Africa, and is spoken a little in Uganda.

The chief characteristic of this class of languages is that all the changes (with scarcely an exception) required to form the grammatical inflexions take place at the beginning of the words. Consequently the learner is at first greatly puzzled by what seems the extreme uncertainty of the words. And especially is this the case with the adjectives and possessive pronouns. For in Luganda and the cognate languages, the forms of these parts of speech are regulated by the class of nouns to which the adjective or pronoun has reference, and there are in these languages from seven to ten, or perhaps even more, classes of nouns, most of which have a distinctive prefix both for the singular and the plural. E.g. in Luganda, lungi means good, and muntu mulungi, a good man; bantu balungi, good men; mti mulungi, a good tree; miti milungi, good trees; nyumba nungi, a good house or houses; kintu kilungi, a good think; bintu bilungi, good things; lusogi lulungi, a good hill; nsogi nungi, good hills; toki dungi, a good banana; matoki malungi, good bananas; wantu walungi, a good place or places, and so on.

Again with the verbs, prefixes are added to prefixes representing person, tense, relative, subject and object, the verb root coming last, so that often what would be the greater part or the whole of a sentence in English, is represented in the Bantu language by a single word. The following instance from the Swahili language will serve to make my meaning clearer: He who will give him the knife, atakayekimpa kisu: here, a = he, taka = will, ye = who, ki = it, m = him, pa = give, kisu = knife.

It need scarcely be said that the Waganda have no written language, and until the establishment of our mission in the country the language had never been studied, and no attempt had been made to reduce it to writing. Now, however, a considerable insight has been obtained into the language, a large number of words have been collected, and the translation of the Bible has been commenced. In reducing Luganda to writing we have adopted the Roman character, as, apart from other reasons, it proves to be well suited to the genius of the language, and by a few simple rules of pronunciation can be made to represent all the sounds found in it, as well as any characters could be expected to do. Only twenty-four letters are used, neither X nor Q being required: the former sound is absolutely wanting, and the latter, though found, is more correctly represented by kw- or ku-.

The Waganda have a number of tales which they relate about the former monarchs of Uganda, many of whom are semi-mythical persons. The hero of most of these stories is Ham or Kintu, the first king of Uganda. The following legend will serve as a specimen. Kintu, when he first settled in Uganda, was a great hunter, and also possessed large herds of cattle. He was, moreover, of a very merciful disposition, and the animals which he caught in his traps used frequently to beg to be let off, saying to him, "You be kind to us in the sunshine (i.e. when you are well off), and we will be kind to you in the rain (i.e. when you are in trouble); and so he would often give them their freedom. On one occasion the pursuit of some wild animals had led him to a greater distance from home than usual, and when he returned he found all his cattle gone. After searching in vain for them for some time, he met a man, who asked him what he was looking for, and Kintu replied that he was seeking his cattle. "Oh, you need not look here for them," was the man's answer, " for the gods came down from heaven and stole them all." So Kintu went up to heaven, and after gaining admittance, demanded his cattle, but was informed by the gods that before he could recover them he must perform certain deeds. He professed his willingness to try, and a large basket of food, enough to satisfy fifty or sixty men, was brought, and he was told that he must eat it all. This was impossible; and while Kintu was wondering how he should accomplish such a feat, a large number of rats whose lives he had spared on earth appeared and ate up the food. So Kintu returned with the empty basket to the gods, hoping to receive his cattle. But the gods took him to a deep well, and, giving him an empty pitcher without a rope, informed him that he must fill it with water from that well. Kintu was again nonplussed, as he had no possible means of procuring or making a rope; but when almost in despair, a flock of swallows, to whom he had formerly shown mercy, flew to him, and taking the pitcher from him, descended the well with it, and brought it up again full of water; so Kintu bore it joyfully to the gods. Then he was conducted to a vast plain, where immense herds of cattle were grazing, and was told that his oxen were amongst them, and that if he could pick out his own cattle from among them without making a single mistake he should be allowed to take them, but if he made one slip he should forfeit the whole. Kintu, who could not distinguish his own oxen, was sorely puzzled; he did not like to try for fear of making a mistake, and yet did not feel inclined to give up after all the trouble he had gone through; when in the midst of his perplexity a large bee, to which he had been kind on a former occasion, came to him and said, "I know which are your cattle, and I will go before and hover over each of your oxen." The bee did so, and Kintu picked out all his own cattle without a single mistake, and returned with them to earth in triumph.

Besides these legends of Kintu and other kings, the Waganda have many stories about animals, similar to Æsop's fables, of which the following is an instance. Once upon a time the hare and the crocodile made a treaty of friendship, and when the ceremony was concluded the hare said to the crocodile, "Take me to your house, my friend, that I may see it." So they crossed over to the other side of the island, and when they reached the place the crocodile said to the hare, "Go into the house while I seek for a present, and let my wife and children come and pay their respects to you." So the hare went in, and the crocodile's wife came with her children and saluted him. Then the wife went into the garden to cut bananas, leaving the children in the house. When she was gone the hare noticed the children under the eaves of the house, and seized and ate them. Then, fearing lest he should be caught, he called to the wife, "Oh, my friend, call your husband, that he may take me to the mainland, for the houses on the other side of the island are on fire." So she called her husband, who took the hare on his shoulders and plunged into the lake. When he was halfway across, the wife came running to the shore, calling out, "Crocodile! crocodile!! crocodile!!!" But her husband, who was making a great splashing in the water, did not hear clearly what she said, and asked the hare, "What does my wife say?" "She says," replied the latter, "that you are to make haste, for the houses are all on fire." So the crocodile swam to the mainland, and the hare ran off into the forest. But when the crocodile got back his wife saluted him with "You fool! I called to you that our guest had eaten the children."

There are also nursery tales, so to speak, of which I give an example in the original with a literal translation. This and similar tales are told to the children on their fingers, like the well-known story of the Five Little Pigs. Wachakusu! Owe. Uvao wa? Mvao kulya mpafu. Zengeddi? Magu magu. Lailao. Semakokilo. Wamlabba? Mpulida biogerri. Parrot! Yes. Where are you coming from? I come from eating mpafu (a fruit of which parrots are very fond). Are they ripe? Ripe, ripe (quite ripe). Swear (so). (Yes by) Semakokilo (a former king of Uganda). Have you seen him? I hear talk (of him).

The Waganda are, in many respects, mentally and physically superior, but morally inferior to most of the negro tribes I have seen. Indeed, morality among negroes seems to be in inverse ratio to the amount of clothing they wear, and the most naked tribes, when uncontaminated by external influence, are the most moral, and the best clothed, the most immoral. Where polygamy is the rule, as in Uganda, woman of course holds an inferior position, being looked upon principally as property, and the more wives a man has the richer he is, for he can have more ground under cultivation. This tends to encourage immorality, which is further increased by the fact, that spite of the large excess of females existing, many of the lower classes cannot obtain wives. In common with all savage tribes, truth is held in very low estimation, and it is never considered wrong to tell lies; indeed, a successful liar is considered a smart, clever fellow, and rather admired. Consequently they judge all travellers by their own standard, and if anything is told them which appears astounding, their reply is "Ulimba!" "What a lie!"

The same applies to theft. The distinctions between *meum* and *tuum* are very ill-defined; and indeed all sin is only relative, the crime consisting in being detected. The average Mganda, while dreadfully shocked if any one steals from him, or murders any of his friends, does not hesitate to do the like if there be a moderate chance of his escaping discovery. Human life is held at a very low estimate, and murder is very common. The following incident will show this. A young page of Mtesa's, son of a subordinate chief, was frequently employed to bring me messages from the palace, and one morning came down to my house, and informed me with great glee that he had just killed his father. I inquired why he had done this, and he said that he was tired of being merely a servant, and wished to become a chief, and said so to Mtesa, who replied, "Oh, kill your father, and you will become a chief;" and the boy did so.

The Waganda put great reliance in charms and "medicine" to make rain, or wind, to make their guns shoot straight, and to protect them in war.

They are a brave, warlike race, but excessively indolent, this being due, no doubt, in a great measure, to the ease with which they can obtain all the necessaries of life. If a gang of men are set to build a house, mend a fence, or do any other manual labour, one or two will work while the rest look on smoking, or " chaffing " each other. The women do the greater part of the hard work, tilling the ground, fetching water, cooking, etc.

The disposition of the Waganda, particularly of the women, is very kindly, and they often take trouble to do a kindness to a traveller, especially if well treated. They generally bring him food on his arrival at a village, and will even light a fire, also offering any delicacies which they think may prove acceptable. The following incident, which happened to my fellow-traveller, Mr. Felkin, will illustrate this. On one occasion he had gathered a number of botanical specimens on the march, and on stopping at a village, some of the women noticed these, and at once went out and brought him a large quantity of flowers; and I have myself had many similar experiences.

They are, moreover, very affectionate, and if properly treated become strongly attached to Europeans, and make very good servants, as they are quick at adopting foreign customs; they soon learn to cook in European style, to wait at table and perform other household duties.

Their skill in imitating articles of European manufacture has already been alluded to. In all kinds of instruction they show remarkable quickness, rapidly picking up a language when they go to a foreign country. They learn to read in a very short time. A large number of boys and young men were under instruction at our mission house in Rubaga, and learnt to read Swahili, and their own language in the Roman character, astonishingly quickly. The Rev. G. Litchfield, one of the Church Missionary Society's missionaries in Uganda, formed a singing class, instructing his pupils by the tonic sol-fa system, and in two or three months they were able to sing any simple tune at sight.

The Waganda have also a high idea of figures. They have native names for all numbers up to thousands, and it is a curious fact that the root of the names of all numbers which are multiples of ten, is the word ten; e.g. kumi is ten; makumi abili (two tens) is twenty; kikumi is one hundred, and lukumi is one thousand. The Waganda are very fond of counting, and whenever they get hold of a book, the first thing they do is to count the leaves. The game of mweso, which has been already mentioned, is one which requires a considerable amount of calculation.

Thus it will be seen the Waganda are by no means

low down in the scale of intellect, and offer a promising field for educational work. Nor is there the fear, which exists with regard to many savage nations, of "improving them off the face of the earth." They have all the vices and most of the diseases of Europeans, and they, in common with the whole Negro race, must possess an enormous amount of vitality to have survived under the constant drain of the iniquitous slave traffic and the fearful losses from constant war. A great future is before the people of Uganda, and from the physical advantages and central position of that country, it is well fitted to be the centre of light and civilisation to the surrounding nations.

CHAPTER IX.

VOYAGE TO KAGEI AND SHIPWRECK.

But to resume the narrative. I remained in Uganda, working at the language, which I was now beginning to speak well, until the beginning of June, when, having heard no further news from the South, and calculating that the caravan which Mackay had talked of sending up to Kagei ought soon to be reaching that place, I decided to go and meet it.

The *Daisy* was at Kagei, having been taken there by the Wang'uána when they left me, so I was obliged to have recourse to the native mode of travelling. Accordingly, having obtained a man from Mtesa to procure canoes for me, I left Rubaga on June 14th. Various delays occurred, and we did not reach the Lake till the 19th, when we crossed over to the island of Busu, which is situated near the entrance to Murchison Bay.

While waiting on the shores of the Lake for the canoes which were to convey me and my party to the island, I saw the most extraordinary swarms of butterflies that I have ever met with. The spot was an open glade in the forest, which here came down to the water's edge. Countless butterflies of all sizes and every hue of the rainbow were flitting about, and on a marshy spot were what I took to be a number of yellow flowers, but, on approaching them, to my astonishment they rose into the air, a perfect cloud of these insects.

On arriving at Busu, I was taken to one of the villages, and a hut was being prepared for my use, when one of the people came and advised me not to stay in it. "Why?" I asked. "Oh! because it has a bad disease in it," was the reply. "What sort of a disease is it?" "It makes a person's fingers and toes drop off." Further inquiry showed that it was a sort of leprosy, and the natives assured me that I should probably catch it by sleeping in the infected hut. This may throw some light on the much-disputed fact mentioned in Leviticus of the leprosy in the house.

This island, in common with most of those forming the Sesse group, was beautifully timbered, and abounded in monkeys and parrots.

The next three weeks were spent in going about from island to island, and occasionally to the mainland, in order to get canoes for the journey. All the different chiefs tried to evade having to provide me with them, as the voyage along the southern shores of the Nyanza is considered a very dangerous one, and is much dreaded by the Waganda canoemen.

When at length we obtained the first instalment

for the journey, the chief of the island from which they were procured came to see us off, followed by a crowd of curious natives. After we had pushed off, he harangued the crews from the beach, bidding them be careful, and exhorting them to avoid the storms, which had shipwrecked so many of their comrades; he concluded his speech with the ominous words, " Lumbi, lumbi, lumbi." (" Death, death, death.") The men promised obedience, and we started, followed by a ringing cheer from the crowd on shore.

The scenery among these islands was of the most fairy-like description. Each island was, for the most part, covered with a dense mass of forest trees, there being frequently a ridge of hills running down its centre. Coasting along (as is the custom of the Waganda) within a short distance of the land, I had ample opportunities of studying the lovely views constantly presented to the eye. The shore was often lined with a thick fringe of the graceful papyrus, like fairy palms, with a beautiful purple convolvolus twining in out amongst the stems; a mass of gigantic forest trees formed a magnificent background to the picture, relieved by occasional openings revealing glimpses of plantain groves and picturesque villages. The water was dotted with pink and blue water-lilies, while in the creeks thick beds of the curious *Pistia stratiotes* were anchored, or drifted about in miniature islands; vast numbers of waterfowl perched in the ambatch bushes or flew swiftly over our heads; the hippos boldly poked up their ugly brown heads to stare at the passing canoes; here and there a crocodile lay basking on the surface of the water, while, perched on some lofty tree, the beautiful black-and-white eagle (*Maliætus vocifer*) calmly surveyed the animated scene below. At other times the shore was clothed for miles with low, dense jungle, having open grassy spots where the crocodiles were wont to lay their eggs, and on the sloping sandy beach the waves of the great Lake broke with ceaseless murmur.

The beginning of July found me only a short distance from the island of Busu, owing to the almost interminable delays which were caused by the various local chiefs who had to furnish the rest of the canoes. These canoes, which are used in war and for travelling, are scattered about among the numerous islands off Uganda, and when the traveller wishes to collect ten or twelve in which to convey his goods and servants, he has to go from island to island, getting one here and another there, till he has made up the requisite number. Most of these canoes are brought from the Archipelago of Sesse, which, according to Mtesa, contains about four hundred islands, varying in size from a couple of acres to several square miles, some of the largest being from ten to fifteen miles in length, and three or four in breadth; most of them are inhabited. I have myself seen between fifty and sixty of this group, and a long list of the names of the islands belonging to Sesse was given me by one of the natives.

These delays, though very vexatious, gave me many opportunities of observing the inhabitants of the country under very favourable circumstances. During the whole time I stayed in their villages I was able to mix freely with them, being unfettered by the restrictions which are in force at the capital, and, as it was my practice to take long walks in search of game and botanical specimens, I obtained a much more accurate estimate of the population of the country, and gained a far better acquaintance with the manners and customs of the people, in these few weeks, than could have been possible in years spent exclusively at the capital. The people also, being at a distance from the dread army of executioners who hover around the court, were not afraid to visit me, and, when sitting under the shade of a tree, reading or writing, I generally had a crowd of women and children watching all my actions. The village chiefs, moreover, used frequently to beg me to protect them from the depredations of the Waganda who, by Mtesa's orders, accompanied me, and who, according to their custom on arriving at a village, began to plunder the huts. On one occasion a chief came to me, complaining that my rascally escort had seized one of the villagers, had bound him, and then imprisoned him in a hut, without food, in order to make the rest of the villagers procure some meat for them, which they were too lazy even to steal for themselves. I at once interfered, but in vain, and a bullock had to be given them before he was released. On another occasion a chief, who had received orders to provide us with a canoe, went off without doing so, whereupon my escort seized his favourite wife, and took her to our next halting-place, remarking that her husband was sure to come after her, and that then they could get him and compel him to send for the canoe.

As we proceeded southwards, the country was more thinly peopled, and there were often long stretches of jungle without a single village. The land, too, became more level, with flat sandy beaches, where the crocodiles were in the habit of basking in the hot sun. On halting once at an open place in the jungle, the canoemen found a crocodile's nest containing eighty-two eggs. This was the largest number I ever saw in one nest, those I have seen generally containing from forty to sixty. The eggs of the crocodile are white, very long in proportion to their breadth, and having thick rough shells; they are about the size of a swan's egg, and are, when fresh, by no means bad eating, having a slight musky favour.

On July 13th we reached Dumo, a fine well-wooded promontory extending some distance into the Lake, and having several large villages. Here I saw some curious rafts, formed of the leaf-stalks of a large palm, which grows abundantly in this locality. These stalks are about nine feet long, and are extremely light. The rafts are made of a double layer of stalks fastened side by side by means of cross pieces of wood which are driven through them horizontally, all the broad ends being together so that at one end the raft tapers almost to a point. Two or three more stalks are secured on either side, one above the other, to form a sort of gunwale to protect the fisherman from the waves, the broad end being left open. These rafts are extremely buoyant, and are employed by the boatmen to carry their fish-baskets out to the spots where they are sunk.

We left Uganda on July 17th, and, having crossed the mouth of the Kagera river, camped in the country of Uzongoro. After passing this river a wonderful change took place in the scenery. North of the Kagera the country was generally low, and densely clothed with forest, while the shore was often fringed with papyrus; now it consisted of high downs, rising often to an altitude of 800 and 900 feet above the Lake, and ending in abrupt precipices 300 to 400 feet in height. These hills sometimes came sheer down to the water, occasionally having a strip of alluvial land along their base, where herds of long-horned cattle grazed, and large villages were found, their level beaches of dazzling white sand affording easy landing-places to my canoes.

We stopped on the night of July 17th, in the district of Keioza. Crowds of people came down to our camp, bringing plenty of provisions for sale. These Wazongora were decidedly inferior to the Waganda in appearance, and were not so well clothed, the men and women wearing dirty skins or grass kilts, while the unmarried girls and boys were nearly naked. Their language was very similar to that of Uganda, and I could understand many of their words.

The following day we continued our voyage, the coast being of the same description, only that the downs were higher, and the capes and headlands bolder. Passing Makongo, where Stanley narrowly escaped a fight with the natives, and where, later on in the same year, I spent two months, we landed on a lofty uninhabited island, whose northern face came precipitously down into the Lake. It was on a sloping piece of open ground, on the western side of this island, that we landed, and made a camp, while some of the canoes went over to the mainland to get food. After seeing all my property safely landed, I climbed to the top of the island, hoping to have a good view of the Lake, but found this impossible, as the denseness of the jungle with which the island was clothed almost shut out the daylight. One peculiar feature of this jungle was the enormous quantities of spiders which it contained; they were mostly a very large black species, beautifully marked with red and yellow; their webs festooned every tree and bush, and one was obliged to stop every few yards to remove the masses of silky fibre from one's face. While climbing along a ledge of rock I came upon several human skeletons lying in a heap. A few steps more revealed other skeletons, and a small cave close by was full of human skulls and bones; judging from the appearance of the teeth and skulls, they were the remains of persons in the prime of life, but whether they had been killed in battle, or were the victims of some of those nameless deeds of blood of which Africa can tell so many, I cannot say.

Our camp was formed on the edge of the forest; three or four large acacias with graceful pinnate leaves stretched their huge arms overhead; in a semicircle facing the Lake were our huts of green boughs and grass; fires were lighted before them on the sward, the blue smoke curling up into the calm evening air, and round them were gathered in picturesque groups the dusky forms of the canoe-men. Flocks of ducks and geese flew by to their roosting-places, hawks and eagles hovered overhead, a solitary crocodile was lazily floating on the surface of the water, while the sun setting behind the purple hills of Uzongora left a broad track of blood-red light across the Lake.

Leaving this place, we pitched our camp on the mainland, on the shore of a magnificent bay opposite the island of Kishaka. We were now in a different district of Uzongora, this part being under the rule of Keitaba. The people were darker than those in the district of Keioza, and the dialect spoken by them varied somewhat from that of the latter province, and had fewer words in common with the Uganda language. The ordinary salutation of the people of Keioza was Kilembé, while here it was Smálige.

We were detained here several days by adverse winds, and left finally on July 30th. We passed along the western side of the island of Bumbire, which rises in the centre to a height of several hundred feet above the Nyanza, and appeared, from the Lake, bare and barren. That night was spent on the uninhabited island of Maiga, and the following day the island of Lubili (also uninhabited) was reached.

Here we remained a whole day, being detained by a storm, and I spent some time in exploring the place. A high ridge runs down its centre, rising almost perpendicularly from the water on the southern side to an altitude of about 150 feet; it is covered with a dense forest and a luxuriant undergrowth of ferns and lycopodia. An open spot on the edge of the precipice afforded a glorious view of vast extent. Immediately below, the tops of the forest trees formed a waving sea of foliage of every shade of green; beyond stretched the blue waters of the Nyanza for many miles, the southern horizon being bounded by the purple hills of Uzinja, while far away on the south-east the summits of two islets of the Kome group were just discernible. The roar of the surf on the rocky shore raised by the morning's storm reached the ear as a faint murmur, the air was filled with the song of birds and the musical hum of countless insects, and occasionally a white-headed eagle startled the echoes with its harsh cry.

Next day, seven and a half hours' good pulling, brought us to the Kome group, a cluster of some twenty islands in the south-west corner of the Nyanza. They are of different sizes, and most of them uninhabited, the people who formerly lived there having been almost annihilated by the Waganda. One of the smallest of these islands is a great breeding-place of the water-fowl which frequent the Lake; it was covered with low bushes, which were filled with the nests of cranes, darters, ibis, and other birds, while on the ground ducks, geese, kingfishers, etc., laid their eggs. When I was there the young birds were mostly about to leave the nest, and the uproar made by the vast flocks of old birds hovering about and the cries of the fledglings for food was perfectly deafening, and could be heard at a great distance. Our canoemen landed and secured a large number of the young darters, which they consider great delicacies, but they had such a powerful odour that I could not bring myself to eat them.

The next two or three days were spent among the Kome group, going from island to island, passing here and there low ridges of rock rising up out of the Lake, often far away from land.

On August 8th we stopped the night on a small island at the entrance to Jordan's Nullah, off the coast of Uzinja. The following day we started early, wishing to reach Kagei before night. It was very foggy, and we lost our way, finding ourselves at length off the coast of Urima, far down Jordan's Nullah. However, turning the canoes in the right direction, we kept along close in shore, passing Great and Little Mwanza. At the latter place the Waganda, attracted by the herds of cattle grazing near the beach, wanted to land and seize some of them, and it was with the utmost difficulty that I prevented them. At length, just as the sun was setting, we came in sight of the familiar Palm Tree Point. The men were tired, and we made but slow progress, so that it was quite dark when we rounded the point, but, guided by the lights in the villages of Kagei, we made for the little cove where we were accustomed to land. These men were new to the place, and, the entrance being difficult to find, I took a seat in the stern, and, paddle in hand, directed the leading canoe, for I knew from long experience every rock and bush about the place. Nearing the village two shots were fired to announce our approach, and a crowd rapidly gathered on the beach. I sprang ashore as the canoe grounded, and inquired of the first man who greeted me if there were any news of the Wazungu (white men). Yes, Mackay had come, and in another minute I had grasped his hand, more than two years having elapsed since I had said good-bye to him at Bagamoyo.

We walked up to the village together, and, after supper, I opened the letters he had brought me. There was much to tell one another; Mackay had his troubles and travels to relate, also how, of the two men who had been sent out to his aid, one had fallen and the other been obliged to return. I had my story to tell of the death of Dr. Smith, the murder of Smith and O'Neill, my work in Uganda, and my voyage to meet him. Time flew by unheeded, and the cocks began to crow, and the first pale flush appeared in the grey east before we retired to rest.

Mackay had started early in the year, with a caravan, for the Lake, and on getting some two-hundred miles from the coast, received the news of the murder of Smith and O'Neill. Leaving the caravan under the charge of one of his companions, he came on rapidly to Kagei, with only a few attendants, and arrived there in June. He had thus been nearly two months at that place when I arrived, having been delayed by sickness and the large amount of repairs required by the *Daisy:* these were now nearly finished, and he was preparing to proceed to Uganda to join me.

A fortnight's work saw our little boat ready for the voyage, and on August 23rd I set off, accompanied by Mackay, for my fifth voyage across the Nyanza, hoping to reach Uganda in three or four days. But we were destined to be disappointed. We made but slow progress the first day, and, the wind having completely died away, we anchored at night off the island of Ukeréwe. Next morning we set sail with a strong S.E. breeze, and ran rapidly up the strait between Wiru and Ukeréwe. This channel is usually a dangerous one, as there is a bar at its eastern entrance, but as the Lake was unusually high, being at least three feet above its normal level, there was water enough on this bar for us to cross it easily. We had a very heavy cargo on board, and being short-handed, I decided not to steer directly for Murchison Bay, as I had hitherto done, but to make for the coast of Uzongora. I intended to fetch the land a little south of the Kagera river, and then run up the coast, so as to escape the heavy seas which are often met with in mid-lake, and which we were especially likely to encounter at this season, as the rains were coming on, and frequent storms were to be expected. Accordingly, on rounding the western side of Ukeréwe, we steered N.W. by W., and on the morning of the 25th sighted Alice Island, and anchored at night in the fine land-locked bay on its N.E. side. We remained there the following day, leaving with a S.E. breeze on the 27th. The wind died away towards evening, and we took to our oars, steering due west for the coast of Uzongora, through a nasty "choppy" sea. Night fell, but we rowed on hour after hour, Mackay and I alternately rowing and steering; but the land seemed as far off as ever. At length some fishermen's fires were seen, and guided by these, we at last reached the coast, and cast anchor in a fine sandy bay about four o'clock in the morning. We were so tired that we lay down and slept for some hours, unconscious of a violent thunderstorm, which burst on us just after we had anchored. The sun was high in the heavens when we awoke, and I found that we were off the village of Makongo. Our food being finished, some of the men offered to go and buy some bananas, if we would go nearer the shore; so, taking up the anchor, we went as near as we dared to the beach, but as it was we ran into too shallow water, and among the breakers raised by the storm of the preceeding night. We were not strong enough to row the boat out of the surf, so cast anchor at once, hoping that the sea would calm down, and, having rigged up a breast-work of awning stanchions and sails, prepared to wait. For a short time the boat rode the waves well; then the wind shifted, and we had great work to keep her head to the breakers; at last, as an unusually large one swept past, the *Daisy* dipped her bowsprit under the anchor cable, and on her rising again, the bowsprit with its supports and several feet of gunwale on the port bow were carried away, so that the water poured in through the gap with every billow. The Waganda whom we had on board were panic-stricken, and, instead of helping to bale out the water, began crying out that they should be drowned. It was no good to remain where we were, the *Daisy* was fast filling, and must soon have foundered; so, getting up the anchor, we ran her on shore, leaping out when the water shoaled, and dragging her up as far as we could. But the beach was steep, and we could not get her out of reach of the waves, which stove in many of the planks in the after section, and inflicted terrible damage upon her. We then set to work to fish up the cargo, and recovered almost everything, excepting a splendid botanical collection which I had made on my voyage to Kagei, and which was irrecoverably lost. As soon as all was got out of the *Daisy*, we made tents of oars and sails, and spread out our saturated clothes to dry. In a short time crowds of natives came from the neighbouring villages to see us; they helped us to haul up the boat, and, on hearing we were hungry, brought us several loads of bananas. Later in the day a chief arrived, bringing a present of a fine bullock, with a message from Keitaba, the king of this district, saying he had heard of our misfortune, and would send men to build huts for us to live in, till we could procure canoes from Uganda to convey us and our property to that country. Two days after, a large number of men arrived, bringing bundles of reeds, sticks and banana-leaves, and in a few hours three huts were built within thirty yards of the Lake. On first examining the *Daisy* we thought her too much damaged ever to be made sea-worthy again, and decided to break her up, meantime sending word to Mtesa of our mishap, and asking him to send canoes to fetch us and our goods to Uganda; so, having procured a canoe from Makongo, we sent some of the Waganda whom we had with us with a note to Mtesa. On second thoughts, however, we decided to cut out the middle section of the boat, and, joining the two end ones together (which we found would, with a little contrivance, be possible), use the timbers of the discarded portion to repair the broken planks of the rest. By this plan she would, of course, be much shortened, and her capacity for carrying cargo much diminished, yet, as her length would be better proportioned to her beam, she would, we hoped, be more seaworthy than before.

So, about a week after the wreck took place, Mackay and I set to work upon the boat, aided by a native carpenter from Zanzibar, who had accompanied Mackay as one of his servants.

The whole of September passed, and found the

Daisy far from being completed, and it was not till October 22nd that we were able to launch her.

During the whole of our stay in this place we were on the best possible terms with the natives, crowds of whom used to come down every day to watch us at work and express their astonishment at the various appliances we employed. We had on board a portable forge, lathe, grindstone, and blacksmith's anvil, and these we fitted up. They were in daily requisition, and were an unfailing source of wonder to the Wazongora, whose constant exclamation was "Choma! choma!" ("Iron! iron!") the ease with which we worked that metal seeming especially to excite their admiration. We had quantities of copper wire, nails, and other things which excite the cupidity of the negro, lying in our tent, yet, to the credit of these natives be it said, nothing was stolen during the whole of our stay amongst them.

We had, of course, been quite unprepared for such a long delay on our journey, and had with us very little of the barter goods necessary for purchasing food, and often had great difficulty in devising means whereby to procure provisions; but we cut up an old sail, which we exchanged for bananas, and once were able to purchase some cowries, from some passing Waganda, for fine calico.

Wild geese frequented the shores of the Bay of Makongo, and a good many of them fell to our guns, though they were very shy and difficult to approach, owing to the total absence of cover; wild guinea-fowl were found in flocks on the downs, and I occasionally bagged one or two of them. Our greatest want was salt, which was not to be had at any price, a deprivation which only those who have themselves experienced it can appreciate.

The scenery of this part of the coast of Uzongora was very fine. Our little camp was on the edge of a flat, sandy, crescent-shaped plain, about a mile at its greatest width, and two miles from point to point where the cliffs approached the water. Facing the sea, the downs formed an amphitheatre of hills, descending steeply some hundreds of feet to the plain, and then rising in gentle undulations towards the uplands of Karagwe, some of the nearer knolls being a thousand feet above the Lake. The face of the cliffs was seamed by deep, narrow ravines, through which sparkling streams of clear cool water ran with a cheerful murmur towards the Nyanza, and fell in beautiful cascades over the steep rocks. These valleys were filled with fine soft grass, and the streams were shaded by fine tree-ferns (*Cyathea Dregei*). On reaching the plain these rivulets dug for themselves deep winding channels, whose banks were festooned with ferns, and shady with dense underwood. A small morass, formed by one of these brooks at the foot of the cliffs, was dotted with a beautiful little purple-and-white orchid, and over the bushes which grew on its margin crept the lovely *Lygodium scandens*, a climbing fern which covered the small trees and bushes with graceful, wavy masses of pale green foliage. I clambered once up the rugged face of the cliff, and was well repaid for the toil. From my feet the grassy plain stretched away to the blue Lake, the course of a stream being marked by a winding ribbon of brilliant green; large herds of cattle, dwarfed by the distance to mere specks, roamed about; the village of Makongo, with its picturesque huts peeping out of a forest of bananas, was visible fringing the shores of the Nyanza far away on the right; and on the distant horizon the outline of Alice Island could be distinguished. On either hand stretched the undulating surface of the downs, varied by plantain groves and patches of verdant corn. The noise of life and the murmur of the brook were both silenced at the height at which I stood, and the calm was only broken by the twitter of the gorgeous sun-birds as they flitted from flower to flower.

This part of Uzongora is densely populated, the people living in large villages of huts very similar to those of the Waganda, and surrounded by immense groves of bananas. They possess considerable herds of long-horned cattle, and frequently brought butter for sale to our camp, but we could never induce them to let us have milk. In physique the Wazongora are decidedly inferior to the Waganda, and, as the nkoba, or bark-cloth tree, does not grow in their country, they are chiefly clothed in the skins of various animals. They catch large quantities of fish in baskets similar to those already described when speaking of the Waganda. Their language belongs to the same family as that of the Waganda, and has some words in common with it. I collected a small vocabulary of words in their language while at Makongo, a selection from which will be found in the Appendix.

Our time was spent very quietly during our stay at Makongo. We were chiefly occupied in repairing the *Daisy*, and the only incidents which broke the monotony of the days were a visit from 120 Waganda canoes *en route* to fight with the people of Bumbire,* and the appearance in the bay of a solitary bull hippo, who kept us on the *qui vive* for two or three nights. For the solitary bulls have the character among the natives of being extremely vicious, and of wantonly destroying canoes, or anything else that may come in their way. Fearing for the safety of the *Daisy*, we kept our rifles loaded and ready to hand, should our visitor appear inclined to come to too close quarters; but he was a

* We subsequently learnt that, in the battle which took place between the people of Bumbire and the Waganda, the former were completely exterminated, with the exception of a few women and children who were made slaves, while the Waganda left more than half their number dead on the field.

wary old fellow, and never gave us the chance of a shot.

On October 11th six Uganda canoes arrived, having been sent by Mtesa to assist us in conveying our goods to his country. But it was not till the 24th that we succeeded in making a start northwards. For the first few days our progress was very slow, owing to a constant succession of headwinds, calms, and thunderstorms. On the evening of the 26th we reached the estuary of the Kagera river, meeting a number of Uganda canoes on their way to Kagei, bearing 200 slaves belonging to one Hamis, a slave of Said bin Salem, the ex-governor of Unyanyembe. The following day we steered for the promontory of Dumo, taking soundings at intervals off the mouth of the Kagera, and found the depth to range from eight to ten fathoms. We kept near the coast of the mainland till some twenty or thirty miles south of the river Katonga, and then threaded our way in a N.E. direction, among the islands, for Ntebbi, our port on the mainland, which we reached on November 1st; and thus ended my last voyage on the Nyanza.

Before, however, bidding a long farewell to the Victoria Lake, some account of its more prominent features may appropriately be given.

The northern and southern limits of the Nyanza have been determined with considerable accuracy, being 0° 27' N., where the Victoria Nile leaves the Lake on the north, and 2° 27' S. (the head of Jordan's Nullah) on the south, the extreme length thus being about 230 miles. The eastern and western limits are not well known, but approximately 30° 40' E. longitude on the west, and 34° 50' E. longitude on the east, thus giving a total breadth of about 220 miles.

The name Nyanza or Nyanja means "sea" in the various lake dialects, and is the distinctive name of the Victoria Lake, never being applied to any other of the great bodies of water of Central Africa, though it is also applied by the Waganda to the Nile between the Victoria and Albert Lakes. This confusion, or rather extension of the term, doubtless gave rise to the accounts given by Musa Mzuri to Speke, by which the northern limit of the Victoria Lake was placed about lat. 3˚ N. The names, "Sea of Ukerewe," "Sea of Ukara," etc., found in some maps, are absolutely unknown to the natives of Central Africa, and are only used by the Arabs, whose nomenclature is often far from trustworthy.

The physical features of the shores of the Nyanza vary much in the different districts. Commencing with Uganda, to the east of Murchison Bay, we find ranges of flat-topped hills coming close to the margin of the Lake. The shores are rocky and the bottom stony, affording but indifferent anchorage, except in some of the bays or opposite the mouths of streams, where there are patches of sand or gravel, and where good holding ground can be found. In some places long mud-banks or sandy spits run far out into the Lake, having only three or four feet of water on them, and marked by a thick growth of water-lilies, reeds, papyrus, and other aquatic plants. Proceeding westwards to the Katonga, the coast-line is broken by deep bays, forming good harbours, the largest being Murchison Bay. South of the Katonga river the country is less hilly, and the shores are often very flat and swampy, with sandy beaches, and clothed with magnificent forest trees. The bed of the Nyanza at this point slopes very gradually down; the fishermen may be seen punting about their rafts a mile or more from shore, and the lead shows a depth of only five fathoms at a distance of between two and three miles from land. Nearing the Kagera river, the hills recede still farther from the Lake, and dense beds of ambatch are found, growing in from four to six feet of water. These ambatch bushes are the resort of numerous water-fowl, especially of the curious darter. These birds have most marvellous powers of diving, but after a time their feathers become saturated, so that they are comparatively helpless in the water; they then betake themselves to these bushes, perching on the boughs with extended wings till the moisture has evaporated, strongly reminding one of old clothes hung out to dry. On the approach of a canoe these rags suddenly become animated, and plunge into the water, to reappear fifty or sixty yards off, only the snaky head and neck of the bird being visible for an instant, as it surveys the position of the intruder.

South of the Kagera river we have the high, fertile downs of Uzongora, already described, with deep water close in shore.

Towards the south-west corner of the Lake, barren stony hills, with a scanty growth of stunted thorns and long grass, take the place of the verdant uplands, and long, bare ridges of rock raise their heads a few feet above the surface of the Nyanza, far away from land, forming serious obstacles to navigation, and necessitating a most careful look-out ahead.

The southern coast is broken by bold headlands formed of huge boulders of igneous rock, hoary and weather-beaten with the storms of centuries, but beautifully variegated with patches of a brilliant orange lichen; between are wide, shallow bays, on whose shores a few villages, inhabited by nearly naked Wazinja and surrounded by banana groves, are to be seen. The western and eastern sides of Jordan's Nullah are of much the same description, having stony hills running down near the coast, while on the eastern side are numerous villages, and large herds of cattle may be seen grazing peacefully on the level alluvial ground between the foot of the hills and the Lake. About Kagei the hills recede farther from the shore, diminishing also in height as the mouth of the river Shimiyu is approached. The beach here is rocky, and the bottom stony, with very bad anchorage. The coast about the mouths of the Shimiyu and Ruana, at the head of Speke Gulf, is flat, and no hills of any magnitude are found till the bold mass of the Magu Mountains is reached at the northern entrance to the Gulf.

Proceding northwards from here through Rugezi Strait along the eastern shore of the Nyanza, the country is mountainous, the huge Majita Mountain rising steeply from the water to a height of 2000 feet above the Lake, and separated by a magnificent bay from Mount Magu. From this point the coast trends in a N.E. direction, the Majita Mountain being separated from another bold headland by a wide and deep inlet, beyond which my personal knowledge of the Nyanza does not extend.

The islands form an important item in an account of this great inland sea. Starting again from Uganda, we find two or three small islands off the entrance to Murchison Bay, then comes the great Archipelago of Sesse, of which a description has already been given. South of this group (with the exception of two little uninhabited islets in the estuary of the Kagera river) we find on more till we come to the long chain which, beginning opposite Mkongo, and including Bumbire, Maiga, and Lubili, extends to the south-west corner of the Lake. Alice Island stands practically alone, rising in solitary grandeur to a height of many hundred feet above the Lake, far away from land.

Off the coast of Uzinja we find the well-wooded, fertile Kome group, most of its members being uninhabited. Then, along the southern side are scattered at long intervals rocky, deserted, and almost inaccessible islands, till we come to Ukeréwe, the largest of all the islands of the Victoria Lake. It is really a peninsula or promontory, running far out into the water and connected with the land by a low swampy neck, through which are one or two narrow channels. North of this is Ukara, and then the Nyanza seems to be almost devoid of islands till we reach Uvuma, off the coast of Usoga, and the scene of many a bloody battle between its brave inhabitants and the Waganda.

There are one or two currents in the Lake which deserve a passing mention. The most important is a strong westerly current, which sets across the entrance to Jordan's Nullah towards the coast of Uzinja. Its speed, as far as I can judge, is about a knot and a half an hour. I first noticed it in my voyage to Kagei in the *Daisy* in January 1877, when, there being no wind, my men had hard work to make way against it with their oars. I also noticed it again in August of that same year, when travelling down to Usukuma in canoes, and I found, on looking over some papers of Lieutenant Smith after his death, that he too had observed it. It is probably caused by the action of the wind, which for the greater part of the year blows from the S.E., on the long, narrow stretch of water extending from the head of Speke Gulf to the end of the island of Ukeréwe. There is also a slight current through the Rugezi Straits, which separate Ukeréwe from the mainland, setting in a southerly direction, thus keeping the channel open.

Storms are frequent on the Nyanza, occurring principally in the months of March, April and May, and September, October and November. They frequently come on with extreme suddenness, and make navigation very dangerous, especially at night. The squalls, however, are often very limited in area, and it is sometimes possible (as I have proved on more than one occasion) to sail out of their path if they are carefully watched. Waterspouts sometimes accompany them, and I have seen as many as three at the same moment in mid-lake, all within a comparatively short distance of my boat. In the shallow waters of the coast of Uddu, a heavy surf is often raised by these storms, sweeping over 200 miles of open water, and great care has to be exercised in approaching the land under these circumstances. The prevailing wind is from the S.E., and blows freshly, as a rule, during the earlier part of the day, dying away in the afternoon ; near the coast it is often modified by the land breezes. When close to land an on-shore breeze can almost always be counted upon in the evening, and an off-shore one early in the morning ; so that, whatever the direction of the wind may be during the greater part of the day, the voyager can always reckon on being able to make some progress at those times. Any boat which is to navigate the waters of the Nyanza in mid-lake with tolerable ease and certainty, in all weathers, should draw not less than four feet of water, and ought to be completely decked, and able to sail pretty near the wind.

The most rapid run I ever made across the Lake was from Bukindo in Ukeréwe to Ntebbi in Uganda, and occupied thirty-four hours; the fastest I accomplished from Kagei to the same place took two days eighteen hours.

The Nyanza abounds in fish, and at least twenty kinds are eaten by the natives on its shores. The study of the various species would, I am sure, amply repay the naturalist for his trouble. Hippopotami, crocodiles, two or three species of water-lizards, otters and large snakes are found in its waters, and multitudes of water-birds of great variety prey on the finny tribes that inhabit it.

Fogs are frequent on the Nyanza, often lasting for weeks together.

CHAPTER X.

FAREWELL TO UGANDA.

MACKAY and I having reached Ntebbi on November the 1st, we waited there two or three days while the news was sent to Mtesa, and then set off for Rubaga, arriving there on the 6th. I introduced Mackay at court, and the king seemed much pleased to see us. He handed over to me a large packet of English newspapers which Dr. Emin had kindly sent me; they were accompanied by a letter from the Doctor, in which he mentioned that three more men were on their way from England to join us. They were coming by the Nile route, and would, he wrote, soon be at Mruli, the most southerly of the Egyptian stations, and distant by road some 180 miles from Rubaga. This was indeed good news for us, and I began to look forward eagerly to the arrival of our new comrades, Messrs. Litchfield, Pearson and Felkin. When I told the news to Mtesa, he seemed gratified, and on my remarking that we should be the largest party of white men ever seen in his country at one time, he replied, "If twenty more Wazungu (Europeans) were coming, I should be glad."

I received a very warm welcome from my old

friend Simbuzi (or, as Stanley spells it, Sambuzi), one of the most intelligent of Mtesa's chiefs. He had been one of the king's servants or pages at the time when Speke was in Uganda, and had been in command of the Waganda warriors who accompanied Stanley on his expedition to "Beatrice Gulf."

On November 13th a report reached us that some white men had arrived at Mruli; so, concluding that it was the reinforcement we were expecting, I decided to go and meet them there. Having told Mtesa of my intention, he expressed his willingness for me to go, and promised to furnish me with 200 porters and an armed escort of 100 men, as part of the road was dangerous.

On November 21st I started for Mruli. The first three or four days' march was in a N.N.W. direction, through inhabited districts with large villages surrounded by the inevitable banana groves, and separated from each other by broad swampy valleys covered with a thick growth of coarse grasses and frequent clumps of wild date palms. On the sixth day we came to jungle, with here and there clearings containing villages. We also passed several villages of the Wahuma herdsmen, and saw numbers of their fine cattle grazing in the open glades of the forest. The huts of the Wahuma are a great contrast to the neat dwellings of the Waganda, being badly and untidily built. They are generally placed in a circle enclosing a large courtyard, where the cattle are housed at night, and are surrounded by stout thorn fences or hedges of a species of euphorbia. As the Wahuma live principally on flesh, and cultivate the ground but little, the plantain groves, which add so much to the picturesqueness of the Waganda villages, are wanting; but, to compensate for this, these hamlets are usually situated just on the edge of the forest, and sometimes have large shady trees growing among the huts.

On the seventh day we arrived at Sumbwi, an extensive village on the edge of the forest, and here we stayed for three days, waiting for some of our porters and collecting food for a six days' journey through the forest. On December 1st we were off again, and soon entered the jungle, passing the sites of some deserted villages; near one of which was a large clump of the thistle-like *Echinus amplexicaulis*, with its large globular heads of rich crimson flowers, forming a striking picture.

We spent the night at some small huts near a group of Borassus palms. The next day's march led us for some distance over low forest-clad ridges and swampy grassy valleys, till, having passed the deserted site of another village, we entered a broad, level, swampy valley with a river, the Lugogo or Ergugu, flowing down the farther side in a westerly direction. This "rush drain," as Speke calls this description of river, was about half a mile wide, it being now the end of the rains (when I again crossed it, two months later, it had contracted to 300 yards), it was five and a half feet deep in the middle, choked with grass and papyrus, and had no perceptible current, but, judging by the marks on its banks and the general slope of the country, I feel convined that it drains into the Kafur.

FOURTH CAMP FROM MRULI, WITH THE MKONO HILLS IN THE DISTANCE.

Two tall young fellows offered to carry me across, and I consented; but, the water coming up to their mouths, I got so wet that, like the Irishman in the sedan-chair without a bottom, I might just as well have walked, but for the appearance of the thing. We left the Ergugu after crossing, but struck it again next day, and camped on its banks. At this, our third camp in the jungle, a snake was killed just outside my hut; it was coiled up in a tuft of grass which a boy sat down on, and out it wriggled to his great horror. Our journey the next day took us along the banks of the Ergugu, which had now widened to a huge swamp, sometimes three miles in breadth. This part of the country is a no-man's land, and fights not unfrequently take place here between the Waganda and Wanyoro, as the road leading from the settlements of the latter, on the east of the Nile, to Unyoro just at this point crosses the road from Mruli to Uganda. The forest about here seemed alive with game; numbers of gazelles and larger antelopes were seen; and one, of a species called by the Waganda "ngubbi," tried to break through the caravan, but was speared by the porters. The soft muddy ground was full of the tracks of rhinoceros, buffalo, and elephant, and we crossed a broad, well-trodden road made by the latter in coming down to drink; while lions, leopards and hyænas kept up a concert round our camp all night. On the following march, after leaving the Ergugu, we saw large quantities of guinea-fowl, which were, however, very wild; I dropped one at sixty yards, but lost it in the long grass. On nearing the camp. I saw two elands standing under a tree not one hundred yards from the road; I signed to my gun-bearer to give me my rifle, and was just raising it to my shoulder when a stupid Mganda, noticing the animals, set up a yell, and they vanished in an instant.

On December 6th we reached Mruli. Before daylight we were on the move, and soon the jungle became thinner, and herds of gazelles were seen scampering off through the open glades. Then we emerged into a wide, open plain, almost treeless, and terribly swampy, being often knee-deep in water. An hour's wading brought us to the banks of the Kafur or Kafa (as the Waganda pronounce it), and shortly after I caught sight of the Egyptian flag marking the station of Mruli. Having collected all our caravan together, we marched on to the station, firing a couple of guns to announce our arrival. Just outside the gate I found a company of soldiers drawn up to receive me, who presented arms as I passed, while the bugles played the "Salaam." Of course I at once inquired for the white men, but there were none there; but a letter was given me from Pearson, asking me to come on to Foweira, another Egyptian station on the Nile, some seventy miles north of Mruli. I was most hospitably received by the officers in charge of Mruli, who cleared out the government divan for my use, and supplied me liberally with food, Dr. Emin, with his usual thoughtful kindness, having given orders that if ever I came to Mruli, or any of the other stations in his province, I was to be treated as his guest.

On December 9th I left Mruli for Foweira, travelling down the Nile in native dug-out canoes. Having embarked from the landing-stage on the bank of the Kafur, a few hundred yards brought us to the Nile. It was my first view of the Nile, as such. I have sailed many hundreds of miles over the lake that gives it birth, and know all its various moods, by day and by night, in cloud and in sunshine, in storm and in calm; I have stood on the watershed that divides the streams which nourish its young life, from those which roll their waters to the Indian Ocean; I have seen it hurl itself, foaming and roaring, through the chasm that forms the eighth cataract; I have seen it winding its way through the sandy desert; I have watched it mingling its waters with those of its sister stream, the Blue Nile; I have seen it flowing past the busy haunts of men, and the mighty Pyramids, and at last lose itself in the blue waters of the Mediterranean, more than 3000 miles from its cradle: but I shall never forget my first sight of it. The river was here half a mile wide, flowing in a northerly direction; the western bank was low, and fringed with papyrus; the eastern bank was higher, and covered with open forest of mimosas and acacias; a delicate convolvulus wove its tangled meshes among the shrubs that bent over the water; purple water-lilies dotted the still creeks; thousands of the little cabbage-like *Pistia stratiotes* floated down the stream, vast numbers of water-birds perched among the reeds, here and there grassy islands divided the current, and a solitary palm reared its lofty crown like a silent sentinel watching the mighty river. Crocodiles lay floating on the surface of the water, and the snort of the hippopotami could be heard in the reeds lining the shore. On we floated, hour after hour, down the broad stream, every turn revealing new scenes of surpassing loveliness. Night fell at length, the full moon rising just as the sun set, and throwing over all a soft veil of silvery light, while the tall papyrus beds were lit up with the lamps of myriads of fireflies, and a gentle breeze sprang up cool and refreshing after the sultry heat of the day, bearing with it the sweet scents of a thousand flowers and all the strange sounds of insect life peculiar to night in a tropical forest. At length, some three hours after sunset, we suddenly heard a bugle-call about a quarter of a mile ahead, and in a few minutes had reached the station of Kodj, where we remained for the night. This is a small station of the Egyptians, close to the village of Rionga, the brother of Kamrasi, the former king of Unyoro, whose name will be familiar to readers of Speke's, Grant's, and Baker's books. He came to see me next morning, and seemed a mild, intelligent man, and kindly dispositioned. On the 11th I went on to Foweira, distant some three hours' journey from Kodj. It is well situated on the steep bank of the Nile, just at the point where it bends away west to the Albert

Lake. I quite hoped to find my friends here, but they had not come, nor could I get any definite information as to their whereabouts. So I decided to wait for news, at the same time sending off letters to tell them of my arrival at Foweira. The officer in charge of the station, Mohammed Aga by name, with whom I afterwards became great friends, gave me a very pleasant hut outside the fortifications, and commanding a glorious view of the Nile and country beyond. At last, on Christmas Day, according to my reckoning (for I found afterwards that I was a day out), letters came from Pearson and Felkin, saying that they had been delayed by sickness, but were now on their way to join me, *viâ* the Albert Lake and Magungo. On January 1st, 1879, I had a note from Pearson, saying they were again delayed at Keroto, three days' journey from Foweira, so, tired of the long delay, I resolved to go and meet them. The next morning I set out, with three porters, three soldiers, and my servants. Our road led in a W.S.W. direction through fine forest, with a few sites of deserted villages, marked only by the bananas (now fast being choked by the dense vegetation) and figtrees. We spent that night at a small village in the jungle, and the next day reached the village of Kissoona, a few hours from Keroto. I had intended to push on to the latter place, but near Kisuna I was met by Amfina, the chief of this district, who told me that my brothers had left Keroto, and would be at Kissoona that evening. Soon after three o'clock the head of their caravan appeared emerging from the forest, and in a few minutes I had welcomed Pearson and Litchfield. Felkin was still at Keroto with their dragoman, who was dying. Both Pearson and Litchfield were suffering from fever, but we sat up talking and smoking for many an hour. The

THE NILE AT FOWEIRA.

following morning we retraced our steps towards Foweira, stopping at the village of the chief Amfina. Felkin was able to join us in the evening (the dragoman having died the previous day), and I have since travelled with him many thousands of miles by land and by sea, and have shared many a toil and danger with him.

On reaching Mruli in December, and finding that

my companions had not arrived, I had dismissed most of the Waganda porters, as food was scarce there, retaining only a small number, three of whom accompanied me to Foweira. After meeting Pearson and Litchfield, I had at once despatched these men with letters, to Mtesa, asking for porters. We decided to await their arrival at Foweira in preference to Mruli, as the latter place was considered unhealthy.

We remained a fortnight at Foweria, moving on to the station of Kodj on January the 21st.

We saw a good deal of Rionga during the three days we remained here. We paid him two or three visits at his own village, where we saw a very neat amputation of the left arm of a small boy (one of Rionga's sons), for a compound fracture of the bones, which had been performed by the chief himself.

On the 25th, news having come that the Waganda porters had reached Mruli, we started in canoes for that place. The journey up the river was a tedious one, taking three days' hard paddling to accomplish. The first night we passed in a large grove of Borassus palms on the eastern bank of the Nile. The next day we met some canoes coming down, and one of their crew handed us a packet of letters, containing, among others, a most flowery epistle from Mtesa, expressing his gratification at the prospect of the arrival of more white men in his kingdom. That afternoon we landed in a forest to cook, and considerable alarm was caused, on the men setting fire to a clump of reeds and grass, by a huge snake, which, rushing out, made its escape into the water. On the evening of the 27th we reached Mruli, receiving quite an ovation from the Waganda, who rushed in crowds to the landing-place to meet us; and we were treated to a long speech from one of the chiefs, who said they had begun to fear that something had happened to me, as I had been away so long.

The 3rd of February saw us once more on the move, and on the 8th we entered Uganda proper, after crossing the Ergugu. This stream had greatly diminished in volume since the beginning of December, and was now only 300 yards in width, with about three feet of water in the middle. The road we followed was nearly the same as that which I traversed on my way north, nearly three months before, and so does not call for any special notice. We arrived at last at Rubaga on February 14th, and found Mackay in good health.

During my absence Mackay had begun a new house, as the small one, which had been built for me more than a year before, was not sufficient for our increased party. The corner poles were up when we arrived, but the work progressed but slowly.

War also had again broken out between the Waganda and the Wasoga, and a portion of the Masai tribe lying on the borders of Usoga: two of the principal chiefs, Sakibobo and Chambalango, together with my friend Simbuzi and a number of other chiefs, had gone into that country with a large army.

Immediately after the arrival of our companions Felkin began treating the king, and paid him frequent professional visits. Mtesa had been laid by for fifteen months with a complication of diseases, and was a terrible contrast to the active, athletic man he was when first I saw him : long confinement to his house and want of exercise, together with constant suffering, had greatly reduced him, and he looked years older than he did in 1877. Some curious scenes took place at first owing to the unwillingness of the chiefs to allow a European doctor to prescribe for their king, and the foremost among those who opposed it was one Kauta, the head cook, a worthless sycophant, who did all in his power to thwart us. A large portion of every bottle of medicine made up for his majesty had to be swallowed by the chiefs who were present when Felkin paid him his professional visits, and also by any of us who might have accompanied him; but after a time, when no harm happened to any one from drinking the medicine, this practice was gradually dropped. The Arab and half-breed traders, however, were very much vexed at the influence which Felkin's successful treatment of Mtesa gave him and us over the monarch, and they redoubled their efforts to poison the king's mind against us.

As the report spread of the improvement of the king's health through the white men's medicine, increasing numbers of chiefs, and also of the poorer classes, presented themselves for treatment. The negro as a rule has great faith in European medicines, and believes that every white man is born a doctor. They are specially partial to strong purges and emetics, and, as a man once told me, they like a medicine " that scratches their throats"; they also consider it most wonderful that we should be able to predict the effects of an emetic.

The Waganda have a curious idea that most diseases are produced by the presence of a snake in their interiors, and when a patient is asked what is the matter with him, his almost invariable reply is that he has a snake inside him. But it must not be supposed that negroes require large doses of medicine as a rule, for frequently they are very sensitive to the action of drugs, especially of quinine. Many cases, however, which are brought to the traveller for treatment are chronic or long-standing diseases, where the patient has tried in vain all the native remedies, and come as a last resource to the European, often, most unreasonably, expecting to be cured with a single dose. For all non-professional travellers, who are only slightly acquainted with medical science, Dr. Livingstone's rule should certainly be always observed, viz., never to treat a case of which one is not pretty certain to effect a cure or give relief. A great deal depends on keeping up one's reputation for medical skill, and care has to be exercised in the way of refusing cases. I rarely directly refused to treat any; I either gave some simple medicine which could do no harm, or imposed some restriction in diet which I knew was not likely to be complied with, making treatment conditional on its being observed.

Medical treatment is the best means of all for winning the affections of the natives of Africa, and all travellers, and especially all missionaries, should, before leaving Europe, make themselves acquainted with the elements of medicine and surgery, such as bandaging, setting broken limbs, tying arteries, and minor operations. They should also be provided with a good stock of medicines, lint and bandages, and should carry with them a small pocket case of surgical instruments. At all stations where Europeans are likely to be permanently settled, an infirmary should be established. Dr. Emin Bey, the governor of the Egyptian Equatorial Provinces, who is a skilful medical man, has one at Lado, with a man to look after it, and two negro boys whom he has himself trained, and who have become really efficient dressers.

On February 21st, two Frenchmen arrived at Rubaga, by name Père Lourdel and Frère Delmonce;

they were members of a party of French Romanists, who had been sent by the Archbishop of Algiers to begin a mission in Uganda. The party had come *viâ* Zanzibar, and having reached Kagei in Usukuma, these two had come on in some Uganda canoes, which they found there, to ask Mtesa's permission to settle in his country, and to procure canoes to bring on the remainder of their party and goods to Uganda, a request which was ultimately granted by Mtesa.

Our new house, which was situated in the same compound as the old one, progressed but slowly, and it was not till towards the end of April that we were able to move into it.

Meanwhile most of us were busy working at various employments. Felkin went frequently to see the king, and two or more of us were almost daily at the palace. A small printing press had been brought from England by the last party, and we were constantly at work with this, printing off the vocabularies and lists of words of the Uganda language which I had collected for the use of the members of the mission. Almost every day, also, we worked at the new house or in the garden, which had been rather neglected, a certain amount of daily manual labour being necessary to health, besides setting a good example to the natives, who look upon manual labour as derogatory to the dignity of men, and fit only for women and slaves. We received frequent visits at this time from chiefs and others. Foremost among these was Mkwenda; his real name was Gabunga, but, his father having been a very well-known chief, the son, who was a mere boy when I arrived in Uganda, is more frequently called by his father's name, Mkwenda, than by his own. This young man is the first in rank of the three hereditary bakungu, who have been already mentioned, though, owing to his youth, he did not take the prominent part in the affairs of the nation to which his rank entitled him. He is a remarkably intelligent young fellow, and always proved himself a good friend to us, standing by us, as far as he dared, when the other chiefs looked coldly upon us.

From the time when Lieutenant Smith and I had our first interview with him, Mtesa had expressed a great wish to send some of his people to England, to learn from their account what our country was really like, and whether it was as great as it had been represented to him. We had encouraged this idea; as, what the chiefs and people of Uganda need, is a better knowledge of their real relation to the outside world and of the comparative insignificance of their own country, and nothing would convince them so strongly of this as a visit to some European country. Those who went would not, probably, have the courage to tell Mtesa all they saw, and how much inferior he was to European potentates, but they would freely tell those of their own rank all they had witnessed, and it would of course be much more readily believed when coming from them than from a foreigner, and creating a much greater respect in their minds towards foreigners than at present exists, would produce a far more favourable opinion of us in the minds of the people generally. As already indicated, Mtesa is by no means an absolute monarch, nor indeed could any king of Uganda be so under the existing régime; the real power lies in the hands of the chiefs. And if a favourable feeling were created in their minds toward Europeans, it would do more towards opening up the country to civilisation than the favour of any number of successive kings merely. For while Mtesa has always been, from various motives, anxious to have Europeans in his country, the leading chiefs have always been more or less opposed to them, principally from fear that they would take Uganda from them, a fear which was increased by the near approach of Egypt. It was, consequently, with a view to producing this change of feeling towards us that we had favoured the idea, first suggested by Mtesa himself, of sending ambassadors to England. This, of course, was bitterly opposed by the Zanzibar traders, who, jealous of all European encroachments on what they looked on as their preserves, were determined to do all in their power to thwart us.

After being several times mooted and again put

off, it was at last decided, in May 1879, that Mtesa should send envoys to England. The Nile route was selected, after some discussion, as being, in our estimation, safer at that time than the southern route by Zanzibar. It was also settled that I should accompany the envoys to England, and that Felkin, who had been for some time in bad health, and who was anxious to consult Dr. Emin, should go with me part of the way. It was necessary that we should send word beforehand of our intention to travel through his province to Dr. Emin Bey, so, after discussing the matter among ourselves and with Mtesa, it was finally decided that Felkin should go on to Mruli first and communicate from there with Dr. Emin, and that I should wait till the envoys were ready, and the presents, which Mtesa intended to send to our Queen, were prepared.

Accordingly Felkin left Rubaga for Mruli on May 17th, 1879, I hoping to follow him in the course of a week or ten days. But, owing to the delays inevitable in African travels, nearly a month elapsed before I could get off, starting finally, with the envoys and an escort of Waganda, on June 16th.

The route which I followed between Rubaga and the jungle on this occasion was to the east of that I had taken on the two previous journeys. On the 21st I reached one of the country establishments of Kangao, who has been already mentioned as one of the three hereditary bakungu; he was renowned as a warrior in Speke's time, but is now quite an old man, and very feeble; he was suffering from rheumatism at the time of my visit, and asked me to prescribe for him, which I did. He had always been one of those most opposed to Europeans, and was a great supporter of the religious system of the

THE MISSION HOUSE, RUBAGA.

Waganda and of their medicine-men. This village of his was a very large one, and one of the cleanest and neatest that I have seen in Uganda, and was shaded by fine forest trees. I stayed a day here owing to an attack of ague, and old Kangao proved very hospitable, sending me presents of a goat, bullock, plantains, sugarcane, and fruit.

The next two or three days' march was through

jungle-covered country with villages at long intervals. The tracks of elephants were very numerous about here, and in several places the gardens had been laid waste by them. For the elephant is a very mischievous animal, destroying trees and plants, apparently for the mere pleasure of doing so, and the track of a herd of these creatures can often be traced through the forest merely by the shrubs torn up by the roots and the huge boughs broken off the trees.

On the 30th of June we entered the real jungle, stopping for the night at an old camp on the edge of the valley of the Ergugu. There were numbers of guinea-fowl about here, and about sunset, being short of meat, I took my gun, and in a few minutes bagged a brace of splendid birds. Next day, July 1st, we crossed the Ergugu, which was rather fuller than when I last saw it in February, and the banks showed that it had been higher a short time previously. We were six days in getting through the jungle, following precisely the same route as before. At our last camp, one of the porters, while gathering fire-wood, came upon a young leopard, which he killed and brought to camp. On July 5th I reached Mruli, and was taken to my old quarters in the government divan. I found letters here from Felkin, saying that he had gone on to Foweira, and asking me to send word on at once of my arrival, and to wait for a reply, as he was expecting shortly to hear from Dr.

Emin Bey. So I despatched all the Waganda with the exception of the envoys, and one or two others whom I kept to send back to Rubaga with letters, as we were expecting a mail from England to arrive shortly. Since I had been last there, Mruli had been much improved and strengthened by a high mound with a deep ditch outside, and was now a really strong place, and if well provisioned could hold its own against a vastly superior force of negros armed only with spears or bows and arrows. The officer in command here was Farag Aga, one of Sir S. Baker's old soldiers, and a very smart officer.

Letters having come from Felkin saying he had gone on to Fatiko, I left Mruli with my party on July 16th, and travelled down the Nile in canoes to Foweira, where I arrived on the 17th, and was most warmly welcomed by my old friend, Mohammed Aga, who had suddenly become a most devout Muslim, and who spent a large part of each day in performing his devotions in the open space in the centre of the station. Two days were spent here waiting for porters, and on the 20th we started for Fatiko. The Waganda with my baggage had been sent across the Nile the previous evening, and after an early breakfast I set off, receiving most affectionate adieux from the officers.

The greater part of the country between Foweira and Fatiko is covered with jungle, and the denseness of the undergrowth made marching very slow, while in the early morning it was so heavy with dew, that in a few hundred yards one's clothes were as completely saturated as if one had plunged into a river. There were enormous quantities of wild vines in this district, and these were now heavily laden with large bunches of grapes which were just ripening. The fruit was small but sweet, and of a very good flavour, and most refreshing after a hot march. On the second day from Foweira we met soldiers coming from Fatiko, and they handed me a letter from Felkin, saying he had started for Lado at Dr. Emin's urgent request. Towards the end of the third day's march we approached the edge of the vast plateau along which we had been travelling, and which here bounds the valley of the Nile, and having descended its western face, encamped at night at its foot.

On July 24th I reached Fatiko, a strong military station, most charmingly situated near hills, among vast fields of corn. I was most courteously and hospitably received by the vakil, Abdul Aga Nimér, a perfect negro gentleman; and indeed in all my journeys through the Soudan and Egypt, extending to several thousands of miles, I always received (with scarcely an exception) the utmost courtesy and kindness from the highest to the lowest of the Egyptian officials.

I stayed more than a fortnight at Fatiko, and was charmed with the place. It possesses many natural advantages, being healthy, and free from mosquitoes; while food is very abundant, and the surrounding natives (the Shulis) are on the best possible terms with the garrison. The neighbourhood of Fatiko is a veritable botanist's paradise, the richness of its flora being unsurpassed by that of any district I have seen in Africa; but unhappily I was debarred from collecting here, as owing to a bad leg, caused by a fall, I was laid up during the whole of my stay.

We left Fatiko on August 8th, the first night being spent in the jungle. The third day we crossed a considerable-sized stream called Khor Djeffi; there had been heavy rain the previous evening, and the river, which was rising when we reached its banks, was almost impassable. I and some of my men got over, but the water rose so rapidly that half my escort was left on the other bank, and they were unable to cross till the following evening. On the 13th we came once more to the Nile, which we had left at Foweira, and crossed over to Dufli, a large military station. From Dufli we marched, through the glorious scenery of the eighth cataract, to Labore, and thence to Mugi and Keri. An account of this part of the journey will be given in the second part of the book. At Keri we obtained a boat and rowed down the Nile to the beautiful island of Bedden, situated among the cataracts of the same name. Were we transhipped our baggage into another boat and proceeded to Regiaf, and from thence to Lado, the capital of the Equatorial Provinces, stopping on our way for half an hour at Gondokoro.

Below Gondokoro we had a narrow escape from an upset, owing to the carelessness of the crew, who allowed our boat to be carried down a narrow side channel, where it was dashed violently against a tree. I reached Lado on August 9th, and was warmly welcomed by Dr. Emin Bey, the governor, and Felkin, who had arrived some three weeks before me.

The subsequent narrative of our journey from Lado to the Bahr-el-Ghazel province, and thence through the vast forest regions between Dem Suliman and the Bahr-el-Arab; our long camel ride through Dafur and Kordofan; our voyage down the Nile to Berber, and the journey thence across the desert to Suakim on the Red Sea, will be detailed in the second part of the book. So I must now bid the reader farewell, and entrust him to other hands to be pioneered through the regions of the Soudan, hoping that I have been able to add something to his knowledge of the people and lands of the mysterious Centre of Africa.

MR. R. W. FELKIN'S NARRATIVE.

CHAPTER I.

SUAKIM TO DUFLI.

A SHORT account of my journey to Uganda is necessary before I begin my description of our homeward travels. I shall merely give a resumé of our journey up the Nile as far as Dufli, that portion of the distance having already been described by other writers. The route from Dufli to Foweira, *viâ* the Albert Lake and Keroto, which is to a great extent new ground to English readers, merits a more detailed account.

In the spring of 1878, the Church Missionary Society received news of the loss of two of the members of their expedition to the Victoria Nyanza; Lieutenant Shergold Smith and Mr. O'Neill had been massacred by Lukongé, king of Ukerewe, and this disaster had left Mr. Wilson alone in Uganda. To strengthen his hands, the Church Missionary Society, in addition to ordering up a reinforcement from the South, determined to send a new party by way of the Nile; a route which was chosen because Colonel Gordon, at that time the Governor-General of the Soudan, had offered to defray the travelling expenses of a party of missionaries, and to forward them through the whole of the vast territory under his rule. This party consisted of the Rev. G. Litchfield, Messrs. Pearson and Hall, and myself.

We left England on May 8, 1878, and landed at Suakim, a port on the Red Sea, on June 9. At this place Mr. Hall was taken ill, and much to his regret was obliged to return to England.

On June 25 we started from Suakim with our caravan of forty camels, and in fifteen days reached Berber, where we stayed until July 21.

Our voyage to Khartoum lasted nineteen days; we took a longer time than is usual, for the engine of the small steamer was out of order, and we also tried to tow four large, heavily-laden boats; to do this against the strong current was too much for the steamer, so that the engine broke down twenty-one times in that short distance. Although the journey was somewhat tedious, it was most interesting. During the enforced delays for the repairs of the engine we were able to make a nearer acquaintance with the people who were at work on the banks of the river; moreover, it was most instructive to see the two modes of irrigation in action. From the banks of the river gullies run in all directions among the newly sown fields, and at the river's brink there are either shádoofs or sákiyehs, which are employed in pumping up the water. The shádoof is a pole weighted at one end, which is slung over a cross-bar, while at the opposite end to the stones there is a line with a bucket at the end, and with this rude contrivance the water is laboriously raised to the required height and poured into the gullies. The sákiyeh is not so often seen, and is a far more complicated machine; it is a large wheel on which water-pots are fixed, or else the wheel is covered by a circular band having pots attached to it at intervals. It is turned by oxen, and being very roughly made, it shrieks and groans in a terrible fashion; and if perchance the steamer is made fast near one of these machines, a sleepless night may be safely anticipated, as the work goes on day and night without ceasing. The reason that the sákiyehs are not more numerous is because of the heavy tax upon them. Instead of the people being encouraged to cultivate as much land as possible, a high tax on each new sákiyeh effectually prevents more cultivation than is absolutely necessary for bare existence.

Between Berber and Khartoum we experienced one of the terrible desert sand-storms; hearing a great confusion and noise on deck, we ran up to see what was the matter, and found that the crew were making the steamer fast to the bank as quickly as possible. We asked the reason for another stoppage, and were told that a sand-storm was coming. On looking to the north we saw on the horizon a thin roll of sand, which soon grew larger and larger, until the whole extent of the northern heavens became dark with sand. A deep yellow hue covered everything, only in the centre of the sky the clouds were broken, and a little blue was visible. In less than half an hour the storm was over us, enveloping us on all sides, but just over the river there was a slight break. The storm, lasting seven minutes, passed over us with a terrific roar, after which came an awful gust of wind, followed by a torrent of rain, which continued with unabated violence for an hour; the cool atmosphere afterwards was most refreshing.

We stayed for five days at Khartoum, and received the kindest possible welcome from Colonel Gordon, of whose generous and ready help it is almost impossible to speak, as words are inadequate to express all that we owe to him. Nothing could exceed his thoughtful and considerate care for our necessities and comforts; everything that was needful for our journey was provided; there was no detail too small or too trivial to be overlooked by him. Amid all the cares and labours of his arduous post as Governor of an immense country, he yet found time to give us the benefit of his counsel on all matters connected with our mission and journey, from the best mode of dealing with King Mtesa down to the duty of seeing that our live-stock was properly fed on the way. Advice drawn from a man of his wisdom and vast experience, given to us freely on precautions in travelling, on the manner of dealing with natives, indeed, on every subject, could not fail to be of the utmost value to travellers inexperienced as we were in all such matters. And not once only, but on many occasions have I had cause to be thankful for the few days I spent in company with one of the noblest men this century has yet produced.

By Colonel Gordon's orders there were provided for us porters for our goods, and, whenever necessary, an escort of soldiers; and at each Egyptian Station houses were prepared for us. Our journey all through Egypt, from the day we landed at Suakim to the day we bade farewell to our escort at Mruli, did not cost the Missionary Society a penny.

We left Khartoum on August 8 in the *Safir*, a larger steamer than the one from Berber; there were a good number of passengers on board, and a large cargo. We arrived on August 23 at Fashoda, the chief town of the Shillook district; we stopped there for a day, and it was at this place that I saw the first native dance. The commandant of the town, a captain, and a major came on board for us, and after we had put on our best helmets and dresses to make as imposing an impression as possible, we accompanied them on shore. On entering the station the company of soldiers presented arms and the cannon fired a salute. We were conducted to a raised platform before the Mudir's house, where seats were prepared for us, and that worthy and his numerous attendants were assembled. On taking our seats the drums and trumpets stationed below on our left began to play, and although the music was good it was rather too near to be enjoyable. A large square was formed by soldiers, their wives, children, and the inhabitants of the town, and soon a noise of bells was heard and a band of Shillooks rushed pell-mell into the square, yelling and leaping in a most extraordinary style. At the same time arrived their young chief, Kaykoum by name, who came up and kissed hands and sat down with us. He is a splendid young man, tall and well built, and his beautiful face was unspoiled by the numerous cuts which so generally disfigure both men and women. He gave me the impression of possessing great power, both of mind and body. His interpreter was quite a study for an artist; he was six feet four inches in height, with a massive face. The warriors came up in a line to the platform and saluted by dropping their lance-points to the ground and half bending the right knee in a very graceful manner. It is difficult to give an adequate description of these men, so fantastic was their appearance. Round each head a band of leather was tied, into which was woven long grass, which stood out all round the head, and waved with each movement. Round the left arm another leather band was tied, to which hung a long black sheep's tail; the ankles and forearms were adorned with rings of copper or brass, and small bits of metal of all shapes were fastened just below the knee, and in some instances bells were tied above the right elbow. The dress of some of the performers was a leopard-skin fastened over one shoulder; others had a skin round the loins; while by others nothing but a belt round the waist was worn, to which rows of iron rings were attached. The Shillook weapons are simple, but very good; a lance, seven feet long, with a broad, sharp head, oval shields made of skins, bows, arrows and clubs, which are carried in the hand, being all they possess.

A circle was formed by the performers round the drum, and they danced round with a long striding step, sinking the whole body at every stride, and at the same time covering it with the shield, then making a lunge forward with the spear. Yells and cries as unearthly as can be imagined were uttered at regular intervals; splendid time being kept to the beats of the drum. Two parties were then formed, attacks and repulses being interchanged, first one party and then the other being chased from the field. Their antics, springs, and contortions while in action are most amusing, and the noise made by the bells and jingling metal is not unpleasant when heard from a distance; at rest they stand leaning on the spear with one leg drawn up. After the warriors had finished their dance, the women performed; they were all clothed and danced in Arab fashion, so there is nothing more to say about them; the dance is a jump, the women falling down on their heels, which sent all the prominent muscles of the body into a quiver. It is by no means elegant, and is accompanied by clapping of hands and shrill cries. The entertainment lasted for about two hours, coffee and sherbet being handed round at intervals; and when we said good-bye we gave them ten dollars as a sign of our appreciation of their efforts for our amusement.

The journey from Fashoda to Lado, the chief town of the Equatorial Provinces, usually occupies twelve or thirteen days, but we were fifty-six days in accomplishing the voyage; we were so much hindered by the large number of "tawfs" or grass islands which were floating down the Nile, and which eventually completely blocked it, that all our wood was exhausted, and for forty days we were held prisoners in the pestilential marshes of this part of the Nile. In another part of this book I give some account of the cause of these obstructions, which are such a serious impediment to the opening up of the river for traffic. Here I will mention some of our experiences during our enforced sojourn in such undesirable surroundings.

Imagine then a space of clear water, a hundred yards broad, and three hundred long, bounded on each side by tall grass and reeds, which grow to a height of twenty or thirty feet above the water, so that nothing but water, grass, and sky could be seen. The river was dark and dirty; supposing you called for a glass of water, you obtained a liquid mixture of mud and water; if a pinch of alum was added to clear it, the result was that about a quarter of an inch of mud was deposited at the bottom of the glass. The sickening smell of tropical plants and of the rotting vegetation oppressed us; now and then dead fish floated past, or at times we saw the decaying body of a native slowly borne down the stream. The air was alive with mosquitoes, whose attacks continued by day as well as by night. The steamer was so crowded that there was no room to walk about the deck, so that want of exercise told upon our health, in addition to the impure water and insufficient food; for all our fresh meat was soon finished, and our principal food was dhurra pancakes, and this was nearly exhausted before we were released, the sailors having to be put on short allowance long before. Nearly every day we had a terrible storm of wind and drenching rain, and the heat of Khartoum having warped the decks, the cabins were not watertight; so that in a storm the driest place was sitting in the paddle-box, but I usually preferred the soaking deck to the smells and mosquitoes which congregated there. About sunset a cold dense fog arose from the river and hung like a pall over the steamer. Even night brought no alleviation to our misery: owing to the frequent storms we were obliged to sleep under cover, and the damp, hot atmosphere below turned the cabins into a vapour bath. Sleep was impossible; the hours passed in a semi-stupor, broken by frightful dreams and horrid nightmare, so that morning found us unrefreshed, and each day less able to contemplate with stoical indifference the outcome of our imprisonment. More than half the crew were down with fever, and the way in which the poor sailors had to work while trying to extricate the steamer was piteous in the extreme. In order to get wood they were obliged to drag the boat through the floating vegetation for nearly three miles, and then work up to their waists in water to reach the little wood procurable. One load of wood was their daily task, and ten hours' work was required to obtain it; however, they never grumbled, but when unloading the boat at night might even be heard singing as they passed the wood up to the steamer. At last, after many days' hard work, our captain thought that he had enough wood, and so we steamed on for a few hours, but found ourselves once more at a full stop and the wood all burnt up. We were in a lake away from the real water channel, and so sent off a few men in a small boat to try and make their way to Shambil, and bring assistance. The days passed wearily, but still the men did not return, and fears were expressed on all sides that they were lost; our provisions were almost at an end, and famine stared us in the face. I confess that on October 4, the forty-second day from leaving Fashoda, I was very down-hearted, and almost gave myself over to despair, all seemed so dark and hopeless. Little was said by any of us, but after an attempt at dinner we retired to our cabins. There the little case containing the photographs of my dear ones at home caught my eye; it was always near at hand, and in times of difficulty the sight of their faces had often cheered and comforted me, and so it was now, they all looked so peaceful and calm; and especially my Father seemed to say, "Trust in God, all will go well." So I took courage, and went on deck in a happier frame of mind, determined not to give up hope; and the reward came sooner than I could have dared to imagine, for very soon I heard the cry of "steamer," or rather "vapour! vapour!" What a rush with telescopes we all made to the paddle-boxes and bridge! and there sure enough in the far distance was something, hardly a steamer, but we could see a mast; every one was almost wild with delight; we ran the flag up to the masthead, and then saw our salute answered by the approching boat, so that at last we dared to believe in the chance of escape. Some of the crew began to pray, some to sing and dance for joy, and there was a general shaking of hands. In about an hour after its first appearance, the boat stopped about six miles off, and we thought that perhaps the block was there, and that we should have still to wait a few days until a small boat could work its way through the grass. In the evening, as we were sitting on the bridge, clad in armour of wraps against mosquitoes, I thought I saw a shadow dart noiselessly across the lake to the steamer, and then a dark figure sprang upon the deck, followed by another and then another. I hastened down the ladder to see who they were, and found to my great surprise that it was our pilot, who had come in a native boat; and so delighted were the sailors to see him again that they nearly hugged him to pieces. He was assailed by such a torrent of questions that some time elapsed before he was able to make himself heard above the tumult; but at last he sat down cross-legged, and a circle was formed round him while he told his tale. It was an interesting sight to watch the group, their eager faces, his graceful gestures, all lit up by the light of the moon, and occasionally by a bright flash of lightning from some clouds in the background. The man told us that after leaving us it had taken three days' hard work to force the boat into the channel of the river, and that then one day's rowing landed them at Shambil. He had brought down a large nuggar, with provisions, soldiers, and wood, to help to extricate us. The next morning the nuggar was able to approach to within a mile and a half of us; it was decided to pull her through the grass barrier which still separated us, and at 7 A.M. the work of bringing her through began. The boat was about ten tons burthen and very heavy, and the way in which the men worked was as follows. First they trampled down the tall grass, which is sufficiently dense and firm to bear their weight; this was done in the direction in which the boat had to be pulled, and a path a little broader than her beam was made. Two ropes were then made fast to the grass fifty yards in advance, and part of the men in the boat pulled at these ropes, part lifted up the bow, and part pushed behind. It took forty-five soldiers and twenty sailors to do this; it was fearful work for them, but by 3 P.M. they managed to get her within two hundred yards of us, when lines were run out from the steamer, and we all had to help, and in about half an hour she floated in our lake. As they worked the men sang a song, finishing with "He! Ho!!" when a great pull is given, and a pause occurs between each haul to enable them to take breath. Coffee-drinking, hand-shaking, and praying followed the accomplishment of this difficult task. Early next morning, the wood from the nuggar having been transferred to the steamer, steam was got up, and we started, towing the nuggar and being piloted by four Kidj (Kitch) natives.

The steamer could hardly make its way through some of the passages, the channel was so narrow and circuitous; sometimes the way seemed quite blocked up, but a sharp turn would suddenly bring us into a large lake, several of which were two or three miles across. About 10 o'clock we could see the real river—that is, the real water channel—in the distance; a most tortuous narrow passage, which we threaded with difficulty, led to it, and at length we managed to get the bow of the steamer into the river, but there we stuck fast; a line was run out and secured, and all hands and passengers pulled away at it, but our efforts were of no avail, for the rope broke. The soldiers then had to work in the water as before, every one on board was obliged to help, and at last the steamer surmounted the obstruction, and the current caught her and carried her down stream with such force that it took us half an hour to get her round.

We steamed back to the nuggar and pulled her into the river, and could hardly believe that we were actually released from our forty days' captivity. On our arrival at Shambil there were great rejoicings, and a large quantity of powder was burnt to celebrate our rescue.

ARRIVAL AT LÁDO.

On October 8 we left Shambil, and late the same evening met a steamer from Ládo, having on board Dr. Emin Bey, the accomplished Governor of the Equatorial Provinces, who proved a good friend to me, and who did much for us on the journey from Ládo to Mruli, the most southern station of his jurisdiction.

News of our difficulties had reached Ládo, and he was on his way with a large number of men to try and assist us; fortunately we had been already released, and so he turned back with us, and we arrived at Ládo on October 9, 1878.

We stayed there for three weeks, the time being occupied in arranging our loads, which should all have been made up into 40 lb. packets before leaving England. We were six days in going from Lado to Dufli. Having had occasion to traverse this part of the route on my return journey, in this place I will only describe the ascent of the Bedden Rapids.

We started from Regiaf at half-past 7 in the morning of November 18, in two nuggars towed by natives, who, in this district, belong to the Bari tribe. The current was very strong, but we went at a better rate than I had expected, and at 10 o'clock changed the twelve natives who were pulling the boats, the number being increased to twenty-five. The rapids at times made the journey most exciting. The men had to walk through the water, the banks being all flooded; the poor fellows were often up to their necks, and sometimes even had to swim short distances, in which cases part of the men held fast the rope, until the others had regained their footing. Two of them were carried off and drowned, and three more would have shared the same fate, but for the exertions of a man in our boat, who swam with a line to them, by means of which we hauled them in. The scenery along the banks was most beautiful, and the river was fringed on each side by splendid trees. The hippopotami kept showing their huge heads within a few yards of the boat, and our men often came to one asleep; who, when disturbed, gave a long stare at the intruders, and then silently slipped into the water and swam away. The natives, in spite of the hard work, laughed and sang as they went, making merry over the mishaps their companions might encounter, such as falls, or knocks, or a tumble into a hole. Each batch of men were to receive an ox at the end of the journey, so probably the prospect of a feast served to keep up their spirits. As we approached each native village, our bugle was sounded, and a new band of natives came down to take their share of the work; hauling up boats, or porterage, is the tax which they pay to the Government. Most of the men wore ornaments of flowers, either stuck into the string which is worn round the waist, or into their earrings, or hung in chains round the neck. At times the men could hardly make headway against the river's force; the water rushed and foamed between the rocks as the first rapid was entered, and for over an hour the struggle continued, and I dare not think of what would have happened if the rope had snapped, which several times seemed likely enough. Rounding the numerous rocks which impeded our progress, was a matter of extreme difficulty; as in bringing the boat broadside against the descending torrent, she heeled over, and, continually dipping her bow, shipped large quantities of water, and made the risk of swamping great. The ascent of the real Bedden rapid is very dangerous. The water roars and foams furiously, enormous rocks jut up on all sides, having only narrow passages between them, through which the boat must pass; and to add to the difficulty, the natives who were hauling the boat had to climb up and down the rocks near the river's edge, and the trees on the bank were also serious obstructions. We bumped the rocks several times, but although we shipped much water, the boat was not quite upset; once, just as we rounded one large mass, the current caught us and dashed us against the bank into the branches of a huge overhanging tree, smashing the awning of the boat to shreds. After sunset the scene was most exciting; the natives lit torches, the ruddy glare of which fell upon their dusky forms, upon the seething water, and the curious fantastically-shaped rocks; while above the roar of the river could be heard, now and again, the straining of the cordage or the shrill cry of the helmsman as he urged the men to extra efforts. "Turr, turr, awafe kawam!" ("Pull, pull quickly, go on!")

In eleven hours after leaving Regiaf we arrived safely at Bedden; an hour and a half only are required to make the return journey.

On reaching Dufli we found that we had the choice of two ways to Foweira, both of which I have had the fortune to traverse. The road *viâ* Fatiko was the one adopted on the return journey; on this occasion we decided to go by Magungo and the Lŭta Nzigé, or Dead Locust, as the Albert Lake is called.

CHAPTER II.

DUFLI TO RUBAGA.

DUFLI (lat. 3° 34′ 35″ N., long. 32° 20′ E., Dr. E.) is a well-built Egyptian station on the banks of the Nile. The streets are wide and clean, and the huts are nicely made of grass, while the Government Houses, which are very roomy, are built of sun-dried brick. There are large magazines made of burnt brick, and a well-ordered boat-building yard is a prominent feature of the place. The whole is surrounded by an excellently constructed wood stockade, and is defended by three field-guns. The officials have good gardens, well stocked with the usual Arab vegetables; and on the east side of the river are large tracts of country overspread with dhurra, which is cultivated to a large extent. The river is broad and navigable as far as the Lŭta Nzigé (Albert Nyanza).

Two steamers have their headquarters at this station, the *Nyanza* and the *Khedive*, the latter being a very strong twin-screw boat, 100 feet in length, built by Samuda Brothers. The steamers are kept in good condition, and in the *Khedive* the passenger finds comfortable cabins, and has the luxury of being able to indulge in a refreshing bath. There is a road along the west side of the river, but as the natives were not friendly, it was not then in use; now, however, it is open, and a new station has been formed at Wadelei, and another at the north-west corner of the Lŭta Nzigé, called Mahehi. The journey by water to Magungo, in Unyoro, takes about three days. Unfortunately for us, about a foot of the steam-piping of the *Khedive* had been lost while she was being carried in pieces to Dufli, and it had not yet been replaced, so we embarked on the *Nyanza*, leaving Dufli on December 21, 1878. The voyage up the Nile, which at this part forms a grand chain of lakes, is one which I shall never forget. The tall papyrus, waving lazily in the soft pure breeze, fringes the shore; beyond lie broad green fields of fast-ripening dhurra; while on either side, in the far distance, are long ranges of hills, with here and there a peak, like Mount Meto, towering up to a height of 1200 feet, and forming sharply defined fantastic outlines against the deep-blue sky.

Right well we steamed along until we came to "Arbatascha" (Fourteen), a curious rock, crowned by a pretty village, which derives its name from the fact that here fourteen chiefs pay in to the Egyptian Government their tax of grain. Here we stopped for a few hours to lay in a fresh supply of wood, which in these regions takes the place of coal as fuel. The wood was carried down to the boat by strong and well-proportioned women, who were gaily ornamented with showy beadwork; and who seemed on the best terms with the sailors, chatting and laughing with them, and evidently regarding their work as mere play.

Leaving Arbatascha we passed numerous villages, at most of which a curious sight presented itself. The natives were as yet unaccustomed to the steamer, and were greatly frightened by its approach, especially whenever the steam-whistle was blown. The warriors rushed down to the water's edge brandishing their spears, while the women and children, carrying as much of their scanty property as possible, ran quickly up the hills, seeking safety in flight.

The next station for obtaining fuel is about half-way between Dufli and Magungo, but here we could not get near the bank, as the river was shallow, so that the wood from the villages had to be brought through the water for about three-quarters of a mile. Only men and boys came, each carrying a load, and receiving as payment a few blue or green beads. The boys carried by far the heaviest loads, and it was strange to see a small child staggering under the weight of a heavy burden, while big strong men brought only light bundles.

We had been led to expect that we should come across a river of considerable size flowing into the Nile on the west side, in the neighbourhood of Wadelei, but, though we used every care, we failed to discover one.

Early on December 23, before sunrise, we approached the Lŭta Nzigé. A thick fog enshrouded everything, completely obscuring the landscape, so that we could distinguish nothing; but, to our delight, soon after the sun rose a rapid change took place. The fog rolled away, revealing a most charming scene. Numerous islands, covered with brushwood and papyrus, stud the mouth of the Lake and the Victoria Nile, while in the distance could be seen the ranges of mountains which guard its western shore. Herds of antelopes, eland (*Oreas Livingstonii*) were grazing on the grassy shore, and forty hippopotami were counted marching in single file along the bank. We had been steaming steadily up stream for some time, when the boat began to pitch and roll unpleasantly. In the distance the high waves of the stormy Lake were visible, their white foam-crowned crests reminding us of the ocean. Neither the natives nor the Arabs enjoyed this part of the journey, as unpleasant sensations arise, and only the well-remembered cry of "steward" was wanted to make the illusion complete!

After steaming for about three-quarters of an

hour across the northern extremity of the Lake we turned into the river proper (the Victoria Nile), and noticed that the current divides at one of the islands, part flowing in a northerly direction, and part diverging to the south-south-west, into the Lake. For this cause Magungo has removed from its old site, as the water is gradually washing away the land at the north-east corner of the Lake, and in consequence the station became so damp and unhealthy as to make a move absolutely necessary. This alteration in the position of Magungo has a connection with the vexed question as to whether or no the Albert Lake is to be regarded as one of the sources of the Nile. This is a matter of such interest and importance that I may be pardoned if I make a digression at this point.

When Dr. Livingstone discovered Lake Tanganyika, he found at no great distance from it a large river. He was unable to trace it to its source, but conjectured that it was the Nile, and that it flowed out of Lake Tanganyika.

Speke was at this time in these parts, and being informed by some missionaries that, according to native report, there was a lake in the centre, he made an excursion as far as Kagei, and then first saw the Victoria Nyanza.

Returning to England, he soon organised a regular expedition for discovering the source of the Nile, and started with Colonel Grant from the south, and proceeded to Kagei. Thence they marched round the Victoria Nyanza, through Karague to Uganda. They discovered that the river flowed out of the Nyanza at the Ripon Falls; and followed its course up to Foweira, where they were compelled to leave it and strike across country to Gondokoro, at which place they met Mr. Baker (afterwards Sir Samuel Baker) and his wife, who were coming from the north to aid them.

Speke and Grant had been told by the natives that there was another lake farther west; this information they gave to Baker, who acted upon it, and continued his journey with the result of discovering the Albert Lake.

Baker struck the Lūta Nzigé at a point called Vacovia, and imagined that the Lake extended far to the south. He was not able to explore the Lake fully, and the true position of Vacovia turns out to be nearly at the end of the Lake, which is only about half as long as was then thought.

The Nile flows from the east into the north corner of the Lake, and flows out in a northerly direction. (See map.) On discovering this, Baker came to the conclusion that the Lake contributed to the supply of water, and ought to be considered as one of the sources of the Nile. A reference to the accompanying map will show the Lake as Baker gave it; and as it really is. Some travellers have

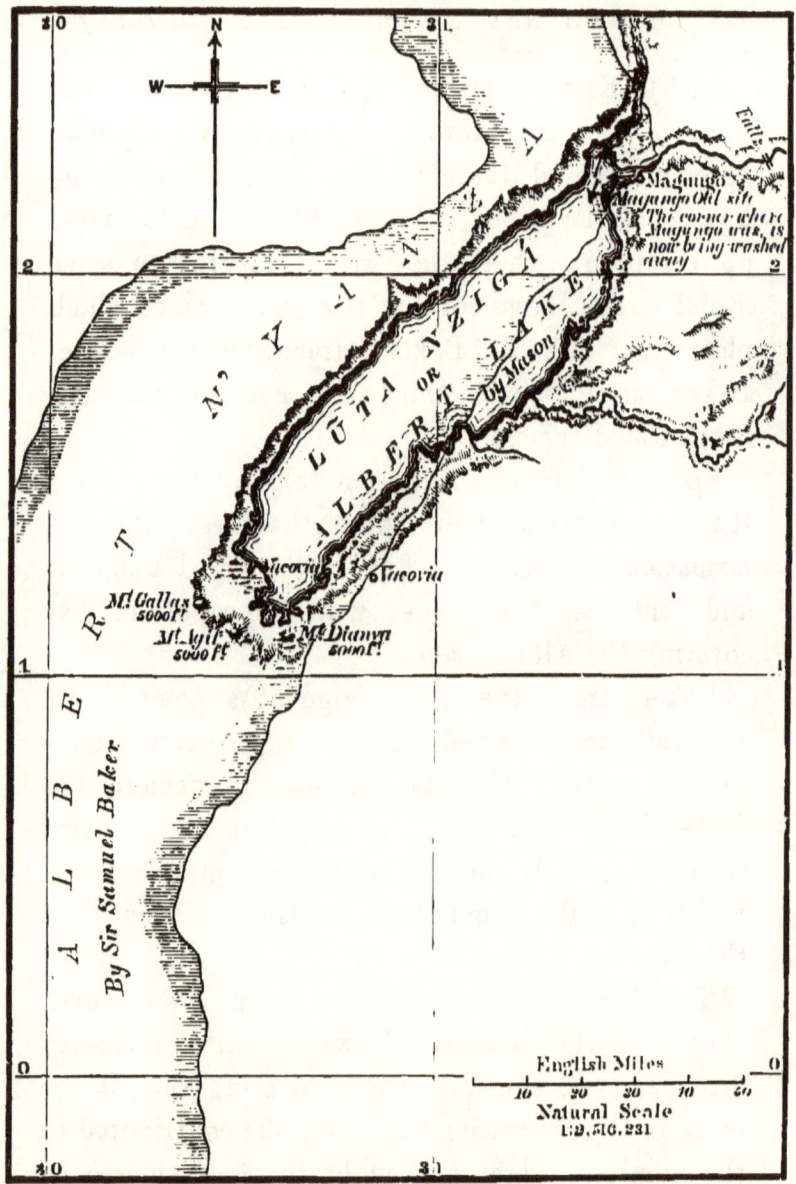

supposed that either the Albert and Tanganyika were the same lake, or that they were joined by a large river such as that seen by Livingstone. If this had been so, Tanganyika might have been regarded as a source of the Nile.

At a later date Mr. Stanley, in the course of his travels, came upon a lake to the north of Tanganyika, which he imagined to be the Albert; but the position he assigns to it makes this to be impossible, as it is much farther south than the extreme limit of the Albert Lake. Since then the Albert Lake has been circumnavigated on three occasions by Gessi Pasha, Mason Bey, and Dr. Emin Bey respectively. They found that Baker had placed Vacovia too far east, that the southern end of the Lake was an ambatch forest, and that there was no large river flowing into it at its extremity. Moreover, on either side of the Lake, there are ranges of hills close at hand, so that the only rivers flowing into it are of very small dimensions; and indeed the water lost by evaporation from the large area of the Lake's surface is greater than the amount of water supplied from these small streams. It is for this reason that there is a current to the south-south-west, *drawn in from the Nile*.

Nevertheless, a lake of this size must exercise a considerable influence on the Nile, and it is that of an immense back-water. At the time of the dry season, there is much less water coming down from the Victoria Nyanza. It is then that the Albert affords water for the Nile, and, as a consequence, the level of its surface sinks until the rains set in and the usual amount of water comes again from the Victoria.

On the whole, I am inclined to think that originally the Albert, Stanley's Lake, and Tanganyika were one, but that owing to volcanic or other causes, they have been divided. Any conjecture on this point must be qualified, until the country between the Albert and Tanganyika has been explored; this need not be a very difficult or lengthy proceeding. I do not think that the Albert can be regarded as one of the sources of the Nile, but that it exercises the influence that has already been described. As far as we know as present, the Victoria Nyanza must be considered as the only source.

I hear that there is a large river flowing into the north-east corner of the Victoria Lake; but if this be so, it has not yet been explored. It may be that the waters from Mount Kilimanjaro do find their way into the Nile; and I shall not be surprised if it be discovered that Lake Baringo does not exist.

Magungo (lat. 2° 14′ 42″ N., long. 31° 31′ 45″ E., 2100 feet above sea-level) is a clean and well-built town, surrounded by a strong earthwork fortification, and a moat which is ten feet in depth. One field-gun and two rocket-tubes are placed in advantageous positions. In addition to the ordinary sentries, a chain of outposts was maintained; good guard being necessary, as the place is coveted by that most treacherous king Kabrega, well known to the readers of Baker's 'Ismäilia.'

The landing-stage is in the form of a horse-shoe, right up to which there is deep water, so that the steamer can be run alongside. On our arrival a body of troops was drawn up round the semicircle; and as we landed the soldiers presented arms, the band struck up the Egyptian "Salaam," and the colours were drooped. As the Mudir, Murjan Aga Donesura, was absent, we were courteously received by the second in command, Mahomet Aga, a young man, and a good and brave soldier. The appearance of the soldiers was excellent, and their spotless white uniforms contrasted well with the gorgeous attire of their officers. Our huts were pleasantly situated under an immense tree, just outside the earthworks.

We were up betime the next day, December 24, for we were to pay a visit to the Murchison Falls. On reaching the landing-stage, we found the steamer prepared to start; the Vakil, Mahomet Aga, had provided a sumptuous luncheon-basket, containing half-a-dozen cold roast fowls, a goodly number of hard-boiled eggs, and a couple of jars of native beer. A large crowd had assembled to see us off, and all being ready, we got under weigh immediately.

The sun was very hot, and a new and agreeable feature presented itself to us, the deep blue of the sky overhead being lightly covered with fleecy white clouds.

We were all in high spirits at the prospect of so pleasant a day, and chatted with the captain and other officers, who " spun long yarns " for our amusement. There were quantities of ripe bananas lying about, and this was the cause of our hearing an interesting fact in gastronomy. It appears that the second engineer has a weakness for this particular fruit, and whenever he is at Magungo, he indulges his taste to the utmost extent. On this occasion, marvellous to relate, not less than a hundred and fifty bananas were required to satisfy his appetite. He was certainly a phenomenon; but, sad to relate, he applied to me for pills the following day.

After leaving Magungo, the river narrowed, while the land on each side rose higher and higher, until we entered a kind of gorge. The hills on either side were covered with great trees, clothed with brilliant foliage, and at each bend of the river the eye fell on natural bowers, formed by tropical creepers drooping in graceful festoons from the mighty branches of huge trees, among which monkeys (the first we had seen in Africa) sported and chattered. Overhead flew birds with magnificent plumage, while gorgeous butterflies, fluttering about in countless swarms, added to the charm of the scene. Here and there we came across sandy, sunburnt patches, forming a striking contrast to the rich colouring of the undergrowth, and affording a pleasant lounge for monster crocodiles. Occasionally the temptation to take a shot at them was irresistible, but whether or no we killed any, I cannot tell, as crocodiles have a knack of falling into the water as soon as hit. In our wake we could see several hippopotami, one of whom, astonished doubtless at the unaccustomed sight, and indignant at such an invasion of his domain, charged the steamer, and made her quiver from stem to stern. This was not an unfrequent occurrence, and occasionally the violent shock does much damage, the screw of our boat having been injured more than once. During our sail, we came near some canoes, the occupants of which tried to race; but when they found we were overtaking them, they ran their canoes to shore, and were soon hidden in the dense vegetation. Through breaks in the trees we could see the natives on the hills looking down on the strange sight of a steamer; they rapidly disappeared when the steam-whistle was blown.

As we passed on we found that the hills closed in ahead of us, shutting out the light, and soon we could hear the roar of the falls in the distance. The water became more and more turbulent as we went on through the gathering gloom, till at last a sudden turn in the river brought us into daylight again. A fissure in the hills admitted the blazing rays of the sun, which fell straight on the fall, now becoming visible. At first we could only perceive the spray, which rose up in clouds and was blown about by the wind; but when we approached nearer, the magnificent fall burst upon our sight, descending in an unbroken column between two rocks, into a seething mass of water some hundred and twenty feet below. The spray, sparkling and flashing in the sunlight like myriads of jewels, is tossed up right to the top of the cliffs, and for several hundred yards the river is a turbulent mass of stormy water. Our captain approached to within half a mile of the fall, the nearest point to which the steamer can with safety be taken, owing to the tremendous force of the current. So she was run in shore; two men, watching their opportunity, leaped out and made her fast to a large tree by means of a stout rope.

We were so fascinated by the fall, the splendour of which I cannot attempt to describe, that we were very unwilling to quit the magnificent scene. Two of our party landed, hoping to advance some way nearer, but the tangled underwood was so thick that they returned defeated, and we were reluctantly obliged to be content with the view from the steamer. Of course, with such a strong current to aid our return to Magungo, the journey down occupied far less time than the voyage up.

At one point, while the men were getting wood,

MURCHISON FALLS.

one of my companions and I ascended the hills on the banks, and were well rewarded for our toil by gaining splendid views over woods and dales, with fine ranges of distant hills. The view of the Murchison Falls is taken from a hill on the southern bank, at a distance of about a mile, and gives but a very slight idea of the grandeur of the scene. It was unfortunately impossible to obtain a better position for a photograph.

It being Christmas Eve we spent as cheerful an evening as we could, although so far from home, and amid such strange surroundings. We had a large fire made under our tree, and sat round it, singing carols, to the great astonishment of a motley throng who formed a ring round us and listened with evident delight to our amateur concert. Of course many a thought was sent across land and sea to our far-distant English homes, where we pictured our friends spending a very different evening.

On Christmas morning the officers of the station called to wish us the customary "El eed Mabarak," or "May you have a blessed feast."

After our Christmas service we repaired to the house of the Mudir, whose head wife Zenab gave us a capital dinner, of which the following were the chief courses: soup, Irish stew, roast fowl, plum-pudding (which we had brought with us from England), and sweets made of honey, butter, ground-nuts and semsem seeds. There was also plantain wine; and tea and coffee followed after dinner. Such excellent cooking we had only once in Africa. After dinner Zenab asked us to stay and see the Mudir's other wives; we accepted the invitation, and they were called in. Three of them were black beauties, and the fourth was a lovely Abyssinian girl of a lighter tint, with expressive gazelle-like eyes. They were neatly and simply attired in print dresses; but Zenab's gaudy colours would have greatly shocked those æsthetic gentlemen who delight in olive-greens and sickly blues, and worship Mr. Whistler's "Harmonies." They sat down on the ground, while Zenab stood and gave us an account of their history.

The next two days were engaged in finding porters, which was a matter of some difficulty, for Kabrega had heard of our journey, and had given strict injunctions to his people not to carry any of our goods. But Mahomet Aga himself went and procured us porters by holding out to them great promises of reward, and perhaps adding a few judicious threats.

At Magungo we were to bid farewell to the steamer and begin marching. It is a great tribute to British enterprise that a traveller can penetrate so far inland in a steamer. The first suggestion for placing one here was made by Sir Samuel Baker, and though many difficulties had to be encountered before his idea could be carried out, Colonel Gordon succeeded in surmounting them, and steamers have been safely transported and reconstructed here, and will doubtless prove to be a great assistance to the work of civilisation in these regions.

On the morning of December 28 we prepared for a start onwards. We were provided with three donkeys. Before receiving the "salaam" I mounted my animal, but, alas, he proved refractory; in spite of my efforts, the beast bolted with me right past the soldiers, who were drawn up in line. I pulled at the bridle, and my legs being too long my feet trailed on the ground, and I presented a most undignified spectacle; the donkey would not stop until seized by two officers who had started in pursuit! They would not let me dismount, but led me ignominiously past the line of troops to receive the parting salaam. After this *contretemps* we finally made our departure, carrying with us most agreeable remembrances of the kind attentions and hospitality of the officials at Magungo.

Three long days' march brought us to Keroto. On the first day the road was for the most part exceedingly bad; the tall tiger-grass and deep underwood impeded the way, and made our progress very slow. It was here that we came for the first time to the banana groves, which were certainly very pleasant and shady, and rested our eyes, which had been much tried by the glare of the sun. We found the Wanyoro porters a wretched set of men.

but we were escorted by a large body of regular troops, who gave valuable assistance. Just before sunset our advance guard was attacked by Kabrega's people. He had not expected such a strong party, so that his men speedily had to retire, leaving one man on the field, upon which our escort advanced and took possession of a small village, where we encamped for the night. The natives showed in force several times, but the sharp fire of the soldiers soon cleared the woods round the village. We found the huts so full of vermin that we were obliged to sleep in the open air. At about 11 o'clock we were aroused from our slumbers by a loud clap of thunder, and a minute or two later a tropical storm broke over us, the like of which I have rarely seen. The rain came pouring down in torrents, soon extinguishing our fires; flash after flash of vivid lightning lit up the dreary scene, and we were almost deafened by the continuous roll of the crashing thunder, which seemed to shake the earth to its very foundations. The storm having made the night as uncomfortable as it well could, we were not sorry to break camp next morning at half-past 5. The road was worse than ever, and we had to cross two streams. The second of these, Khor El Pasha, is a very rapid torrent, which we reached about mid-day. We had to cross it by springing from stone to stone, the natives catching us as we landed on each rock. It was a matter of some danger, for if a slip had sent us into the rapid stream, no human power could have saved us. After a tiring march of twelve hours we pitched our camp on a hill near another rocky stream, and a second violent storm coming on, we passed another sleepless and miserable night.

It may be well to mention that, when in camp, no one is permitted to go beyond the line of sentries without a firebrand. Any one who is so reckless as to disobey this regulation stands a good chance of getting an ounce of lead from one of the sentries on his return.

We were glad to arrive at Keroto, and to be under the protection of its strong stockade, for all along the route the signals of the hostile natives, such as shrill cries, whistles, blowing of horns, and the war-drum, had kept us continually on the alert.

Exposure to the rain during the past two nights had prostrated my two companions with fever, and was "the last straw" in the case of our poor Syrian dragoman, Nicola, who had been ill for some time, and he died at this place in the course of a few days. Poor fellow! He little thought that this journey would cost him his life.

Keroto (lat. 4° 18' 10" N., long. 31° 40' 28" E., 3451 feet above sea-level) has generally been placed on maps too far east. The above position will, I believe, be found accurate; the altitude has not before been determined. A more picturesque spot can hardly be imagined. There is a large clearing in an immense forest, in the centre of which stands the town; an open space of about 200 yards being left all round to prevent an enemy finding shelter near the stockade. As the garrison is not large enough for the purpose of working as well as mounting guard, and as there are no friendly natives here, it is a matter of some difficulty to obtain the necessary amount of provisions. Kabrega is constantly harassing the station. It is to be regretted that an end had not been put to his tyrannical rule, as would have happened some time ago but for the strong opposition excited in England by some people who look with jealous eyes at the extension southwards of Egyptian territory; but I can confidently state that in those parts of the country which are under Egyptian rule, and where the government is conducted as it is by the present Governor of the Equatorial Provinces, the natives are in far better circumstances than under their own despotic and brutal kings.

To my thinking, those who know so little of the *facts* of the case would effect more good by keeping silence, which we have high authority for knowing to be at times "golden," than by dogmatising concerning matters of which they can have but an imperfect and scanty knowledge; whilst those who are in a position to practically assist the cause, are hampered and often thwarted in their self-sacrificing efforts to raise the people by the ignorance and folly of sentimentalists. There is unfortunately in Europe a class of philanthropists who are wise in their own conceit, who have a number of pet theories, which are well adapted for board-rooms and newspaper articles, but, when put to the test of practical experience, are found to be utterly worthless. It would be well if some of them were to pay a flying visit to Central Africa. They would probably learn a few lessons which would well repay the cost of the journey; and would confer a great boon on thousands, who in those far regions are to this day suffering from the force of the "fixed ideas" which these well-intentioned but misguided gentlemen, having once originated on insufficient data, so obstinately maintain.

At Keroto we saw Amfina, one of Kabrega's cousins, who had come to meet us. His pedigree may prove a matter of some interest:

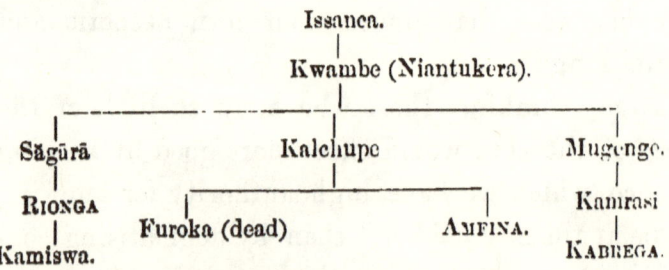

This table, which shows the relationship of Kabrega, Rionga, and Amfina, all of whom will be frequently mentioned, was kindly given to me by Dr. Emin

Bey, and as my own inquiries confirm its accuracy, I can repeat it with every confidence.

It was at this station that we saw the curious Wanyoro dance. I was sitting in my hut at night, when a messenger came from Amfina asking me to go over to see him. I was very glad to accept his invitation, and followed the guide. I found Amfina sitting in front of his hut, surrounded by three or four of his head men, with a huge bowl of merissa (native beer) in front of him. He told me that his people had made friends with our porters, and as they had a good brew of merissa, they were intending to make a night of it and have a dance; so he thought I might like to see it. I thanked him, sat down, and lit my pipe. He gave me some merissa, a sour, muddy compound, not a very agreeable beverage, and entered into conversation with me about the manners and customs of his people. After which, at my request, they danced their war-dance to the accompaniment of drums and the clapping of hands. Seizing their spears with their right hand and their shields with their left, they advanced with a crouching kind of spring in a zigzag towards Amfina, and then retired, uttering their war-cry. Those who have seen the performance of the friendly Zulus will be able to form a good idea of this dance, which is very similar. They then, for their own pleasure, danced the peculiar dance of the tribe, which is a wonderful performance, but so indecent that a description of it cannot be given.

The next day, January 4, a long and rapid march brought me to Amfina's residence, Panyatole, passing *en route* the village Kissuna. The road from Keroto first descends and then winds up hill for a long way, the land rising and falling, thus forming several ridges, one above the other, until Panyatole is reached. From each of these elevations there are most picturesque views. The eye wanders down the glades of the forest; and among the trees, herds of graceful antelopes may be seen lying down or grazing at will. As we neared Panyatole, the birds flew hither and thither, telling us, by their shrill screams, that a storm was at hand, even if the heavy masses of cloud and the growing darkness had not already warned us. Our pace quickened; the soldiers and boys broke into a jog-trot, as they did not relish the idea of a drenching. Our progress was all the faster as Amfina had caused the grass along the road to be cut down. But our efforts were in vain. The storm broke over us, and before we reached shelter, we had a thorough soaking. During this march one of my boys fell ill, and I gave orders for him to be carried on an angereb. My men made great objections, for though they are willing to carry a *white* man, they draw the line at those of their own colour. They wanted the boy to be left behind, to catch us up on recovery, if he could, and they seemed quite unable to understand my anxiety for a mere boy.

It was at Amfina's that I had the pleasure of meeting the Rev. Mr. Wilson, who had come from Uganda to meet our party, and who has been my companion and friend through many a danger, and many a long month of wearisome travel.

All the villages here are well fortified by a thick thorn fence, partly as protection against Kabrega, and partly to prevent the entrance of leopards. There is only one gateway, just wide enough for a cow to get through; and it is closed at night by a massive door, which slides between the walls and two upright posts, thus forming an impassable barrier.

The way in which the Wanyoro build their houses is as follows: a long stout pole is fixed into the ground; around this, at the distance of some ten feet, is placed a circle of saplings, which are bent over and securely fastened to the centre pole, thus forming a dome. The whole is thatched with grass; a doorway and porch are made, and the hut is finished as far as its externals are concerned. Inside there are two partitions, dividing the hut into three parts, as shown in the diagram. In one of these is the fire, in another the beds, while the third is used as a sitting-room.

There is no arrangement made to permit the smoke to escape, and so the huts are not very comfortable for Europeans, who find that a very little smoke goes a long way. In addition to this discomfort, the traveller who is particular on these little points may have rather a strong objection to the fleas which find their way into the hut in the grass that bestrews the floor. The sanitary arrangements in Unyoro are not so good as in Uganda, where the people are most particular about such matters.

In Unyoro, it is the custom for the near relatives of the late king to fight for the throne; this has caused much bloodshed; and now a continual succession of small raids goes on between Kabrega, Rionga, and Amfina. The two latter certainly do not bear any brotherly feeling to the former; indeed, Amfina begged us to help him to fight for what he considers his own land.

Amfina has a remarkably intelligent face, a fine soldierly bearing, and is a thoroughly polished man. Doubtless he has learnt much from the Arabs, though, unlike Mtesa, he does not speak their language well. He was very friendly, and gave us plenty of provisions; but, like all the natives, he—*alieni appetens*—wanted us to make him presents of all we possessed. As in Cairo, so in these parts, there is a continual cry of backsheesh — backsheesh! His reception of us was very pleasing; the divan was overspread with Turkish carpets, the seats and bolsters being covered with spotless linen. Coffee and cigarettes were gravely handed round in the most decorous style by smartly dressed boys. The chief's old mother came to see us; but she was quite thrown into the shade by her ten daughters-in-law, Amfina's wives, such a bevy of beauty as one does not often see. They were all modestly dressed in robes made either of skins, or of the native bark-cloth. They were very pleased at being allowed to inspect our clothes, stockings, and boots, and asked as an especial favour to see our hair. Their wonder and admiration at Mr. Wilson's hair, which happened to be rather long, knew no bounds, and only after considerable pulling from their fair—no, I am forgetting—their *dusky hands*, would they believe that it was real and would not come off. Of course we were asked the usual stock of questions: they were very much surprised and disgusted to find that we had no wives, but Amfina offered to supply the deficiency in any quantity we might desire. It is hardly necessary to say that we refused on this, as on all such occasions; but it is well to state, that it is a great disadvantage to be unmarried in Africa; bachelors at once lose caste with the natives, who cannot understand it. All missionaries would do well to remember this, and to bring out a wife each with them; for I feel persuaded that the fact of their being unmarried does much to set the natives against religion. In Africa, as elsewhere, the example of the life led by the professors of Christianity is the thing which teaches most; and how can a man inveigh against the evils of polygamy unless he can show to the natives the possibility of living with one wife?

After spending a pleasant hour and a half with Amfina we retired at sunset to our huts, hoping to prepare ourselves by a long night's rest for the march to Foweira. We were cheated out of this by the natives making such frightful noises, that sleep was an impossibility.

From Amfina's seriba the road to Foweira was through a dense jungle; the high reeds and the thick tiger-grass made marching exceedingly difficult and fatiguing. Dead trunks of trees lay rotting across the path, and we often got our feet entangled in the creepers which grow so luxuriantly, and give great trouble to the unsuspecting traveller. In Africa it is needful to be always on the look-out, and to walk warily, for danger lurks on all sides. It is out of the question to ride; the venturesome wight who attempts this daring feat soon finds that his donkey has a knack of stumbling among the many impediments; and while the rider, to his great disgust, finds himself and his saddle in an inglorious position on the ground, the donkey wanders on, usually away from the path, and probably gets stuck in a swamp. The rescue of the animal, and the raising up of the bruised and indignant rider, of course, hinder the caravan for some time. Nevertheless we persevered through all these little annoyances, and at night camped out in the forest. The soldiers built huts for themselves, and offered to do the same for us, but we foolishly refused. Next morning we discovered that it is best in Africa to take advice; for as we had only our mosquito curtains to protect us, we were drenched to the skin by the heavy dew that had fallen. This jungle is the resort of herds of wild animals, among which are plenty of wart-hogs (*Choiropotamus Africanus*). As this animal is unclean according to the law of the Prophet, we had some difficulty in getting it cooked, for no Moslem will dare to touch it. And indeed, when cooked, we did not find the flesh at all good.

In course of time we arrived at Foweira, a town situated on a high bank, at a curve in the river, which thus forms a natural protection on two sides. The Nile here is 850 yards broad, and is deep, so that it could be navigated by steamers of considerable draught as far as Urondogani; after that place there are rapids which bar the way into the Victoria Nyanza. Between Foweira and Magungo porterage would be always necessary, as the river falls 700 feet in its course between these places. Just opposite Foweira, a small river, the Kubuli, flows into the Nile from the east, then turning north I was told it is navigable for small boats for a good many miles inland.

The natives here catch a great quantity of fish, chiefly the large-headed silurus, though there is a kind of carp, weighing from one to three pounds, which is very palatable. The way they catch fish is by means of a basketwork trap as in the picture.

We left Foweira in native canoes, and after six days arrived at Mruli on January 27, 1879.

Mruli (lat. 1° 37' 43" N., long. 32° 19' 49" E.; 3513 feet above sea-level) was at that time the most southern of the Egyptian stations. Since we were there, the garrisons both from this place and from Keroto have been withdrawn, and now Foweira, Magungo, and a new station on the Nile exactly north of Panyatole, form the southern boundary of Egyptian territory.

At Mruli our Egyptian escort left us; we parted from such faithful attendants with much regret, and felt as we bid them good-bye that we were saying farewell to civilisation.

Mtesa had sent an escort of 1500 men in addition to 400 porters, and we left Mruli on February 3; in five days afterwards we crossed the Ergugu, the most northern boundary of Uganda, and arrived in Rubaga, Mtesa's capital, on February 14; a curious valentine for him!

We had such a large escort from Mruli to Rubaga, for the following reason. Just north of the Ergugu, between Uganda and Mruli, there is a strip of land, about thirty miles broad, which belongs to Kabrega, and along this there are two roads from east to west which are used by his men; the road leading to Uganda crossing these at different points. The first batch of porters who had been sent for our goods, had been attacked in this border-land; and Mtesa heard from Kabrega of his intention to try and capture us, his former attempt to do so between Magungo and Keroto having been unsuccessful.

I shall not soon forget our march across this piece of country. We were encamped in a forest, and soon after midnight the drums began to beat and we were told we must start again. Being wearied with the previous day's journey we refused, but it was useless to try to sleep longer, the noise was too great. Drums were beating, horns were blowing, men were shouting and crying, so we made a virtue of necessity, and prepared to start. On coming out of our huts we saw a strange scene; the whole wood was lit up by the bright moonlight and the lurid glare of many huts which had been fired to give sufficient light to the porters who were collecting the goods and arranging themselves into different bands, while the soldiers of each chief rallied to his standard. At last all was ready, and the drums of the head chief gave the signal to march. The other chiefs took up positions to see their men pass, and as each warrior went by he saluted his chief by brandishing his spear and shield, uttering at the same time a fierce yell, and then vanished into the darkness. Some 200 men thus rushed forward as the advance guard, and the others fell into three long lines and proceeded. If there had been noise and confusion before, all was quiet now, hardly a sound broke the stillness of the night as we silently threaded our way along the circuitous path. Now and then there was a whispered word, or slight blow of a stick on a stump, as the man in front gave us warning of a branch of a tree or hole in the ground. This precaution was most necessary, for there were many obstructions, and the light of the moon was not powerful enough to penetrate through the trees and dense undergrowth. The moon shone brightly as we marched through the sombre, silent forest, casting long deep shadows from every tree, while millions of dewdrops sparkled like diamonds on every tree and bush, or fell in silver rain as the dusky forms glided weirdly beneath them. At last the faint line of dawn became visible on the horizon, and presently the sun burst forth in all his power, dispelling darkness, but his fierce rays made us regret the refreshing coolness of the night.

It was only then that we understood all the precautions which had been taken to prevent a surprise. On each side of the path, at the distance of about half a mile, were chains of sentries moving parallel to our column; whilst on each ant-hill, or other high ground, some men were placed as sentries, having with them a drummer to give the alarm should the enemy appear ; as soon as the body of the caravan passed, these men rushed forward to the front to attain some fresh point of vantage. No Wanyoro were seen, and we crossed the no-man's land in safety. These arrangements are very interesting, as they show the high state of efficiency of the Waganda army.

We were heartily welcomed by Mr. Mackay, who had reached Uganda from the south, and for three months had been alone in Rubaga. The king sent down messengers with presents of food to bid us welcome.

Before we left England many ridiculed the idea of the possibility of our reaching Uganda by the Nile route ; indeed Mr. Stanley assured us that we should not get half our goods to the Lake. From Suakim to Rubaga we lost none of our party, excepting our dragoman, and not a single load or package ; I doubt whether any travellers from Zanzibar to the Victoria Nyanza have been so fortunate.

APPENDIX I.

BY REV. C. T. WILSON.

THE question of opening up commerce with the tribes inhabiting Central Africa is becoming every year of greater importance to Great Britain; as in many markets where our merchants had formerly a monopoly, formidable rivals have entered into competition with us, and as some countries which used to be large consumers of our manufactures are now manufacturing for themselves, it is manifest that new markets and fresh fields for commerce must be sought if we are to have a continuance of the commercial prosperity which our country has formerly enjoyed. No region of our earth presents so virgin a field for enterprise of this sort as Central Africa, with its vast lakes, fertile soil, and teeming population.

Several projects have been set on foot with the object of establishing trading stations in, and opening up trade with, the interior of Africa; notably one promoted by the late Mr. J. Bradshaw, of Manchester; but his scheme was far too vast and visionary, and he asked much too large a capital (10,000,000*l.*) to start the undertaking. Central Africa is no El Dorado, as some people seem to imagine, where gold is to be had in unlimited quantities for the trouble of picking it up. Yet a properly organised company, under the guidance of men possessing the ordinary qualities necessary for commercial success, prudence, a willingness to learn, and not to stick by preconceived notions, and not in too great a hurry to become rich, would in a few years get a fair return for the money invested, and would do more (by promoting lawful trade) than a score of gunboats towards suppressing the horrible trade in human beings still unhappily carried on to a large extent.

But one great obstacle has to be encountered at the very outset of the enterprise, viz. the difficulty of transport from the great lakes to the sea. No one who has studied the question of trade-routes to the great lakes would select the Nile for that purpose. The eight cataracts which are found in its course from the Albert Lake to the Mediterranean, the liability of the narrow channels in the great marsh-land between Bohr and the Sobat to be blocked by the tawfs, the floating islands of grass which have so often proved such terrible obstacles to navigation, and the ever-shifting sandbanks, upon which even the light-draughted native boats frequently get stranded during the dry season, present engineering difficulties which are practically insurmountable for the purpose in hand; not to mention the Murchison Falls, where the Nile springs at one leap over a ledge of rock 120 feet in perpendicular height, or the long succession of rapids between these falls and Foweira, where in some thirty miles the river falls more than 800 feet. Another serious difficulty has to be encountered in using the Nile as a great waterway for steamers, and that is the question of fuel. For hundreds of miles south of Khartoum trees are scarcely to be met with in the valley of the Nile, and fuel is already becoming scarce under the demands of the scanty traffic now carried on by the government of the Soudan; while if any considerable increase in the traffic should occur, it would have to be brought from increasing distances, till it would be as costly as coal brought from Europe, unless that mineral should be discovered anywhere within a reasonable distance of the Nile Valley, of which however there is little hope.

The unsuitability of the Nile route for trade purposes being granted, the alternative route from the East Coast naturally suggests itself.

The great obstacle here has always been the difficulty of transport. There is no large navigable river; the presence of the tsetse fly (*Glossina morsitans*) prevents the employment of the system of bullock-waggons in vogue in South Africa, and renders the use of pack-horses impossible. The country is quite unsuited for camels (even if they were proof against the tsetse, which they are not), and the African elephant, not having been yet trained like his Indian brother, the sole method of transport hitherto has been by means of the Wapagazi, or negro porters. This system is, however, slow, cumbrous, and costly, and utterly inadequate to any extension of trade.

As already mentioned, the ordinary baggage animals are useless on account of the tsetse fly, though, it is true, it has been suggested that possibly a line of country might be found north of the 7th parallel of S. latitude where this fly would not be met with; but this is far too vague an hypothesis on which to found any project.

The only alternative, then, seems to be some kind of railway; and I feel, for my own part, convinced that Central Africa can only be opened up by steam-power. It would be premature for any one to say that any particular kind of railway was *the one* for Central Africa; but of all those I have seen or read of, that described by Mr. J. B. Fell, in a paper read before the Society of Arts, on April 29th, 1879, seems to me the best suited for Africa. One of its great advantages is that it obviates the necessity of having large embankments or deep cuttings, the rails being carried over the inequalities of the ground on viaducts of wood or iron, much, I imagine, like the American trestle bridges.

Such a railway, which would cost only a small amount per mile for construction, which could be laid with tolerable rapidity, and which would admit of moderately heavy trains running at a speed of from twelve to twenty miles an hour, would do wonders towards opening up these regions to commerce.

In laying the line of rail the neighbourhood of large rivers should be avoided as much as possible, as they change their beds and alter their course so frequently and with such rapidity during the rain, that they would carry away the track completely on either side of their beds, and thus necessitate the relaying of large portions of it after each rainy season, besides suspending communication altogether for a considerable period.

The route for such a line should also be, as far as compatible with directness and slight gradients, through an inhabited district, so that trade might at once be begun with the natives. For my own feeling is that it would be very unwise to attempt to carry the line of rail at first as far as the Victoria Lake. A line of 100 miles or so in length would connect the East Coast range of mountains with the seaboard, would open up a considerable area of country to commerce, and afford the Europeans of Zanzibar an easy means of retreat to the healthy uplands of Usugara during the more trying parts of the year. Its terminus, moreover, would form an advantageous *point de depart* for the traveller, the trader, and the missionary; the long delays in the deadly coast region, which has proved so fatal to many a traveller, being thus obviated.

The experience also which would be gained by a modest enterprise such as this would be invaluable when the time came for extending the line, and penetrating into the remoter regions of the interior.

If such a line were laid down, trading depôts should be formed at intervals of twenty or thirty miles, or even less in thickly populated districts, where two or more Europeans should reside for the purpose of encouraging trade with the natives. For it must never be forgotten that, if a line is ever to pay, trade must be made. The average African negro has hardly a want now which he cannot himself satisfy; his land produces grain enough to supply him and his family with food, or his bow and arrows or spear kills a sufficiency of wild animals to furnish him with meat. He manufactures his own weapons, and his hoes, axes, and knives, from iron obtained from native ores; he moulds and bakes his own cooking-pots and tobacco-pipes, while the bottle-gourd, which he trains over his hut, supplies him with all else he needs in the way of domestic utensils. Tobacco (his sole luxury) he either grows himself, or, as in the case of the Wagogo, obtains it by barter from neighbouring tribes. He either discards clothing altogether, walking about in primitive nakedness, or the jungle grasses or the skins of wild animals furnish him with a scanty kilt. Should he, however, have made such an advance towards civilisation as to require cloth, he can obtain a sufficiency, in exchange for grain, from passing caravans, or for the tusks of the elephants he has killed for food.

That it is possible to create wants, and thus stimulate trade, may be seen in the case of the Waganda, who have had a variety of wants created through contact with Arabs, Egyptians, and Europeans, and with whom, consequently, a considerable trade (as such things are reckoned in Africa) is carried on by the Arabs and half-breed traders from Zanzibar.

In the case of Uganda, ivory and slaves are the only products obtainable, as nothing else at present pays for transport to Zanzibar; but many things, even under the present costly system of porterage, might be made to pay in districts within 200 miles of the coast, as the cost of transport increases with the distance in almost geometrical progression. When the negro has had a fresh want created he will be found ready enough to exert himself to supply it. Slaves and ivory come most readily to hand at first, but trade in the former being prohibited, and the supply of the latter being not only limited, but even on the decrease, he will soon turn his attention to other articles which may be exchanged for cloth or whatever else he may need. Consequently the most important work which a pioneer trading enterprise has to accomplish is to discover what native products, or other articles obtainable or capable of being produced in the various countries, are most likely to bring a fair profit, and to induce the natives to bring or produce these things for sale. Nor will the natives be found slow in taking advantage of such discoveries, when once the need of articles of foreign manufacture is felt. Thus in Ugogo a large trade might be done in beeswax, if once the Wagogo became aware of its value. In the regions lying nearer the coast, cotton cultivation might be advantageously promoted. While in Uganda vast quantities of rice might be grown in its swampy valleys, and on the hill-slopes chinchona and the tea-plant would probably flourish. Indiarubber, gum-arabic, hides, and possibly other natural products as yet unknown to Europeans, would, in many districts, form important articles of commerce. The natives, however, in almost every case, must be taught the value of these things, and then they themselves, with their interest quickened by the necessity of supplying their wants, will discover other articles which Europeans alone might have been long in discovering, and which may prove very valuable.

I would, however, again insist that any trade to be remunerative, must be developed by Europeans among the various tribes of the interior; and this will, I believe, be most readily accomplished by a system of depôts at intervals along the line of railway. Settlements of negroes would soon form round these depôts for the sake of protection, and the natives could be employed in cultivating the ground and collecting articles of trade. This is somewhat the system adopted by the Arabs; they form trading centres in the interior, and send out their slaves from there to more distant regions.

So, too, with these proposed depôts, as opportunities offered other trading stations might be formed at some distance from the line of railway, communication being kept up by porters or donkeys, or, in districts free from the tsetse fly, by bullock-waggons; these stations would gradually be extended, and so larger and larger areas would be opened out to commerce. When at length the Victoria Lake is reached, two or three small steamers placed on that lake would give the trader access with but small cost and labour to a vast area.

But to return to the subject of the construction of a line of railway into the interior.

One question which will very naturally be asked is, "How would you find labour to construct a line?" My answer is, "Employ Chinese," for I believe that they will be found to be best suited for the work. Negro workmen are, as a rule, very unsatisfactory, and from the account given of the Zanzibar mofundi or artisans, in the first chapter of this book, it will be seen how unreliable they are, and what constant supervision they require. While, on the other hand, the capabilities of the Chinese for work are too well known to need mention here. The question is how far they would stand the climate; but following the opinions which have been given me by men who have been both in China and on the East Coast of Africa, there is not much to be feared on this score; added to which, rice can be got cheaply and in large quantities for their food. The expense at first for getting a number of Chinese labourers to the East Coast of Africa might be considerable. I believe, nevertheless, that owing to the much greater expedition with which the work would be accomplished, and its superiority, it will be found cheaper to employ them, at least for any work requiring skilled labour, in preference to negro workmen, especially when the comparatively high rate of pay which obtains at Zanzibar is taken into account.

In the first instance, of course, only a single pair of rails would be laid, of tolerably narrow gauge, with passing places at the various depôts. The rolling stock should be small in quantity at first, so that if it should prove unsuited to the country, no great loss would be incurred by having to provide fresh waggons, etc. Negroes might be educated to act as firemen, pointsmen, etc., but the engine-drivers, as is the case on the Egyptian railways, must, for a time at least, be Europeans.

But whatever plan of railroad be adopted, it must be remembered that at the commencement all must be experimental, and that it by no means follows that systems which have succeeded in India or other tropical countries will succeed here, or *vice versâ*, that systems which have failed in those countries will fail also here. The managers of the enterprise should start prepared to abandon many of their ideas and preconceived notions, and to adapt themselves to the circumstances.

Another very important factor in the success or failure of any such enterprise, is the manner in which the natives of the various tribes on the proposed line of traffic are treated. Everything should be done to conciliate them. The passing traveller can often afford to disregard the feelings of the natives towards himself: not so the trader. His desideratum is a safe road to the coast and a ready market for his goods, and these can only be obtained by winning the goodwill of the people. The Arab traders are sure to try to arouse vigorous opposition against such an enterprise, and they will stoop to any means, however vile, of poisoning the minds of the natives against the white trader.

It must always be borne in mind that the negroes are the owners of the soil, and that therefore they should be conciliated as far as possible. As a rule it would be best to purchase, for a nominal sum, the right to make the line of rail through the territory of different chiefs, and this should be done even where no opposition may be encountered, as it gives one a right to the land which even negroes, as a rule, recognise. The friendly relations thus established with the various tribes would be of more value to the trader than any amount of land won at the muzzle of the rifle. The natives in such a case would soon learn the value of the line to themselves, and would, I believe, readily aid in protecting and maintaining it.

Some such enterprise as here indicated, with a moderate

capital, would before long be able to do a fair trade with the interior, would pave the way for a larger enterprise, and above all, would contribute much towards stopping the slave-trade.

This is a point which I specially commend to the notice of philanthropists and the Anti-Slavery Society, as one in which they might greatly further both directly and indirectly the suppression of slavery and the slave-trade. If legitimate trade were introduced, the need, so to speak, for the slave-trade would cease. As mentioned in the case of Uganda, the chiefs have often nothing else to sell in order to supply their wants, but show them that they may become rich by cultivating their land and collecting the produce of their forests, they will soon cease to sell their subjects, as it will pay them better to keep them at home to cultivate their land.

Great Britain has a special interest moreover in thus suppressing the slave-trade at its source. A handsome fortune is spent every year by our country in maintaining gunboats and their crews to put down the slave-trade on the East Coast of Africa and the Red Sea, but two years' expenditure on this armament, if employed to start a company which would open up the interior of Africa to legitimate commerce, would do more to heal "the open sore of the world," than ten times the amount spent on capturing cargoes of slaves at sea.

The promotion of trade by missionaries would be of immense assistance in improving and raising the negro races. It would provide an outlet for the natives' superabundant energies which are at present spent in wars with their neighbours; and one of the surest ways of putting a stop to these desolating wars will be to find the people plenty of lawful employment at home. Some will think, no doubt, that this is secularising the missionary's work too much; but if he is to gather villages or communities of converts round him, he must find them plenty to do, or they will be sure to get into mischief; and one of the surest ways to do this, and one which would add greatly to their material comfort, is to encourage and foster legitimate trade among them.

All who have read Dr. Livingstone's life and works will see what importance he, who was *facile princeps* among African missionaries and explorers, attached to this matter, and one may be well content to follow such a leader on a question of this kind.

In any enterprise to such a *terra incognita* as Africa still is, as far as trade is concerned, some reverses must be expected, and a large return of profit must not be looked for at first; but a properly organised enterprise, where too much would not be attempted at first, might look in a few years to the payment of very respectable dividends, and to an unlimited field for future operations.

APPENDIX II.

LIST OF PLANTS COLLECTED BY REV. C. T. WILSON.

THE plants enumerated in the following list were collected by the Rev. C. T. Wilson in Uganda and Uzongora, and the islands off their coasts; they were brought to England and deposited in the Herbarium at Kew, where they were examined by Professor Oliver and other botanists, who have furnished the accompanying catalogue. It will be seen that though only nineteen species of ferns are given below, that fifty species or varieties are mentioned in the former part of this book as occurring in this region. The collection of these specimens were all destroyed in the wreck of the *Daisy* at Makongo, in September, 1878, together with many other specimens of flowering plants, so that nearly all the plants enumerated in this list were collected subsequent to that date.

Nymphæa Lotus.
Nymphæa stellata.
Cleome monophylla.
Gynandropsis pentaphylla.
Wissadula rostrata.
Abutilon indicum? (imperfect).
Sida Schimperiana.
Sida cordifolia.
Triumfetta.
Chonchorus olitorius.
Oxalis corniculata.
Psorospermum febrifugum.
Celastrus senegalensis.
Cardiospermum Halicacabum.
Combretum; sp. ?
Osbeckia.
Dissotis; sp. nov. ?
Tassiæa diffusa.
Ludwigia prostrata.
Mukia scabrella.
Diplolophium abyssinicum.
Crotolaria recta.
Crotolaria incana.
Crotolaria var. laburnifolia and capensis.
Crotolaria striata.
Crotolaria; sp. ?
Indigofera; sp. ?
Tephrosia (Reineria); new species.
Tephrosia var. T. Anselii.

Tephrosia longipes.
Vigna; sp.?
Rhynchosia viscosa.
Glycine javanica.
Desmodium; sp.?
Desmodium; sp.?
Pseudarthria; sp.?
Pseudarthria Hookeri.
Zornia diphylla.
Acacia, n. v. Acacia Seyal.
Bauhinia reticulata.
Cassia Kirkii.
Cassia didymobotrya.
Cassia Tora.
Rutidea; sp.?
Rubia cordifolia.
Gardenia Thunbergia.
Spermacoce (Hypodematium) sphærostigma?
Hedyotis; sp.?
Pentas, v. P. carneæ?
Vernonia; sp. nov.?
Vernonia; sp.?
Vernonia; new species? var. V. Unonis.
Vernonia pumila.
Vernonia cinerea.
Vernonia violacea.
Bothriocline Schimperi.
Adenostemma viscosum.
Ageratum conyzoides.
Blumea lacera.
Conyza, conf. C. Hochstetteri.
Aspilia, conf. A. linearifolium.
Aspilia Kotschyi.
Helichrysum undatum.
Helichrysum bidens? (too young).
Chrysanthellum procumbens.

Siegesbeckia orientalis.
Senecio discifolius.
Notonia abyssinica.
Gynura vitellina.
Berkheya Spekeana.
Echinops amplexicaulis.
Faroa, new species? near F. salutaris.
Gomphocarpus; sp.?
Gomphocarpus physocarpus.
Asclepias, near A. macrantha.
Margaretta rosea.
Landolphia florida.
Carissa, near C. edulis.
Euclea divinorum.
Striga Fombesii.
Rhamphicarpa, near R. tubulosa.
Cycnium adonense.
Sopubia ramosa.
Physalis, var. P. angulata?
Withania somnifera.
Solanum giganteum.
Solanum melongena, var.?
Solanum (imperfect).
Solanum nigrum.
Evolvulus alsinoides, var.
Ipomœa sessiliflora.
Acanthus arboreus.
Spathodea; sp.?
Justicia; sp.?
Acanthacea (left doubtful).
Clerodendron (Cyclonema myricoides).
Lippia; sp.?
Lantana; sp.?
Coleus barbatus.
Hoslandia decumbens.
Geniosporum; sp.?

Acrocephalus lilacinus.
Leucas velutinus ?
Polygonum barbatum.
Chenopodium album.
Ackyranthes argentea.
Celosia trigyna.
Celosia argentea.
Phytolacca abyssinica.
Arthrosolen ; sp. ?
Acalypha villicaulis.
Phyllanthus ; Pseudo-Nirani ?

Phyllanthus ; sp. ?
Eriocaulon ; sp. ?
Canna indica.
Gloriosa virescens.
Gladiolus Quartinianus.
Scilla (Ledebouria) minima.
Eulopia ; sp. ?
Lissochilus ; sp. ?
Lissochilus off. L. Oliverianæ.
Lissochilus, near L. arenarius.

FERNS.

Gleichenia dichotoma.
Cyathea Dregei.
Davallia elegans.
Lonchitis pubescens.
Pellæa geraniæfolia.
Pellæa hastata.
Pteris incisa.
Pteris quadriaurita.
Asplenium longicauda.
Asplenium furcatum. Two varieties.

Asplenium (Athyrium) nigripes.
Oleandra articulata.
Nephrodium Wilsoni ; new species.
Nephrodium Filix-mas, var.
Polypodium Phymatodes.
Polypodium lycopodioides.
Acrostichum punctulatum.
Lygodium scandens.

APPENDIX III.

Itinerary of a Journey from Bagamoyo to Kagei, by Rev. C. T. Wilson, July 1876 to January 1877.

Date.	Place.	Days.	Hours.	Miles.	Remarks.
1876					
July 28	Shamba Gonera	1	$1\frac{1}{2}$	$2\frac{3}{4}$	
Aug. 1	Kingani River	1	6	$6\frac{3}{4}$	We crossed the K— in dug-outs.
,, 2	Kekoku	1	$2\frac{1}{2}$	$5\frac{3}{4}$	
,, 4	Camp	1	3	7	
,, 5	Rosako	1	$2\frac{1}{2}$	8	
,, 7	Paskweni	1	4	10	
,, 8	Ibrahim's Vill.	1	2	6	
,, 10	Mezizi	1	5	$9\frac{1}{2}$	
,, 12	Pongwe	1	$4\frac{3}{4}$	$10\frac{1}{4}$	
,, 14	Funi	1	$4\frac{1}{4}$	10	
,, 17	Hidalima	1	2	4	
,, 18	Mba	1	4	10	
,, 21	Wedigumba	1	$4\frac{1}{2}$	10	We struck the W— this point.
,, 22	Mbuumi	1	$3\frac{1}{2}$	8	
,, 24	Camp	1	5	$11\frac{1}{2}$	
,, 25	Kwedibago	1	3	8	
,, 26	Camp	1	4	3	Crossed the Wan— bridge.
,, 28	Camp	1	4	$9\frac{1}{2}$	
,, 29	Camp	1	3	$7\frac{1}{2}$	
Sept. 1	Camp	1	$4\frac{1}{2}$	$9\frac{1}{2}$	Crossed the M— River and enc— on its banks the Usagara H—
,, 2	Camp	1	5	$10\frac{1}{2}$	
,, 4	Magubika	1	$4\frac{1}{2}$	11	
,, 6	Camp	1	$2\frac{1}{2}$	6	
,, 7	Camp	1	3	6	
,, 8	Kitango	1	3	$7\frac{1}{4}$	
,, 13	Camp	1	3	7	
,, 14	Camp	1	8	20	
,, 15	Tubugwe	1	$2\frac{1}{2}$	7	
,, 17	Mpwapwa	1	8	19	
Oct. 8	Chunyo	1	3	8	
,, 9, 10	Debwe	2	20	42	We crossed the M— Mkali durin— march.

APPENDIX III.

ITINERARY of a JOURNEY from BAGAMOYO to KAGEI—*continued.*

Date.	Place.	Days.	Hours.	Miles.	Remarks.
1876					
Oct. 12	Mvumi	1	4	10½	
,, 14	Matamburu	1	4	9½	Ugogo.
,, 17	Bihawana	1	5	12	
,, 18	Kididimo	1	1½	4¼	
,, 20	Camp	1	8½	22	
,, 21	Kitararu	1	4½	11	
,, 23	Mbahi	1	2¼	6½	
,, 26	Puna	1	3¾	11	
,, 28	Unyanguira	1	2¼	6½	Left Ugogo.
Nov. 1	Mtine	1	3¾	10¼	
,, 3	Camp	1	6	14½	
,, 4	Gange	1	2	5	⎫
,, 6	Camp	1	8	19	⎪
,, 7	Camp	1	6½	16	⎬ Forest Region.
,, 8, 9	Camp	1	23¾	35	⎪
,, 10	Camp	1	8	20	⎪
,, 11	Camp	1	4½	13	⎪
,, 12	Camp	1	4½	13	⎭
,, 13	Usuri	1	3	8	Iramba.
,, 15	Ushuri	1	4	9	
Dec. 6	Camp	1	5	13	⎫
,, 7	Camp	1	5	13	⎬ Forest Region.
,, 8	Camp	1	8	21	⎪
,, 9	Camp	1	8½	25	⎭
,, 10	Hambu	1	9½	20	Unyamwezi.
,, 11	Ng'uru	1	1	3	
,, 30	Masimbo	1	2½	6	
1877					
Jan. 2	Camp	1	6	18	
,, 3	Semwi	1	3½	8	
,, 5	Senanga	1	3½	9	
,, 6	Wandu	1	1½	4½	
,, 8	Amagunguri	1	2¼	7	
,, 10	Mondui	1	3	7½	
,, 11	Balaku	1	3	8	
,, 13	Uvika	1	4	10	
,, 15	Mamaro	1	4	10	
,, 17	Asonge	1	4½	10	
,, 19	Wama	1	5	11½	
,, 22	Mamwamba	1	2	5	
,, 23	Ungwe	1	3½	9	
,, 24	Wara	1	3½	9	
,, 26	Wambwa	1	2¼	7	⎫
,, 27	Village	1	3	8	⎬ Ueukuma.
,, 28	Gungwa	1	3	9	⎪
,, 29	Kagei	1	3	9	⎭

(351)

APPENDIX IV.

Vocabularies of Native Languages.

	Luganda.	Fur.	Madi.	Kederu.
Antelope			Kulă	
Arm	Mkono	Donah	Kallah	Dri.
Arrow	Kasali; mwambi		Etu	Atu.
Axe	Mbadzi; kabadzi	Bo	Loggo	Kolongo.
Banana	Toki			
Bedstead	Kitanda	Pidi	Surah	Surah.
Beer	Mlamba; marwa			
Beads	Nkwanzi	Badiana	Biallah	Biallah.
Beard	Kilevu; busoga	Dulan		
Bow	Mtegu		Keiuyah	Korsu.
Boy	Mlenzi	Kwatin	Uiskorah	Manungwa
Brother	Mganda	Bein	Undŭ	Odrupi.
Brook	Kaga	Kura soruba	Ranga	
Buffalo	Mbogo		Kobi	
Cat	Kapa	Bis	Yow	Guru
Canoe	Lyato			
Camel	Ngamira	Gamal (?)	Karasse	
Calf of leg	Lutumbwe	Toringdolgoin	Wistissi	
Child	Mwana	Kwatin	Sisi	Sisi.
Chin	Kilevu	Karu		
Cloth	Lugoi	Guri		
Clouds	Kili	Kuttu		
Cow	Anti nkazi	U	Isah	Isah.
Chief	Mkungu; mton-goli	Sagal	Wisyerra	Meinenga yerra.
Coffee	Mwanyi			
Copper	Chikomo			
Crocodile	Gonya		Tamorah	
Dog	Mbwa	Assă	Wihi	Kortcher.
Drum	Ng'oma	Kisŭ	Datteï (large) Kurai (small)	Datteï. Laari.
Ear	Kutu	Dilo	Mbilli	Bi.
Earth	Insi; taka	Du	Kang-u	Jini.
Elephant	Njovu	Engri	Kidi	Kidi.
Eye	Liso	Nui	Komang	Mi.
Father	Baba; kitangi	Babă	Dadă	Turpi.
Face	Maso	Kumi	Komommah	Mimaru.
Fire	Mulilo	Utŏ	Wado	Asi.
Fence	Kisakati	Giabl		
Fish	Chenyanja	Puu	Censa	Kisebi.

VOCABULARIES OF NATIVE LANGUAGES—*continued.*

	Luganda	Fur.	Madi.	Kederu.
Fish-hook	Roba	Nyamdam	Mongo	
Finger	Ngallu	Toringa	Denjerida	
„ Fore	„ ya vimumbu			
„ Middle	„ ya kati			
„ Little	„ ya nasu			
Flute	Ng'ombe		Traüli	
Foot	Kigerri	Tarintŭ	Mindima	Mipah.
Forest	Kibila	Kuruma	Wevu	Wevu.
Forehead	Chenyi; teni	Evi muji	Memi	Tau.
Fowls	Nkoko		Yaru	
Gazelle	Mpeo	Pra	Lelu	
Giraffe	Ntuga		Kerri	
Girl	Mwala	Kwanŭ	Ui-yo	Ngoiti.
Goat	Mbuzi; kabuzi	Din	Wanya	Indri.
Grass	Subi	Dei	Lomah	Keyi.
Ground-nuts	Chinwewa			
Gun	Mundu	Bundu		
Gunpowder	Buganga			
Hand	Mkono		Kalamah	
„ Palm of	Kubutu	Domandin	Mikosma	Mikala.
Head	Mtwe	Tabbu	Do	Dri.
Heaven	Gulu	Gioul	Miri	Bu.
Harp	Nanga		Taumu	
Hippopotamus	Mvubo		Wari	
Hair of head	Mvwili; vili	Tabbu nilu	Iavu	Iavu.
Horse	Mbrasi	Murta		
Hoe	Nkumbi		Chabu	
House	Nyumba	Dana	Loko	Sowa.
Iron	Chuma	Doura	Kor-hi	Loggo.
Ivory	Sanga	Engri dagi (elephant's tusk)		
King	Kabakka	Abbakuri	Yerra	Nyerra.
Knife	Nkambi	Sagin	Evu	Eŭli.
Lake	Kidiwa; nyanja	Birga	Ulu	
Leg	Mugulu	Tar	Ndi	Pa.
Leopard	Ngo	Giara	Tukiara	
Lion	Mporogoma	Muru	Ubiu	
Man	Muntu	Dua	Kurah	Agwa.
Millet	Mwembe	Kam	Nyenyo	Inya.
Moon	Mwezi	Duāl	Niahoa	Imbah.
Mother	Mawe; nyabu	Mina	Ma	Eudra.
Mouth	Mumwa	Udŏ	Haw	Si.
Monkey	Nkima	Karou		
Mouse	Messe	Moni	Lusiĕ	
Moustache		Purru		

APPENDIX IV.

VOCABULARIES OF NATIVE LANGUAGES—continued.

	Luganda.	Fur.	Madi.	Kederu.
Mountain	Lusozi	Puga	Doku	Berengo.
Morning	Incha	Losari	Demindo	Ondo.
Night	Chiro	Lodikoin	Endo	Ngetchi.
Nail, finger	Dwala	Karu	Koïnyi	Koïnyi.
Nose	Nyindo	Dormi	Kano	Kornvo.
Neck	Nsingo	Ku-i	Gu	Teemba.
Ox	Nti	Nu	Dangmo	Dangmo.
Paddle	Nkasi			
Pipe	Mindi		Tuku-taba	
Rat	Messe	Gummul	Warku	
Rain	Nkuba	Kwi	Mirē	Ei.
Rice	Mpunga	Rus (?)		
River	Mugga	Bow	Rodi	
Rope	Mugwa; lugoi		Kordi	Kabi; lorli.
Sandal	Ngato	Dowla	Kamuka	Kamuka.
Serpent	Njoka	Num	Wiri	Eni.
Sister	Mwanyanya	Dadā	Emi	Omwopi.
Shield	Ngubbi	Kerbi		
Sun	Njuba	Dule	Kadroa	Kitu.
Star	Munyenye	Uri	Calu	Kedu.
Sheep	Ndiga	Urī	Kemelli	Temelli.
Slave (M.)	Muddu			
Spear	Fumo	Kori	Waha	Azu.
Sword	Upanga: kitalu	Sarr		
Tobacco	Taba	Tabā	Taba	Taba.
Tooth	Linyo	Dagi	Tisi	Tisi.
Tent	Gulu	Tong		
Thigh	Chiinja	Diuil	Lusi	
Tongue	Ndimi; lulimi	Dali	Ndeuda	Ladra.
Tree	Mti	Kurum	Kaga	Ishe.
Wood (timber)	Lubau	Kir		
„ (fire)	Luku	Eira	Yerri	Tisa.
Water	Madzi	Korŏ	Weni	Ji.
Well	Ludzi	Irohr		
Wheat	Ng'ano	Karu	Nyeniu	Enya.
Woman	Mkazi	Dunyan	Mbara	Toko.
Zebra	Ntrege			
Bad	—bi	Tulabā	Emeddi	Lenjiko.
Big	—anvu	Apah	Kiedra	Ambah.
Black	Dagavu	Diko	Korndu	Oui.
Blue	Sama		Muri	
Clean	—ungi	Tay		
Dear	—kalubo			
Dirty		Kusay		
Fat	—ene			

VOL. I.   2 A

APPENDIX IV.

Vocabularies of Native Languages—*continued*.

	Luganda.	Fur.	Madi.	Kederu.
Good	—ungi		Emettukin	Lenji.
Green	—a noandagala	Kiro	Yowi	
Heavy	Zitoa		E-ettu	Elenji.
Little	—tono; —ana	Iting	Tissi	Pare.
No	Nedda	Kei-elba	Lah	Maleku.
Red	Myufu	Puka	Ei-hi	Akā.
Short	—impi			
Shallow	Madzi matono			
White	—eru	Puta	Einyi	Oenre.
Yellow	Chenvu			
Yes	Wampa		Wah	Wah.
1	Mo	Dik	Korlo	Orlo.
2	Bili	Go	Irio	Rri.
3	Satu	Is	Utah	Na.
4	Nya	Ungal	Suwor	Su.
5	Tano	Ors	Mwi	Nzi.
6	Mkaga	Sundi	Dakka	Driolah.
7	Msamvu	Servi	Demrio	Driari.
8	Mnana	Tuman	Dumta	Driana.
9	Mwenda	Tisi	Dumsor	Driasu.
10	Kumi	Wei	Bu-te	Bute.
11	Kuminemu	Weni dik	Dumte	Bute Orlo.
12	Kumi nabili		Dumte Irio	,, Rri.
13	,, satu		Dumte Utah	,, Na.
14	,, nya		,, Suwor	,, Su.
15	,, tuno		,, Mwi	,, Nzi.
16	,, nkaya		,, Dakka	,, Driolah.
17	,, msunvu		,, Demrio	,, Drian.
18	,, mnane		,, Dumta	,, Driana.
19	,, mwenda		,, Dumsor	,, Driasu.
20	Abili		Bute Irio	,, Rri.
30	Asatu		,, Otah	,, Na.
40	Anya			
50	Atano			
60	Nkaga			
70	Nsamvu			
80	Chinane			
90	Chenda			
100	Chikumi			
200	Bikumibibili			
1000	Lukumi			

Note.—The Luganda vocabulary was collected by Rev. C. T. Wilson, and the Fur, Madi, and Kederu vocabularies by R. W. Felkin.

APPENDIX V.

MR. WILSON'S AND MR. FELKIN'S METEOROLOGICAL AND HYPSOMETRICAL OBSERVATIONS.

By E. G. Ravenstein, F.R.G.S.

SUMMARIES of the greater part of the following observations have already been published by Dr. Hann, in Petermann's 'Mittheilungen' (1879, p. 64, 1880, p. 143), and most of the altitudes have been computed by the gentlemen named, or by Dr. Zöppritz. It appeared to me, however, that a summary of these most valuable observations would form an appropriate appendix to a work in which an account is given of Mr. Wilson's and Mr. Felkin's journeys in Africa. In the course of my search for materials to aid me in the compilation of the large Map of Equatorial Africa, upon which I am now engaged, the authors kindly placed at my service their journals and diaries. I then found that these contained a mass of information which had not been utilised by Dr. Hann. This determined me to sift the whole of the facts collected, and to embody the results in a series of tables, accompanied by such notes as are required for their elucidation.

Mr. Mackay's observations at Rubaga have not been embodied in this memoir. That gentleman, however, continues to record the various atmospheric phenomena, and his results will contribute in still further enlarging our meteorological knowledge of the Victorian Lake region.

In Tables I. and II. the observations are given as recorded. When beyond Keroto Mr. Felkin put back the hand of his aneroid 1·07 in. This has been allowed for, and the record appears as if the instrument had not been interfered with.

The temperatures are given in all cases as recorded. Dr. Emin's means of max. and min. temperatures are deduced from observations made at 7 A.M. and 2 P.M.

The aneroid observations by Mr. Wilson and Mr. Felkin, for March, April, and May, 1879, have been reduced to the aneroid "J. Browning, No. 952." This instrument was verified at Kew in June 1880, and the error then determined (-0.28 in. for the average pressure at Rubaga) has been applied to all the readings recorded.

Dr. Emin Bey's results, however, are given in their original shape, as there are no synchronous observations on record, to enable us to reduce his "Naudet, No. 1339," to the "Browning," as a standard. From observations made during four corresponding months, but not in the same years, Dr. Emin's "Naudet" appears to give readings 0·10 in. higher than Mr. Wilson's "Browning." This, of course, applies only to Rubaga, for at Lado, which lies about 3000 feet lower, the relative readings of the two instruments may be very different.

The rain was measured by Mr. Wilson in a circular gauge having a diameter of 3·5 inches. Our means have been computed for whole days of 24 hours.

I. Mr. Felkin's Observations between Khartoum and the Albert Nyanza, 1877.

Locality.	Period.	Temperature (F.)					Pressure of Atmosphere.				
		8 A.M.	Noon.	4 P.M.	8 P.M.	Daily Mean.	8 A.M.	Noon.	4 P.M.	8 P.M.	Daily Mean.
Khartoum	8–12 Aug.	79	95	96	89	88	Inches. 28·50	Inches. 28·44	Inches. 28·40	Inches. 28·46	Inches. 28·45
Shambil	5–7 Oct.	83	89	92	85	84	·50	·48	·39	·48	·46
Bohr	9–11 ,,	85	89	89	83	86	·48	·48	·38	·40	·43
Laldo	20–23 ,,	80	88	85	79	81	·48	·41	·40	·47	·44
Gondokoro	2 Nov.	78	83	82	78	80	·52	·45	·30	·35	·41
Regiaf	3–17 Nov.	77	85	85	78	80	·52	·44	·41	·45	·45
Kerrie	20–26 ,,	78	91	90	81	82	·39	·32	·28	·31	·325
Labore	29 Nov.–1 Dec.	77	88	86	80	81	·30	·19	·13	·20	·21
Duffi	3–20 Dec.	75	89	90	80	81	27·98	27·86	27·80	27·86	27·85
Magungo	25–27 ,,	73	80	80	70	77	·97	·88	·83	·89	·89

II. Mr. Felkin's Observations on the Road to Rubaga, 1878.

Locality.	Period.	Temperature (F.)					Pressure of Atmosphere.				
		9 A.M.	Noon.	4 P.M.	9 P.M.	Daily Mean.	9 A.M.	Noon.	4 P.M.	9 P.M.	Daily Mean.
Keroto	30 Dec.–3 Jan.	69	82	84	72	71	Inches. 26·34	Inches. 26·62	Inches. 26·57	Inches. 26·51	Inches. 26·52
Foweira	7–20 Jan.	74	84	84	71	73	·41	·35	·29	·34	·34
Mruli	27 Jan.–2 Feb.	79	86	87	76	78	·46	·37	·33	·39	·38
Rubaga	14–24 Feb.	72	81	87	78	75	·87	·82	·76	·80	·80

APPENDIX V.

III. Mr. WILSON'S, Mr. FELKIN'S, and Dr. EMIN BEY'S OBSERVATIONS at RUBAGA, in UGANDA, 1876-79.

Month.		Observer.	Days.	Temperature (F.)							Rain.			Cloud (1-10).
				Extremes.			Means.							
				Max.	Min.	Range.	Max.	Min.	Range.	Computed Mean.	Amount.	Probability.		
Jan.	1878	Emin	..	94·8	60·8	34·0	83·3*	65·8*	17·5*	71·2	Inches.	·51		4·9
,,	1879	Wilson	31	86·0	53·8	32·2	81·9	56·8	25·1	69·3	5·6	·36		3·0
Feb.	1878	Emin	..	94·8	61·8	33·0	85·3*	65·3*	20·0*	71·2	..	·43		..
,,	1879	Wilson	28	86·4	53·8	32·6	80·4	58·6	21·8	69·5	3·6	·40		..
March,	1878	Emin	31	91·8	62·6	32·2	85·5*	67·3*	18·2*	72·8	..	·42		5·5
,,	1879	Wilson and Felkin	31	88·0	54·8	33·2	78·4	58·9	19·5	69·9	4·9	·87		..
April,	1878	Wilson	24	88·0	61·5	25·5	84·0	64·4	20·6	72·0	5·4	·57		..
,,	1879	Wilson and Felkin	30	88·0	54·8	33·8	81·8	58·0	23·8	70·2	5·7	·45		6·0
May,	1878	Wilson	31	88·6	60·0	28·6	84·0	62·5	21·5	71·0	1·5	·53		..
,,	1879	Wilson and Felkin	15	81·5	46·0	35·5	77·6	56·8	20·8	70·2	3·4	·75		7·7
June,	1878	Wilson	12	85·5	60·0	25·5	82·0	62·0	20·0	70·0	1·5	·51		..
Aug.	1876	Emin	25	86·0	51·4	34·6	78·5*	61·7*	16·8*	66·6	..	·42		4·8
Sept.	1877	Wilson	31	81·0	60·1	20·9	75·4	63·9	11·5	69·6	Some	·66		..
Oct.	1877	,,	30	81·0	57·9	23·1	76·8	62·2	14·6	68·5	Much	·74		..
Nov.	1877	,,	31	82·0	63·0	19·0	76·3	64·9	11·4	70·5	Much	·80		..
,,	1878	,,	30	82·9	63·0	19·9	76·5	64·9	11·6	70·8	Much	·53		2·1
Dec.	1878	,,	15	86·0	57·0	29·0	82·8	59·4	23·4	71·1	Less	·68		..
,,	1878	,,	31	85·8	61·0	24·8	78·8	64·6	14·2	71·6	..	·26		3·4
,,	1878	,,	27	85·6	53·4	32·2	81·0	57·9	23·1	69·4				

* See remarks above.

APPENDIX V.

TABLE III —continued.

Period.		Aneroid.			Tension of Vapour. Mean.	Moisture. Noon.
		Max.	Min.	Computed Mean.		
					Inches.	
Jan.	1878	25·70	25·55	25·63	..	..
,,	1879	..	..	·57	..	..
Feb.	1878	·73	·57	·65	..	..
,,	1879	..	..	·50	..	..
March,	1878	·73	·59	·65	..	..
,,	1879	·67	·46	·55	·700	76
April,	1878	·64	·46	·55	·744	77
,,	1879	·67	·42	·55	·712	79
May,	1878	·68	·48	·59	·709	74
,,	1879	·67	·47	·55	·677	83
June	1878	·70	·55	·51	·704	79
Aug.	1876	·77	·59	·70	..	..
,,	1877	·64 ?	·54	·60	·628	80
Sept.	1877	·62	·47	·53	·560	67
Oct.	,,	·60	·42	·52	·600	68
Nov.	,,	·57	·42	·50	·615	72
,,	1878	..	..	·67	..	..
Dec.	1877	·55	·42	·48 ?	605	65
,,	1878	..	..	·58	..	..

Relative Moisture (Additional Observations).

8 A.M. in 1878: March , April 90, May 91, June 93.
9 P.M. in 1879: ,, 87, ,, 90, ,, 84, ,, .
4 P.M. in 1879: ,, 77, ,, 82, ,, 84, ,, .
6 P.M, in 1878: ,,   , ,, 92, ,, 84, ,, 88.
9 P.M. in 1879: ,, 93, ,, 91, ,, 83, ,, .
Lowest in 1877: Aug. 49, Sept. 53, Oct. 56, Nov. 59, Dec. 49.

TABLE III.—concluded.

Period.		Winds (in Per Cent. of Total Observed).							
		N.	N.E.	E.	S.E.	S.	S.W.	W.	N.W.
Jan.	1878	4·5	19·8	25·7	13·6	..	9·1	9·1	18·2
"	1879	35·7	2·5	2·5	14·7	34·6	5·0	2·5	2·5
Feb.	1878	..	..	..	..	..	..	...	..
"	1879	7·0	5·8	..	..	74·4	9·3	3·5	..
March,	1878	..	..	..	..	..	..	..	..
"	1879	7·6	3·3	..	50·0	31·5	5·4	2·2	..
April,	1878	..	..	1·5	27·2	58·1	11·7	..	1·5
"	1879	1·8	3·5	4·4	24·6	50·8	9·6	3·5	1·8
May,	1878	1·8	12·4	2·6	21·3	43·4	13·2	1·8	3·5
"	1879	..	4·4	..	3·3	54·4	8·8	..	..
June,	1878	..	15·0	..	20·0	52·5	12·5	..	..
Aug.	1876	..	12	20	52	4	12	..	..
"	1877	{Southerly breezes during day. Thunderstorms from N. and N.W.							
Sept.	1877	Southerly.							
Oct.	1877	Southerly; thunderstorms from N.E., N., or N.W.							
Nov.	1877	Southerly.							
"	1878	16·7	5·5	..	11·1	22·2	11·1	16·7	16·7
Dec.	1877	Southerly up to 21st; then northerly.							
"	1878	..	20·0	6·7	..	13·3	33·3	13·3	13·3

SUMMARY.

Month.	Pressure of Atmosphere.	Temperature (F.)		Rain. Probability Per Cent.
		Mean.	Range.	
January	Inches. 25·57	70·2	25·1	43
February	·50	70·3	21·8	41
March	·55	71·2	19·5	42
April	·55	71·1	22·2	62
May	·57	70·6	21·1	49
June	·61	70·0	20·0	75
July	(·61)	(9·0)	..	?
August	·60	68·0	11·5	46
September	·53	68·5	14·5	66
October	·52	70·5	11·4	74
November	·58	70·9	17·0	66
December	·53?	70·5	18·5	47
Year	25·56	70·1	..	56?

APPENDIX V.

TABLE IV. VARIATIONS from the DAILY MEAN PRESSURE.

The following table is deduced from the observations made by Mr. Wilson and Mr. Felkin at Rubaga, and by the former at Makongo, 10 feet above the level of the Victoria Nyanza. For the sake of comparison we have added the results obtained by Dr. Emin at Ládo, on the Upper Nile, and by Dr. Robb at Zanzibar.

On examining this table it will be found that if the barometer be read at 6 A.M., or about 9 o'clock in the evening, a very fair approach to the daily mean will be obtained. At 10 A.M., and again late in the night, the barometer stands highest, whilst at 4 or 5 in the afternoon it reaches its extreme minimum. The range on the shores of the lake is more considerable than either at Ládo or Zanzibar, being almost identical with that observed at Calcutta, viz., 0·116 in.

Time.	Rubaga. (March–May, 1879.)		Makongo. (Oct. and Sept., 1878.)		Ládo. (4 days.)	Zanzibar. (Year.)
	No. of Obser.	In.	No. of Obser.	In.	In.	In.
Mean Press.	—	25·560	—	25·746	27·906	29·954
6 am.	—	—	1	0·000	—	+ 0·004
7 ,,	12	+ 0·017	17	+ ·022	+ 0·016	·021
8 ,,	10	·034	19	·039	·035	·038
9 ,,	107	·059	12	·074	·055	·041
10 ,,	17	·064	11	·075	·067	·045
11 ,,	—	—	11	·056	·047	·033
noon	110	+ ·011	17	+ ·033	·035	·021
1 p.m.	27	·000	15	·000	+ ·016	+ ·002
2 ,,	7	− ·047	11	− ·017	− ·012	− ·017
3 ,,	—	—	13	− ·037	·031	·027
4 ,,	142	− ·052	14	− ·041	·043	·037
5 ,,	6	+ ·006	19	− ·044	·039	·033
6 ,,	—	—	16	− ·035	·035	·028
7 ,,	—	—	3	− ·031	·027	·017
8 ,,	5	− ·016	6	+ ·009	− ·012	− ·007
9 ,,	119	+ ·018	2	·009	0·000	0·000
10 ,,	5	+ ·001	2	·009	+ ·008	+ ·007
11 ,,	2	− ·025?	—	—	—	·005
midnt.	2	+ ·040	—	—	—	·003
Range	—	·116	—	·119	·110	·094

ALTITUDES.

The number of trustworthy altitudes resulting from these observations is not large, but amongst the localities determined in a satisfactory manner are Rubaga, the capital of Uganda, and the level of the Victoria Nyanza. For Rubaga Mr. Wilson and Mr. Felkin have supplied satisfactory sets of observations for thirteen months, whilst at Makongo, on the shore of the lake, Mr. Wilson observed during nearly two months. Two instruments were used at Rubaga, viz., Mr. Wilson's "J. Browning, No. 952," and Mr. Felkin's "Newton, No. 1137." They both kept pace well together, the "Newton" keeping uniformly 1·05 (with correction, 1·34) in. ahead of the "Browning." The latter, on its return to England in June 1880, was tested at Kew, when it was found to need a correction of − 0·28 in. under a pressure corresponding to that prevailing at Rubaga. This quantity we have deducted throughout Table III.

The resultant altitudes (computed from Guyot's and Radau's tables), under the assumption of a mean pressure of 29·9 in. at the sea-level, are as follows:—

	Feet above sea-level.
Rubaga (Mission House, 1 mile to the S.W. of the King's Residence)	4510
Makongo (260 feet below Rubaga)	4250
Victoria Nyanza	4244

This result agrees in a remarkable manner with that obtained by Mr. Stanley, according to whose

APPENDIX V. 363

9 boiling-point observations, computed by Lieut. Sugden, R.N., the lake-level lies at an elevation of 4366 feet. Speke, on the other hand, gives the lake an altitude of only 3400 feet.

The computation of altitudes from Mr. Felkin's observations while journeying out to Uganda presents great difficulties. The aneroid used ("Newton, No. 8137") has not been verified at Kew. The comparisons with one of Dr. Emin's aneroids ("Naudet") at Ládo, and with Mr. Wilson's "Browning" at Rubaga, though both undoubtedly trustworthy for the locality, and under the pressure at which they were made, furnish conflicting results which we are quite unable to reconcile or to reduce to a common standard.

At Rubaga Mr. Felkin's "Newton" uniformly ranged 1·34 in. higher than the corrected "Browning." If we were to deduct this quantity from Mr. Felkin's previous readings they would place Magungo (on the Albert Nyanza) about 1100 feet lower than Rubaga, or at an elevation of at least a thousand feet in excess of the truth.

Mr. Felkin's observations at Ládo, on the outward journey, exhibit an error of + ·03 in., as compared with the mean pressure during the corresponding month, as determined by Mr. Dovyak.* On his

---

* But at Gondokoro, where Mr. Felkin, however, observed only for one day, his aneroid exhibits no error at all! This shows the

return journey, in August 1878, Dr. Emin carefully compared Mr. Felkin's "Newton" with his own "Naudet," and it was then found that the correction which had to be applied to the former, in order to reduce it to the "Naudet" as a standard, amounted to -0.32 in. Dr. Emin's aneroid is no doubt an excellent instrument, but no opportunity has occurred hitherto for trustworthily determining its index error. At Rubaga, where Dr. Emin observed during four months, as shown in Table III., his recorded readings are 0.101 in. higher than those of Mr. Wilson's "Browning"; whilst, as compared with Dovyak's mercurial barometer readings at Gondokoro, they are 0.11 in. too low for the whole year, and 0.07 too low for the month of August. It results from this that if we would reduce Mr. Felkin's readings to Dovyak's barometer, 0.25 in. ($0.32 - .07$) must be deducted from them. The altitudes then found by reference to Dovyak's observations at Gondokoro, are shown in the columns marked a in the following table. Altitudes computed on the assumption that a correction of only $-.02$ in. should be applied fall about 250 feet short of the figures given.

We have, in addition to this, corrected Mr. Felkin's readings on the assumption that the error,

---

futility of deducing trustworthy corrections from observations limited to a few days, and made with instruments the errors of which, under variable conditions, are not thoroughly well known.

which on starting from Lado amounted to +·25 in., gradually increased until it attained its maximum at Rubaga, with 1·34 in. The resultant altitudes are given in the columns marked *b*. It will be seen, however, that this assumption is altogether inadmissible. That the aneroid underwent a change is undeniable, but this change clearly did not occur whilst Mr. Felkin travelled up the Nile to the Albert Nyanza. It took place undoubtedly after he had scaled the plateau, and probably not until after he had left Mruli behind him, and moved the hand of his aneroid!

The results are as follows:—

	Height above Gondokoro.		Height above the Sea.	
	a.	b.	a.	b.
Gondokoro (assumed)	—	—	1526	1526
Magungo (Albert Nyanza)	767	1276	2293	2802
Kiroto	2233	3684	3759	5210
Foweira	2413	4036	3939	5562
Mruli	2367	2960	3893	4486
Rubaga	1840	2984	3366	4510

The altitudes of most of these places have been determined by Dr. Emin, at Buchta, with the following results:—

      Magungo, 2330 ft. (Emin), 2384 ft. (Buchta).
      Kiroto,   4213 ft. (Buchta).
      Foweira, 3763 ft. (Buchta).
      Mruli,   3946 ft. (Emin, a single observation referred to Rubaga).

Hypsometrical observations considerably reduce these altitudes.

>Foweira, 3432 ft. (Emin), 3542 ft. (Lt. Baker).
>Mruli, 3513 ft. (Emin).

We are inclined to accept 3950 ft. as the altitude of Mruli, and 3760 ft. as that of Foweira.

As respects Gondokoro we have thought it best to retain the altitude assigned to it by Dr. Hann, viz. 1526 feet or 465 metres, as numerous published altitudes are dependent upon it. Our own computations have yielded the following results:—

>Gondokoro (Dovyak) .. .. 1507 feet.
>„ (Capt. Watson) .. .. 1443 „
>Ládo (Dr. Emin Bey) .. .. .. 1618 „

In conclusion, we give a list of altitudes calculated by Dr. Zöppritz from aneroid observations made daily at 6 A.M., and published in Petermann's 'Mittheilungen.' As far as the "village on the Tonj," the altitudes are referred to Ládo, where corresponding observations were taken by Dr. Emin. The heights beyond that place were referred by Dr. Zöppritz to the average of the mean monthly pressures at Ládo and Khartoum, but we have amended his results so as to give Dara a height of 495 m. (as determined by Colonel Mason), instead of the 565 m. resulting from the method of computation referred to.

APPENDIX V. 367

	Feet.		Feet.
Ládo (assumed)	1525	Kerimu	1893
Khurji	1595	Camp, 2-3 Oct. ..	1801
Waniyetti	1585	Lake	1676
Camp, 19-20 Sept. ..	1949	Agar	1637
Khor Koda	1844	Kok	1696
Niambara	2014	Rumbehk, or Rohl ..	1585
Camp, 21-22 Sept. ..	2201	Jau (Jur)	1578
Zanga	2185	Mukhta	1545
Kederu, No. 1	2096	Gohk or Abreal	1539
„ No. 2	2228	Boit	1558
Madi	1788	Tonj (military post) ..	1558
Bakina	1778	Village on Tonj, 14-15	
Takka	1903	Oct.	1486
Kudukeri, swamp ..	1830	(Djour Ghattas	*1650)

	Feet.		Feet.
Abugurun	1520	Gondu	1680
Kutchuk Ali's	1570	Mt. Saffa, Camp near	1710
Zeriba Waou	1540	Foroga	1680
„ Pizelia	1560	Rahad ez Zurzur ..	1600
Camp, 19 Nov.	1560	El Brak	1570
„ 20 „	1600	Atraha (Pond)	1570
Dem Idris	1740	Alugur	1530
Camp, 22 Nov.	1680	Kalaka	1510
Dem Suleiman	1690	Agarab	1580
Sabu river	1690	Sigela	1590
Ngaru's village	1760	Fasko	1600
Liffi	1640	Ilummi	1590
		Dara (assumed)	1624

* Computed from 3 days' observation by Mr. Wilson, referred to sea-level.

INDEX.

REV. C. T. WILSON'S NARRATIVE.

Albinos, 149
Alice Island, 119, 242
Arab merchants, 13
Arab physicians, 7
Arab slave-dealers, 21

Bagamoyo, 29
Baobab tree, 80
Beads, 47
Bukindo, 88, 122
Bumbire, Island of, 237
Busu, Islands of, 228

Castor-oil tree, 33
Christmas Day, 265
Cloth as money, 46

Daisy, The, 92, 94, 98, 103, 117, 122, 140, 241, 243, 248

Emin Effendi (Dr.), 113, 116, 141, 271, 281
Envoys from Uganda, 274

Fatiko, 278
Felkin, R. W., 257, 266, 269, 275, 281
Foweira, 264, 267
French Romanists, 272

Gange, 64

Gordon, Colonel, 113
Guides, 43

Hassáni, 114, 123
Highland Lassie, 3
Holmwood, Vice-consul, 23
Hongo, 58, 63

Iramba, 69
Ivory, 9

Jordan's Nullah, 81, 239

Kadúma, 81, 84
Kagei, 81, 120, 127, 139
Kagera River, 234, 241
Kekoka, 32
Kiganda language, 108
Kingani River, 23, 30
Kintu, 219
Kitánge, 40
Kodj, 264
Kome Islands, 238

Leopards, 56
Litchfield, Rev. G., 257, 266
Livingstone, Dr., 3
Livingstone's house, 6
Livúmbu River, 79
Loads, 44

370 INDEX.

London, H.M.S., 2, 3, 19, 21
Lugogo or Ergugu, 259, 268, 277
Lukonge, 86, 89, 115, 121
Lourdel, Père, 271

Mackay, A., 23, 126, 141, 240, 268
Magubíka, district of, 39
Majita Mount, 253
Makongo, 242, 247, 248
Masimbo, 129
Mirambo, 130, 135
Mkúndi River, 39
Monungu River, 129, 136
Morton, Mr., 112, 132
Mpwapwa, 53
Mruli, 262, 268, 278
Mtesa, 97, 104, 108, 141, 197
Mtinginya, 130
Mufta, 108
Murchison Bay, 103
Mvúmi, 57

Nange River, 74
Nile, 263
Ng'uru, 75, 78
Ntebbi, 117, 140

O'Neill, 25, 50, 65, 74, 77, 85, 90, 97, 114, 120, 124

Packing, 24
Pearson, C. W., 267
Pemba, Island of, 1
Pongwe Hills, 32
Porters, 29, 42

Rionga, 267
River-crossing, 35
Rubaga, 103
Rubeho Mountains, 55
Ruga Ruga, 77, 80

Said-bin-Salim, 131, 134
Semwi, 79, 127, 136
Sesse, 143, 229, 230
Seyyid Burgash, 18
Sheik bin Nasib, 133
Slave trade, 22
Smith, Dr., 26, 68, 91, 93
Smith, Lieutenant, 23, 26, 57, 68, 76, 91, 97, 100, 106, 112, 114, 120, 124
Small-pox, 33
Songoro, 85, 89, 92, 115, 121
Swahili language, 13

Tabora, 76, 133
Témbes, 54
Thunderstorms, 70
Tsetse fly, 42
Tubúgwe, 51

Uganda, 97, 102, 143.
  Climate of, 146
  Fauna of, 144
  Geology of, 147
  Population of, 150
  Roads of, 147
  Tribes of, 148
  Vegetation of, 144
Ugogo, Plateau of, 53
Ukara, 98
Ukeréwe, 83, 87, 94, 241
Umyangogo, bed of, 63
Unyanyembe, 76
Ushuri, 67
Usmao, 80
Usuri, 66
Uyui, 132, 134, 135
Uzinja, 238
Uzongora, 118, 234, 242, 246

INDEX.

Vezi, Island of, 86
Victoria Nyanza, 83, 144, 249, 256
  Coasts of, 250
  Currents of, 254
  Islands of, 253

Waganda, 148
  Their arms, 153
  Animals, 163
  Administration of Justice, 201
  Birds, 169
  Cooking, 161
  Customs, 182–189
  Classes, 193
  Chiefs, 193, 273
  Character, 225
  Dress, 151
  Diseases, 183
  Food, 158
  Government, 193
  Houses, 172
  Insects, 170
  Influence of foreigners, 209, 212
  Language, 217
  Legends, 219

Waganda.—*Continued.*
  Music, 154, 215
  Manufacturers, 176
  Morals, 223
  Navy, 203
  Occupations, 171
  Royal family, 196
  Religion, 206
  Tools, 157
  Trade, 189
  War system, 201
Wahuma, 148
Wahudimu, 18
Wami River (of Usagara), 23, 31
Wami River, 81
Wanyambo, 149
Wanguana, 14, 137
Wasoga, 149

Zanzibar, 1, 4, 11
  Coinage of, 19
  Market of, 5
  Town of, 2, 4
  Trade of, 12, 20
  Workmen of, 17

MR. FELKIN'S NARRATIVE.

Albert Lake, 302, 303, 306
Amfina, 325, 329
Arbatascha, 304

Baker, Sir S., 310, 320
Baringo Lake, 312
Bari natives, 299
Bedden Rapids, 299, 301
Berber, 286
Block in Nile, 292, 294

Camels, 286
Christmas Eve, 319
Church Missionary Society, 285, 289
Crocodiles, 315

Dufli, 299, 302, 303

Eland, 306
Emin Bey, Dr., 299, 311
Equatorial Provinces, 292

Fashoda, 289, 292
Foweira, 332

Gessi Pasha, 311
Gordon Pasha, 286, 288, 324
Grant, Col., 307, 310

Hall, J. W., 286
Hippopotamus, 300, 315

K. Kabrega, 313, 322, 324, 325, 329, 334
Kaykoum, 290
Keroto, 321, 323
Kidj natives, 298
Khartoum, 286, 288
Khor El Pasha, 322
Kilimanjaro, 312
Kissuna, 327
Kubuli River, 332

Ládo, 292, 299
Litchfield, Rev. G., 286
Livingstone, Dr., 307

Magungo, 307, 312
Mahomet Aga, 313, 320
Mason Bey, 311
Monkeys, 314
Mosquitoes, 293
Mount Meto, 304
Mruli,* 289, 333, 334
Murchison Falls, 318

Native dance, 291, 326

Nicola, 323
Nile marshes, 292
Scenery, 300

Packages, 299
Panyatole, 327
Pearson, C. W., 286

Regiaf, 299
Rionga, 325, 329
Rubaga, 333

Sandstorm, 287
Shádoofs, 287
Shambil, 295, 297
Shillooks, 290, 291
Speke, T. H., 307, 310
Stanley, 311, 336
Stanley's Lake, 312
Steamers, 286, 289, 303
Suakim, 286

Tanganyika, 307, 311
Thunderstorm, 322

Victoria Nile, 306
Victoria Nyanza, 312, 336

Waganda escort, 334
Wanyoro huts, 328
Wart-hogs, 332
Wilson, Rev. C. T., 285, 330
Wives, 331

Zanzibar, 336
Zenab, 319

* On map Mrooli.

LONDON: PRINTED BY WILLIAM CLOWES AND SONS, LIMITED,
STAMFORD STREET AND CHARING CROSS.

www.ingramcontent.com/pod-product-compliance
Lightning Source LLC
Chambersburg PA
CBHW030400230426
43664CB00007BB/671